A Special Issue of
Cognitive Neuropsychiatry

Voices in the Brain: The Cognitive Neuropsychiatry
of Auditory Verbal Hallucinations

Edited by

Sean A. Spence
University of Sheffield, UK

and

Anthony S. David
Institute of Psychiatry and GKT School of Medicine, UK

Psychology Press
Taylor & Francis Group
HOVE AND NEW YORK

First published 2004 by Psychology Press Ltd

Psychology Press
Taylor and Francis Group
27 Church Road
Hove
East Sussex BN3 2FA

Psychology Press
Taylor & Francis Group
711 Third Avenue,
New York, NY 10017

Psychology Press is an imprint of the Taylor & Francis Group, an informa business

© 2004 by Psychology Press Ltd

All rights reserved. No part of this book may be reprinted or reproduced or utilised in any form or by any electronic, mechanical, or other means, now known or hereafter invented, including photocopying and recording, or in any information storage or retrieval system, without permission in writing from the publishers.

British Library Cataloguing in Publication Data
A catalogue record for this book is available from the British Library

ISBN 1-84169-963-2 (hbk)
ISSN 1354-6805

Cover design by Joyce Chester
Typeset by DP Photosetting, Aylesbury, Bucks

Contents*

Voices in the brain
Sean A. Spence   1

Choices for voices: A voice hearer's perspective on hearing voices
Graham Cockshutt   9

Hearing voices: A phenomenological-hermeneutic approach
Philip Thomas, Patrick Bracken, and Ivan Leudar   13

Psychological treatment for voices in psychosis
Til Wykes   25

Compelling imagery, unanticipated speech and deceptive memory: Neurocognitive models of auditory verbal hallucinations in schizophrenia
Marc L. Seal, Andre Aleman, and Philip K. McGuire   43

Auditory hallucinations: Insights and questions from neuroimaging
P.W.R. Woodruff   73

Locating voices in space: A perceptual model for auditory hallucinations?
Michael D. Hunter   93

The cognitive neuropsychiatry of auditory verbal hallucinations: An overview
Anthony S. David   107

Auditory hallucinations as primary disorders of syntax: An evolutionary theory of the origins of language
Timothy J. Crow   125

Subject Index   147

---

*This book is also a special issue of the journal *Cognitive Neuropsychiatry*, and forms issues 1 & 2 of Volume 9 (2004). The page numbers are taken from the journal and begin with p. 1.

Voices in the brain

Sean A. Spence
University of Sheffield, UK

This special issue of *Cognitive Neuropsychiatry* is devoted to the problem of auditory verbal hallucinations (AVHs): the experience of "hearing voices". Here, the word "problem" might imply a symptom and/or an intellectual puzzle. Throughout human history AVHs have been variously construed, sometimes as a sign of divine inspiration, sometimes as a symptom of mental illness (Leudar & Thomas, 2000). In this issue we sample some contemporary accounts of this strange aspect of human experience. Such a concentration of material, devoted to this single topic, is, we think, unusual and provides a unique opportunity for weighing up alternative strands of data and debate. The committed investigator, and the interested reader, should, we hope, find much that is stimulating and provocative. In the final analysis, we are attempting to understand a phenomenon that may be said to have profound effects upon many people's lives: Whether they hear voices themselves or care for (and about) those who hear them. Let us begin with a brief case study.

J: a case of AVH

When I was thirteen years old, I had a voice from God to help me govern my conduct... The first time I was very fearful. And came this voice, about the hour of noon, in the summer-time, in my father's garden... I heard the voice on the right-hand side, towards the church; and rarely do I hear it without a brightness. This

---

Correspondence should be addressed to Sean A. Spence, Reader in Psychiatry, University of Sheffield, The Longley Centre, Norwood Grange Drive, Sheffield, S5 7JT, UK.

Thanks to my co-editor Professor Tony David for comments on an earlier draft of this paper; to all the authors whose work is included in this volume for their timely contributions; and to Dr Colin Rhodes for alerting me to references relating to visionary artists.

The *Second Sheffield Psychopathology Symposium—Voices in the Brain* was supported by the Department of Academic Clinical Psychiatry, University of Sheffield. We are grateful to all for their support and to Mrs Jean Woodhead, Ms Beverly Nesbitt, Mrs Kathryn Pursall and Mr Martin Brook for their organisational and technical assistance. Details of future meetings are available at www.psychopathology.co.uk

The quote from Joan of Arc, which appears in this paper, is reproduced in many sources but this abridged version was taken from: Regine Pernoud's *Joan of Arc by Herself and Her Witnesses*, published by Scarborough House, Lanham, Maryland (1994).

brightness comes from the same side as the voice is heard. It is usually a great light... This voice was sent to me by God and, after I had thrice heard this voice, I knew that it was the voice of an angel. This voice has always guided me well and I have always understood it clearly.

(From Pernoud, 1994)

What do we make of such an account? It is provided by a 19-year-old; looking back six years to the experience described. The phenomenology seems clear enough, a voice in external space, specifically to the right and associated with a light. We might infer that the voice is heard in the second person (it has "guided me well"). We might then consider localising signs: The confluence of auditory and visual experience, implicating the posterior left hemisphere. Is this sufficient? Probably not, we might wish to consider "diagnoses": The presence of a light has prompted some to consider migraine; the possibility of epilepsy has also been entertained, as has schizophrenia. Indeed, the range of proffered diagnoses has also included psychopathy, hysteria, and cerebral tuberculosis.

Context is important, of course. In this case, the account is recorded in the transcript of a trial, a trial for heresy. And part of the reason the informant is held to account is because of a military career. And this is also unusual (especially for the time) because the informant is a young woman. By this stage she has led an army, or at least contributed significantly to its progress, through an initially successful campaign. The informant is, of course, Joan of Arc.

One aspect of this case that makes it so compelling is the very clear account remaining of the phenomenology. Because of the literally life-and-death nature of the decisions that would follow, verbatim accounts were set down, questioned and re-clarified, and are still preserved from the 1430s (see the website of the St Joan centre: http://www.stjoan-center.com/Trials and Sullivan, 1996). We know more about Joan's life than possibly any other medieval figure (see Wheeler & Wood, 1996). And at the centre of proceedings is a clear account of AVHs.

Perhaps the story of Joan of Arc sets up some problems pertinent to this volume of *Cognitive Neuropsychiatry*; for the bald description of the form of an auditory verbal hallucination, a voice perceived, to the right, in external space, does not seem to do justice to Joan's experiences, her actions, and their consequences. If there is a cognitive neurobiological account of such phenomena, to what extent is it sufficient unto itself?

The story of Joan of Arc is that she grew up in the context of the Hundred Years War between France and England; a time of immense social dislocation, in which she began to hear voices when she was aged 13. When she was 17 years old, she sought out the Dauphin (the future Charles VII of France), her voices having told her that she would lift the siege of Orleans and see the Dauphin crowned king. She gained access to Charles and, after an assessment by his advisers (both physical, to establish her virginity, and theological, to establish her legitimacy; Wood, 1996), he provided her with access to his army. We can only speculate upon his view of Joan. Would Charles have regarded her as inspired or insane? He is unlikely to have been naïve where madness is concerned. The reason Charles' father (Charles VI) had lost his throne was because of his own chronic psychosis (probably schizophrenia; Waley & Denley, 2001, p. 137, pp. 174–176; Gordon, 2000, pp. 29–31). So the Dauphin had seen psychosis at close quarters, in his "father" (his paternity remains an issue); would he lightly have granted Joan access to his forces if he had thought her insane?

In due course, Joan did indeed lift the siege of Orleans and did see the Dauphin crowned King Charles VII. Her own military career lasted about a year in all and ended with her capture. She was sold to the English, and eventually tried by the Inquisition. Despite being cross-examined in rooms of sometimes 50 or 60 "assessors" at a time (see http://www.stjoan-center.com/Trials), Joan's account of herself is subtle and measured; she was clearly not thought-disordered. However, Charles did not come to her rescue and she was burned at the stake in Rouen in 1431. Joan was 19. It was the nature of her relationship to, and avowal of, her voices that led to her death; "direct contact" with God, unmediated by the Church, being construed as heretical. Some years later Joan was exonerated at a second (posthumous) trial, her "nullification", and later still, in 1920, she was canonised, becoming a saint of the Roman Catholic Church. At the trial for her canonisation, it was one of the Devil's Advocates who proffered the diagnosis of hysteria (above), to counter the legitimacy of Joan's experiences (Ansgar Kelly, 1996, p.221). Today, there is a website devoted to translations of her trials and emerging scholarship (above). On 16 June 2003 an Internet search, performed by the author, revealed 113,996 websites mentioning Joan of Arc. Not bad for a possibly illiterate 19-year-old who heard voices and lived half a millennium ago.

What we think we know

Staying with the present day and this issue of *Cognitive Neuropsychiatry*, all but one of the papers published here is derived from a meeting which took place in Sheffield, England, in September 2002: The *Second Sheffield Psychopathology Symposium—Voices in the Brain*. The purpose of that meeting was to investigate the current state of our knowledge of "voices"—AVHs. We began by considering the contemporary "voice hearer's" perspective. What is it like to hear voices? What do voice hearers ask of others? Though the experience of individuals is likely to vary greatly, some common themes emerged: The desire for phenomena to be taken seriously, for the hearer to be treated with respect; the need for timely assistance, often under very trying circumstances; and a certain agnosticism with respect to the etiology of "voices". Cockshutt (this issue) is conversant with the medical model, and has retained some positive perspectives on it, but doubtless there will be other voice hearers whose experiences of services have been less than positive.

While much that follows will dwell upon the "form" of phenomenological experience (the "physical" attributes of the "voice", its location in space), an alternative perspective is that of Thomas and colleagues (this issue) who address the hermeneutics, the meaning and interpretation of verbal material. They demonstrate the relations that exist between the "content" of AVH speech and the life and circumstances of the hearer. Explicit in their account is a social relatedness, not merely to the content of the "voice" but to its perceived author. Notwithstanding the excesses of an earlier "psychodynamic" age, this hermeneutic perspective has been much neglected with the subsequent return to a more "biological" psychiatry. However, it (hermeneutics) provides an interesting challenge to the cognitive paradigm, as instantiated in models of "internal monitoring" below (and see Thornton, 2002).

This leads us on to a mode of support that many voice hearers have found helpful: Group work. It is often a feature of nonstatutory settings, in the self-help and voluntary sectors, as well as an aspect of hospital or other "professional" environments (not that these sectors need be mutually exclusive). Wykes, in this issue, considers the evidence that formal group interventions utilising cognitive models can help in psychosis, specifically in alleviating AVH. This is a detailed and rigorous account, forming a baseline for future service evaluations. We await the outcome of randomised trials of this intervention.

While the former account examines the application of a cognitive model in helping to *treat* symptoms, Seal and colleagues present a structured literature review of empirical findings relating to three cognitive models that have been used to *explain* AVH: Those implicating defective auditory imagery, verbal self-monitoring and episodic memory. Their data derive from a host of carefully designed studies, undertaken in the hope of locating those cognitive "breaks" which might underpin the phenomenology of the hallucinated voice. This contribution will, one hopes, assist future investigators in the search for candidate cognitive *processes*.

Next, we come to the application of biological research methods that have substantially impacted upon our understanding of AVHs in recent years. In the latter decades of the 20th century, functional neuroimaging techniques, such as SPECT, PET, and fMRI, allowed investigators to image the neural correlates of cognitive function. No longer reliant upon interesting but necessarily idiosyncratic neuropsychological single case studies, such investigators could study the normal brain *in vivo*. These methods also provided psychiatric researchers with a means of examining the brain states underlying abnormal mental experience; hence, the AVH emerged as a suitable candidate for investigation. Initially, such studies identified areas of the brain where activity correlated with the experience of AVH (commonly implicating the temporal lobes). Subsequently, investigators have applied increasingly sophisticated instantiations of the cognitive paradigm, to "image" functions not symptoms, specifically the functions that might support symptoms: "inner speech", "verbal imagery", "object recognition", and so on. These studies have helped to identify candidate *systems* whose dysfunction might generate psychopathology.

In this issue, Woodruff outlines the findings from neuroimaging studies of patients who experience AVH (and who are mostly diagnosed as having schizophrenia); studies which implicate plausible regions in frontotemporal and subcortical structures in particular. However, he rightly indicates that multiple systems will be engaged in supporting different aspects of the AVH experience (perception, impulse control, etc.). Hunter (this issue) then takes this methodology back into the "normal" state, in an original attempt to model those systems that engage when a psychotic symptom (hearing a voice outside the head) is simulated in healthy volunteers. Coming to Hunter's work after a consideration of the phenomenology reported by Joan of Arc (above), one is impressed that a purely biological account of the *form* of her experience might confine itself to really quite specific brain regions. With ever more sensitive neuroimaging methodologies emerging, and more sophisticated data analytic procedures becoming widely available, it seems likely that the neural correlates of AVH will increasingly be understood, from a biological/biomedical perspective.

David, my co-editor, then takes up the baton to examine and critique the cognitive neuropsychiatric paradigm itself: How good are the "box and arrow" models of AVH? Do they explain anything? This is an opportunity to take stock of the very paradigm that provides the rationale for this journal. In fact, David's account of the empirical literature points quite specifically to those areas of the model that have potential for future exploitation and those that are pretty much exhausted. This expert summary of the state of the art should assist future investigators in choosing fruitful areas of study.

A biological perspective that few readers would question is that of the evolutionary advantage conveyed by cognitive adaptations of the human brain. Perhaps language is the defining characteristic of the human condition, and perhaps (more controversially) language is at the heart of schizophrenia: Certainly many of the symptoms of the disorder are expressed via its mediation (not least "voices"), and some signs are quintessentially disorders of speech (such as formal thought disorder and alogia). Thus, the final paper in this special issue is provided by Crow, who sets out an elegant case for his theory that schizophrenia is inherently related to the human attribute of language, not in a trivial way, but through a specific, genetically mediated, confluence of genes for language, brain asymmetry, and the propensity for insanity. The persistence of schizophrenia in the human population is thus attributed to its inherent link to the capacity for language. Seen through the prism of recorded history, this is one of many perspectives that have attempted to relate "voices" to the human condition.

What we know we don't know

Implicit in the cognitive neuropsychiatric paradigm, exemplified by most of the papers in this special issue, is the premise that a discrete functional system is defective; its defect manifest in the heard, sometimes external, voice. In time, this approach may reveal a pathophysiology of AVH, informing accounts of the etiology of psychosis itself (cf. below). However, at the present time, the biological treatment interventions available to us relate not to this level of analysis, but instead to a mostly neurochemical understanding of psychosis. Hence, they seem to indirectly implicate the dopaminergic and serotonergic systems in the neurochemistry of AVH, though it remains unclear how such knowledge explicates a single voice. We might plausibly claim that changes in neurotransmitter levels facilitate hallucinations under conditions of stress but we cannot invoke chemistry to explain their content (what the voices "say"). Some readers may recall the early iterations of Chris Frith's model of positive symptoms, in which he hypothesised that (typical) antipsychotics worked to reduce positive symptoms (including AVHs) by essentially preventing action-generation (Frith, 1987, p. 644). Hence, the parkinsonism induced by these drugs was constitutive of their therapeutic efficacy. If internally generated actions cannot be generated then their preceding intentions are not available to be misperceived by a faulty "internal monitor"; hence, they cannot give rise to voices (or passivity phenomena; see David, this issue). This remains the nearest thing we have to a synthesis of the cognitive and the chemical but it still does not account for the content of a voice (other than to suggest that dopamine is, in some way, permissive).

Meanwhile, in the contemporary clinical arena, there is the increasing application of talking therapies to treat what might otherwise be regarded as "biological" symptoms. Cognitive behavioural therapy (CBT) is accruing published evidence for its efficacy as a treatment of positive symptoms, and service users, often outside the statutory realm, are employing their own strategies to counter voices, through group work and peer support (see above; Wykes, this issue). Hence, in the clinic, it is not a question of using one or the other methodology, biological or psychological, but more a case of forging a synthesis that is appropriate: A search after those strategies that assist a given individual. But consider the implication of at least one of these strategies: If CBT can be shown to alleviate AVHs, what would this mean for the cognitive neuropsychiatric model? Are boxes and arrows rewired by speaking? Is faulty internal monitoring "fixed"? Perhaps we need not address these questions just yet, as the evidence for CBT is still susceptible to critique (see the debate between Turkington & McKenna, 2003).

Of course, much of the foregoing takes for granted the pathological status of hearing voices. Yet, voices may be construed in other ways, and increasingly these perspectives have relevance to the clinical/applied realm. It matters whether we see such experiences as inherently abnormal, justifying treatment interventions, or as an aspect of the (normal) human condition. Hence, there are recent accounts stressing the occurrence of these phenomena in "normal" populations (e.g., Jackson & Fulford, 1997, cf. David, this issue). It may be that for every person diagnosed with schizophrenia, who hears voices, there are ten in the population who hear a voice but yet do not seek or receive psychiatric intervention (Bentall, 2003, pp. 96–98). In another context, it has been remarked that "visionary artists" characteristically commence their careers in response to a voice (Cardinal, 1989), reminiscent of the mission of Joan of Arc (above). This raises many questions, which space will not allow us to enumerate here, but one might suffice: If voices are not (in themselves) a justification for treatment, then those whom we treat (and study) in clinical settings may be ascertained for reasons other than their "voices". In other words, we might be studying "special cases" (the "1 in 10"). Yet, there must also be an antidote to an overly romanticised view of AVH. Many of those whom we see have suffered greatly; some of those whom we do not see may suffer also; and both Joan of Arc and some of the visionary artists described by Cardinal (1989) were "led" toward ultimate destruction. Indeed, was this not also true of Socrates, who expressed surprise that his "voice", his "daemon", became silent once his fate had been sealed (Jaspers, 1957/1985, pp. 10–11)?

As if to illustrate the latter point, the author has recently seen a patient who worked in a clinical discipline for many years while experiencing AVHs on an almost daily basis. Her voices were experienced as coming from external space, from right and left, and were as loud as veridical speech. She did not present for medical attention until the "character" of her voices changed. Throughout her twenties the patient had heard voices that soothed and encouraged her, they seemed to prompt her to do things; objectively, her life was going well. But after about ten years, and in the context of a promotion, the character of these AVHs changed substantially: instead of encouraging the individual they denigrated her, and instead of "adopting" a soothing tone they began to laugh and jeer at her. Subsequently, they urged her to cut herself, severely, "promising" that they would leave her if she obeyed their commands. In fact, she came to medical attention in the context of severe attempts at self-destruction and the AVHs have resisted those antipsychotic medications administered to date (including some "atypicals"). So, the presence of AVHs *per se* was insufficient for distress or medical attention, and the application of the current dopaminergic/serotonergic paradigm has not caused these symptoms to remit. We clearly have much need of progress in our understanding of these perplexing phenomena.

Manuscript accepted 15 July 2003

REFERENCES

Ansgar Kelly, H. (1996). Joan of Arc's last trial: The attack of the Devil's Advocate. In B. Wheeler & C. T. Wood (Eds.), *Fresh verdicts on Joan of Arc* (3rd ed., pp. 205–236). New York: Garland.

Bentall, R. P. (2003). *Madness explained: Psychosis and human nature.* London: Allen Lane, Penguin Press.

Cardinal, R. (1989). The art of entrancement. *Raw Vision*, Winter, 22–31.

Cockshutt, G. (2004). Choices for voices: A voice hearer's perspective on hearing voices. *Cognitive Neuropsychiatry, 9*(1/2), 9–11.

Crow, T. J. (2004). Auditory hallucinations as primary disorders of syntax: An evolutionary theory of the origins of language. *Cognitive Neuropsychiatry, 9*(1/2), 125–145.

David, A. S. (2004). The cognitive neuropsychiatry of auditory verbal hallucinations: An overview. *Cognitive Neuropsychiatry, 9*(1/2), 107–123.

Frith, C. D. (1987). The positive and negative symptoms of schizophrenia reflect impairment in the perception and initiation of action. *Psychological Medicine, 17*, 631–648.

Gordon, M. (2000). *Joan of Arc.* London: Weidenfeld & Nicolson.

Hunter, M. D. (2004). Locating voices in space: A perceptual model for auditory hallucinations? *Cognitive Neuropsychiatry, 9*(1/2), 93–105.

Jackson, M. C., & Fulford, K. W. M. (1997). Spiritual experience and psychopathology. *Philosophy, Psychiatry and Psychology, 4*, 41–65.

Jaspers, K. (1985). *Socrates, Buddha, Confucius, Jesus: The paradigmatic individuals.* San Diego: Harvest. (Original work published 1957)

Leudar, I., & Thomas, P. (2000). *Voices of reason, voices of insanity. Studies of verbal hallucinations.* London: Routledge.

Pernoud, R. (1994). *Joan of Arc by herself and her witnesses.* Lanham, MD: Scarborough House.

Seal, M. L., Aleman, A., & McGuire, P. K. (2004). Compelling imagery, unanticipated speech and deceptive memory: Neurocognitive models of auditory verbal hallucinations in schizophrenia. *Cognitive Neuropsychiatry, 9*(1/2), 43–72.

Spence, S. A. (2004). Voices in the brain. *Cognitive Neuropsychiatry, 9*(1/2), 1–8.

Sullivan, K. (1996). Joan of Arc's voices. In B. Wheeler & C. T. Wood (Eds.), *Fresh verdicts on Joan of Arc* (3rd ed., pp. 85–111). New York: Garland.

Thomas, P., Bracken, P., & Leudar, I. (2004). Hearing voices: A phenomenological-hermeneutic approach. *Cognitive Neuropsychiatry, 9*(1/2), 13–23.

Thornton, T. (2002). Thought insertion, cognitivism, and inner space. *Cognitive Neuropsychiatry, 7*, 237–249.

Turkington, D., & McKenna, P. (2003). In Debate: Is cognitive-behavioural therapy a worthwhile treatment for psychosis? *British Journal of Psychiatry, 182*, 477–479.

Waley, D., & Denley, P. (2001). *Later medieval Europe* (3rd ed.). London: Longman.

Wheeler, B., & Wood, C. T. (1996). *Fresh verdicts on Joan of Arc.* New York: Garland.

Wood, C. T. (1996). Joan of Arc's mission and the lost record of her interrogation at Poitiers. In B. Wheeler & C. T. Wood (Eds.), *Fresh verdicts on Joan of Arc* (3rd ed., pp. 19–29). New York: Garland.

Woodruff, P. W. R. (2004). Auditory hallucinations: Insights and questions from neuroimaging. *Cognitive Neuropsychiatry, 9*(1/2), 73–91.

Wykes, T. (2004). Psychological treatment for voices in psychosis. *Cognitive Neuropsychiatry, 9*(1/2), 25–41.

Choices for voices: A voice hearer's perspective on hearing voices

Graham Cockshutt

User Support and Employment Service, Sheffield, UK

To many people the mere concept that a person "hears voices" is enough to convince them that the individual concerned is violent, unstable, and should be locked away. The media continually regenerate this view and invariably we, as voice hearers, are portrayed as being involved in murder, rape, mutilation, and devil worship.

The reality, however, is somewhat different. Yes, I hear voices. Yes, at times, my reality and that of non-voice hearers are different. I am, for the most part, aware of what is happening to me and I have developed a variety of coping strategies—although some would say distraction techniques—to try to allow me to cope with day-to-day life. These are not unique to me. Voice hearers have developed them and each of us adopts and adapts them to suit our particular situation. The reason for this is simple. Although I am not unique in hearing voices, my voices are unique to me.

What is it like hearing voices?

For me, and I can only speak for myself, the voices are externalised ... and real. There is no point in pretending otherwise. I could say that I understand that they are a false manifestation of my internal thoughts. The truth is that for me that is the unreal aspect of it all because by pretending to believe that the voices are unreal I am, in essence, creating a false reality. A reality in which what I say, and what I believe, are different. I realise that this is how most people live their lives, as a compromise between the two aspects, but for many voice hearers it is not that easy. Many people would meet me and think: "There's someone in control of the situation". We have to develop specific ways of coping.

Correspondence should be addressed to Graham Cockshutt, Sheffield Care Trust, Fulwood House, Old Fulwood Road, Fulwood, Sheffield S10 3TH, UK.

© 2004 Psychology Press Ltd
http://www.tandf.co.uk/journals/pp/13546805.html   DOI:10.1080/13546800344000129

So how do we cope?

The first thing that I have to do is accept that I hear voices and that I might go through periods of being unwell. As John Cleese said in the film *Clockwise*:

> I can cope with the despair. It's the constant hope I can't stand.

The constant hope, in my case, is that the voices will suddenly disappear. If I wake up each morning with that as a hope then I am, at the present time, always disappointed. So begins another day with a failure. The voices will start and another long day will ensue. Far better is to accept that the voices will be there and try to deal with them. Acceptance—rather than denial—is therefore the first step.

My second strategy is one that frequently causes shock-horror amongst other voice hearers: Medication. I know (because like a majority of voice hearers I have tried it) that if I stop taking my medication my condition deteriorates. This normally happens over a period of about 3 weeks. Knowing that this is the case I try to be rigorous in my "compliance regime". You will notice that I said "try". I do take drug breaks—how irresponsible—for 2, 3 or even 4 days. Not because I feel that it makes a significant difference but to show that I am in control. Yes I know, just another delusion!

What else works?

None of what follows is either original or of guaranteed success. These are strategies that I, and others, have used and found effective. "Compartmentalising" is the name I give to trying to keep my voices separate from other thoughts and actions. It involves breaking down what I think is happening and then dealing with each part individually. It allows the voices to be "ignored" in the sense that the compartment they are in does not have to be visited. This does not mean that I do not hear the voices, only that I am not focusing on that particular compartment so it becomes background noise.

Another technique I use is what I call my pub approach. This is not the well known self-medication process that many of us have tried (although that one does have some attractions). The comparison I use is that of a party of people in a pub. They split into two groups but you hear your name mentioned in the other half. You have the capacity to either ignore it and remain in your conversation or listen to the other group whilst appearing to be with yours. I use a similar approach trying to keep the voices in the background.

There are, of course, many other well known, and for some people effective, ways of coping. The use of a Walkman—although these days people tend to want a CD or mini-disc player—can help. The suggestion that this is a sign that people are coping less well is not one to which I would subscribe. It is certainly a coping strategy that is used in the early stages but it can help people to begin to focus on something other than the voices and should not be dismissed lightly. Relaxation techniques, coping with stress, forward planning and an assortment of alternative/complementary approaches are successfully used by people. I suppose it is a case of "horses for courses" or more accurately "choices for voices".

A place for doctors?

So where does the medical profession fit in? Well it may surprise some people to know that I believe they have a vital role to play. One of the problems I have always faced as a voice hearer is that of wanting an explanation. Not a medical explanation because in many ways that means little to me. I need an explanation that accommodates the reality of the voices: one that acknowledges that they are there. I am sure that at this point a number of people reading this are reaching for their pens to write and suggest that maybe I am once again a suitable case for treatment, having lost touch with reality. This is not the case. My reality is clear; I just need help to explain it. Thomas and colleagues' suggestion of phenomenology (this special issue) has certain attractions because it is a tangible explanation for what happens to us. The idea that the voices have a spiritual connection will certainly appeal to many—can anyone explain why Doris Stokes was revered and I'm not? Anything that allows us to explain our voices is important. Similarly, any research that takes place should have a fundamental benefit for voice hearers. The pursuit of academic knowledge for its own sake does us no favours. An example that springs to mind is that of psychosocial intervention (PSI). This began as a practical attempt to merge psychological approaches with the consideration of social imperatives but what appears to have happened in some areas is that it has become an academic process where the qualification is more important than the proliferation of the approach. This does not apply in all cases, I admit, but probably in more than is good for services. Sending people (service providers) on the course is fine but the opportunity to utilise the skills acquired is also important. The creation of a supportive environment that allows the PSI approach to be effectively used is vital for it to be of benefit to service users. If you, as doctors and health professionals, are aware that this could happen maybe it can be avoided.

We need your help to try and explain the unexplainable. Maybe we should set up an X-file?

Other information is available from:

www.hearing-voices.org.uk; www.unlocking-potential.com; www.rethink.org
User Support and Employment Service
Sheffield Hearing Voices Group
Unlocking Potential (A service user led self-help group).
All are based at St George's CMHC, Winter Street, Sheffield, S3 7ND, UK

Manuscript accepted 17 January 2003

Hearing voices:
A phenomenological-hermeneutic approach

Philip Thomas and Patrick Bracken
Centre for Citizenship and Community Mental Health, University of Bradford, UK

Ivan Leudar
University of Manchester, UK

The word "phenomenology" has a number of meanings. In this paper we briefly contrast the different meanings of the word in psychiatry and philosophy. We then consider the work of the philosophers Heidegger and Merleau-Ponty, as examples of what Hubert Dreyfus calls ontological phenomenology, in contrast to an epistemological approach. We present a brief outline of Merleau-Ponty's theory of embodiment, and contrast this with the dominant, epistemological (or Cartesian) view of experience. Through the example of a woman who experienced bereavement hallucinations, we try to show how this approach can open up a hermeneutic approach to the experience of hearing voices. An understanding of embodiment can help to counter reductionism, whether biological or social, and dualism (body/mind and mind/society). It is only when we consider the *totality* of human experience that we can understand its meaning. This has two main benefits. First, it legitimates the claims made by those who hear voices that their experiences are intrinsically meaningful. Second, it can provide a framework for those who work with voice hearers and who are interested in understanding these experiences. In this sense, phenomenology can become a valuable clinical tool.

There is, one hopes, a sense of irony in the title of the conference at which this paper was originally presented.[1] The expression, *Voices in the Brain*, is problematic. Voice hearers talk of voices being inside or outside their heads.

---

[1] This paper was originally given as an invited talk at the *Second Sheffield Psychopathology Symposium—Voices in the Brain*, Sheffield, England in September 2002.

Correspondence should be addressed to Philip Thomas, Centre for Citizenship and Community Mental Health, School of Health Studies, 25 Trinity Road, Bradford BD7 0BB, UK; p.thomas@bradford.ac.uk

Psychologists talk of voices in the mind, but how is it possible to speak of voices in the brain? The problem concerns assumptions implicit in cognitivism about the relationship between mind, body and world. We shall examine these assumptions using by way of illustration that branch of philosophy called phenomenology, a word to which philosophers, psychologists, and psychiatrists apply different meanings. These meanings reflect different ways of orientating ourselves to mind, body and world, and this is important when we approach the person who hears voices. We shall argue that the "situation" of voices, or their positioning, extends beyond spatial metaphors and includes their position in culture, history, and the individual's life history. We will begin by describing briefly our recent work in this area, and then relate this to the view of phenomenology that continues to dominate psychiatry. We shall then demonstrate the value of a hermeneutic phenomenology using bereavement hallucinations as an example.

The influence of Cartesianism runs deep in psychiatry, and is found both in cognitivism and the variant of phenomenology popular in psychiatry. Most philosophers, psychologists, and psychiatrists now reject Descartes' separation of mind from the body, the *Res Cogitans* from the *Res Extensa*. Baker, Kale, & Menken (2002) have recently declared that the ontological separation of mind and body is unsustainable. Neuroscientists claim that mental life can be explained by neuroscience, their ultimate goal being to replace the language of psychology with the languages of the natural sciences. Cognitive scientists make the claim for a distinct psychological realm in which mental life cannot be reductively explained by natural sciences, but which can be explained through analogy with computers, making the operation of the mind amenable to scientific study. In reply, we (Bracken & Thomas, 2002) have argued that although cognitive science and neuroscience claim to move us beyond ontological dualism, they perpetuate the essential features of Descartes' philosophy. In particular, they uphold the epistemological separation of inner mind from outer world. They fail to acknowledge the problems that arise if we regard the mind as a "thing" (Descartes' *Res*). We have also argued that psychiatry (and medicine) need a different philosophical framework if we are to move beyond the limitations of Cartesianism (Bracken & Thomas, 2001). The question of meaning lies at the heart of this framework.

Where *are* voices situated?

The need to ask this question arises from a number of critiques of cognitivism that have emerged within academic psychology over the last 25 years, for example the work of Harré (1979). What has been called the discursive turn in psychology (Harré & Gillett, 1994), deeply influenced by the later philosophy of Wittgenstein and the work of Lev Vygotsky, stresses the importance of understanding human action by virtue of the fact that it is embedded in an infinite variety of social, cultural, historical, and political contexts. In contrast, cognitivism accounts for human experience and behaviour in terms of inner mental processes that represent external social reality. This divorces human experience and action from these contexts, and renders it meaningless. For example, cognitive models of auditory hallucinations relate voices to disturbances in discourse planning (Hoffman, 1986), or deficits in self-awareness due to a failure of the internal monitoring of thought (Frith, 1992). This removes the experience from the contexts in which they occur, and explains them in terms of disordered inner mental processes. Our recent work has shown the value of these contexts in understanding the possible meanings of voices.

For example, let us consider the case of Socrates and his daemon. The French protopsychiatrists applied their emerging understanding of hallucinations to Socrates' experience, claiming that he was mentally ill. Leudar (2001) has shown that Socrates' experience was situated in a culture (Athens, 4th century BC) in which the experience of daemons was controversial. Younger Athenians regarded the experience as superstitious and contrary to reason, whereas for Socrates it indicated that he was gifted to have such an experience. The important point here concerns how Socrates' experience was negotiated and situated in his culture. This is formulated in Leudar and Thomas (2000) as a question: What would Socrates have to relinquish of his own worldview if, as the protopsychiatrists claimed, his experience was a hallucination? We cannot answer this without considering the meaning that Socrates and his contemporaries attached to the experience. We have to conclude that if Socrates accepted his experience as a hallucination he would be forced to accept that there were no such things as Gods and daemons, because these beliefs were an integral aspect of his culture.

Our work with Peg Davies, a voice hearer, has shown that we can also understand the meaning of voices through the person's life history and spiritual belief system (Davies, Thomas, & Leudar, 1999; Leudar & Thomas, 2000). Peg had a diagnosis of paranoid schizophrenia, and heard voices for 25 years despite regular neuroleptic medication. Her life was constrained by her fear of her voices and their influence on her. She was puzzled by her experiences, and believed that if she could understand their meaning she could cope better with them. We used the Pragmatics of Voices Interview (Leudar, Thomas, McNally, & Glinki, 1996) to help her describe the identities of her voices in detail, while at the same time she wrote her life story. Consequently she was able to understand her experiences in terms of her strongly held Catholic faith (her voices' identities were of devils and angels), and her need for love and unconditional acceptance from others, which she related to the fact that she was adopted as a baby.

Two radically different conceptions of phenomenology

It should now be clear that we are dealing with very different ways of thinking about voices, and at this point we shall explore these differences more fully with reference to phenomenology. In psychiatry, phenomenology has come to be synonymous with the listing of symptoms and their nosological significance. In this sense it refers to the description of abnormal mental states, a view deeply influenced by the work of Jaspers (1963). Bracken (1999) has described the limitations of this view, which was heavily influenced by Husserl's early philosophy. Husserl intended phenomenology to be a rigorous science of human experience, an approach that involved bracketing out background contexts, and an intense form of self-examination. Husserl was immersed in the traditions of Cartesianism and its assumptions about the nature of the mind-world relationship, which divorces the inner world of mind and the external world. Phenomenology was an account of the structure of the representations realised through this method of internal reflection. The philosopher Hubert Dreyfus contrasts what he calls epistemological (or Husserlian) phenomenology, with ontological phenomenology. Rather than speaking of how the mind represents external reality, which is of course a key concern of cognitivism, ontological phenomenology attempts to understand how human beings relate to the world. Indeed, Dreyfus qualifies this because it implies that mind and world are separate entities. Thus, the phenomenologies of Heidegger and Merleau-Ponty replace the epistemological relationship of subject and object with the ontological "being-in-the-world". The emphasis here is on human contexts in which objects and events stand out and make sense to us. For Heidegger the context arises out of culture, which provides a shared understanding of what is real, and what counts as being human. Understanding Being creates a space or clearing (*Lichtung*) in which events or phenomena stand out as meaningful for us. Merleau-Ponty compares this clearing with the light in a room. We may not be able to detect its source, but its presence makes objects in the room stand out for us. This is important because reality is not determined universally in terms of distinctions between inner and external worlds, but is influenced by cultural factors that make it possible for us to understand and make sense of our experiences in particular ways. This view of phenomenology differs markedly from that adopted by psychiatry, which is largely (though not exclusively) influenced by epistemological phenomenology. In this sense the ontological phenomenology of Heidegger and Merleau-Ponty represents an alternative to reductionist and positivist accounts of human consciousness. In *Being and Time*, Heidegger (1962) broke free of the influence of Husserl and developed a hermeneutic approach to phenomenology. Experience can be understood precisely because being-in-the-world is contextualised and engaged in the everyday, social world. Heidegger attempted to unite phenomenology and hermeneutics, that aspect of philosophy concerned with interpretation in human affairs, work which inspired existentialism and critical theory. These movements are influencing psychiatry through the use of narrative in qualitative research and the theoretical grounding of a critical sociological approach to psychiatric practice. Ontological phenomenology questions the assumption that it is possible to explain experience or predict behaviour through causal accounts of mind. It also questions whether this is to be desired. In other words, it raises political and ethical concerns. It has close affinities with the sociocultural approaches to mind that informed our recent work on voices (Leudar & Thomas, 2000).

Merleau-Ponty and Embodiment

In *Phenomenology of Perception*, Merleau-Ponty (1962) draws on the experience of people with neurological disorders such as anosognosia and phantom limb pain to delve in depth into the problems of body-mind dualism. He argues that neither neurological nor psychological accounts of these experiences can fully account for the complexity of these experiences. We might be able to explain phantom limb experiences in terms of neurological or psychological disturbances, but the Cartesian split between the "psychological" and "neurological" is so profound that we simply cannot understand experience by adding the two together. To put it another way, if we reduce human experience to fragments of behaviour or perception in order to explain how the mind represents the external world, we simply cannot recreate experience by reassembling the fragments. He proposes a phenomenological approach that situates human experience *between* the physiological and the psychological, which he finds in being-in-the-world and embodiment. For example, phantom limb experiences sometimes reappear as memories are recalled to the amputee. How might this happen? Merleau-Ponty proposes that memory operates not through association, but because it reopens the time lost to us and invites us to recapture the situation evoked. He puts it the following way:

> In so far as emotion and memory can call up the phantom limb, this is not comparable to the action of one *cogitatio* which necessitates another *cogitatio*, or that of one condition bringing about its consequences. It is not that an ideal causality imposes itself on a physiological one, *it is that an existential attitude motivates another and that memory, emotion and phantom limb are equivalents in terms of being-in-the-world*.
>
> (Merleau-Ponty 1962, p. 86, emphasis added)

Occasionally, amputees appear to be unaware of the physical loss of a limb, and attempt to walk on a phantom limb as they would a real one. We can understand this through embodiment. Having a body is to exist in a particular culture for a particular time, and to identify with and commit oneself to particular projects. Our bodies define our spatiality and draw us into the physical world. Our bodies also define our temporality, especially our finitude. The body is the locus of past, present, and future. The amputee in projecting his/her past embodiment into the present may be prompted to walk on his/her amputated leg. Merleau-Ponty uses the expression "quasi-present" to refer to this projection of past embodiment into the present. It is because we carry the past with us, as Langer (1989) puts it "sedimented" in our bodies, that we may be haunted by past experiences.

Ontological phenomenology situates human experience in personal, historical, and cultural contexts, and it is through these contexts that experience can be understood as meaningful. This can be seen in the work of the anthropologist Csordas, and the social psychologist Blackman, both of whom have used Merleau-Ponty's philosophy to explore hermeneutic approaches to the experience of hearing voices. Csordas (1994) considers the experience of a young Navajo Indian, Dan, who developed a psychosis after the removal of a left temporal-parietal astrocytoma. In addition to hearing voices, he also developed a pronounced expressive aphasia. Dan's first language was English, and although he regained the ability to use English, he lost what little Navajo he had. He coped with this through his relationship with the "Holy People", who wanted him to address a younger Navajo generation who were unable to understand prayer in Navajo. Dan describes coping with these problems in what he calls the "Navajo way", by becoming a medicine man (traditional healer). His own attempts to overcome his expressive language problems were ineffective, but by attending to the words of the Holy People (his voices), his speech was inspired, and he was able to make himself understood to others in his community. Peyote ingestion played an important part in this process. From Dan's account, his inspiration arose from having the peyote spirit enter him, and the Holy People who put the words to him. Csordas suggests that there was a phenomenological fusion of what Dan heard (the voices say) to what he said. In other words, for Dan, becoming a medicine man and developing the power of prayer allowed the "domestication" of his experiences into intentional utterances. So, we might understand it as a coping mechanism. Csordas provides a particularly interesting view of the boundaries between neurology and phenomenology (pp. 278–285). Language disturbances and "hyperreligiosity" are not infrequently observed clinical features of people with epilepsy, as are verbosity and circumstantial speech. It has been argued that such speech is actually a coping mechanism to deal with expressive aphasia. This means that verbosity is neither a direct effect of the lesion, nor part of a "personality change", but may better be understood as part of a series of processes that are reconstitutive of the self. In other words, it is important that we consider the part played by human intentionality in understanding "symptoms". This is particularly important in understanding how people cope with symptoms and recover from illness.

For Blackman, Merleau-Ponty's philosophy is a powerful way of combating determinism, whether biological, psychological or cultural. Like Csordas, she finds in embodiment a valuable way of thinking about how we might integrate experiences such as hearing voices into our lives. She is concerned with the situatedness of such experiences, their contexts, and how these contexts render the experience admissible or inadmissible. This has ethical implications. For example, the work of the Hearing Voices Network (Romme & Escher, 1993) offers an alternative ethical context in which voice hearers may share their different understanding of their experiences. Local understandings of voices in hearing voices groups would be regarded as pathological within psychiatric discourse, but become an "ethic of expansion" in such situations.

Voices in bereavement

Merleau-Ponty's work indicates that the experience of neurological disorders is understandable in terms of the individual's life history, because memories of our past experiences are embodied. Embodiment entails an awareness of past and present action, as well as possibilities for future action. If "To have a phantom arm is to remain open to all the actions of which the arm alone is capable..." (Merleau-Ponty, 1962, p. 81), then can we extend this to hearing voices? Can we think of voices, like phantom limbs, as "quasi-presents"? Can we, as Blackman (2001) suggests, use embodiment and the situatedness of these experiences as a way of opening up the possible meanings of voices? Our earlier work has shown how the experience of hearing voices is situated socially and culturally. In the following account taken from an interview with a subject in Leudar and Thomas (2000, Ch. 9), we re-examine the transcript from the perspective of Merleau-Ponty's philosophy. Although the purpose of the original interview was to describe the interactions between voice hearer and voices, not to explore voices and embodiment, the subject's experiences are moving and meaningful and show the value of an embodied approach to voices.

Sue is a 46-year-old woman with three children, interviewed by PT and IL. Her partner, Alan, died suddenly 7 years prior to the interview, after a heart attack. They had lived together for 14 years. She described her relationship with Alan as difficult. He was a domineering man who was critical of the way she brought up the children. Shortly after his death she began to sense his physical presence, an experience that comforted her. But later, when she started to hear his voice, his words brought alive difficult aspects of their past relationship in her present. This is her response to a question about the sort of things that Alan's voices tells her not to do:

> *Sue*: Well, it changes. Initially, just after he died, it was always, it was like a comforting voice I thought thought initially perhaps that was me projecting, wanting him to comfort me. But then he would do it in anger and he he was a very angry man and he'd be angry and irritated by me and say "you're being *stupid*".

For Sue, experiencing the past negative aspects of her relationship with Alan was vivid. His hallucinatory voice carried for her what were the most important hallmarks of his disapproval and criticism of her, when he was alive:

PT: How does Alan's voice respond to your attempts to challenge or defend yourself?
Sue: It'd be like a gasp. I'd hear him, not so much saying anything, but it would be a (sharp intake of breath) kind of sound, where, it would be his, because his would always end on a "tut"
PT: Right, so is that
Sue: so it would be ("ahh, tut")
PT: and is that
Sue: kind of sound
PT: Right, right. And is that how he was in real life?
Sue: Often.
PT: Right, not always.
Sue: No, often.

It is worth noting that in real life it was a nonverbal gesture (a sharp intake of breath and a "tut") that signified Alan's disapproval so powerfully for Sue. His hallucinatory voice had exactly the same feature, and was associated with the same sense of being criticised. The following passage indicates that this aspect of her past relationship with Alan is still very much alive for her in the present. For now, in situations where she felt he would have criticised her in the past, especially where her children are concerned, she experienced his critical sigh and "tut". In other words, her experience of Alan's voice is situated. His responses to her lived experiences in the present are socially situated, and they are exactly as they would have been had he been there:

Sue: Erm, in the, more, more recently erm I got into trouble erm in the last three weeks and I actually, Alan, oh wrong, Stephen, my son said to me "Dad wouldn't have been impressed with this would he?" and I heard him say "No, I wouldn't"
PT: Oh right, so he does sometimes comment on other things that people say to you.
Sue: Yeah, and I didn't you know, apart from Stephen reminding me of that, he would never even come into my mind but I heard him say it.
PT: Right,
Sue: "No, I wouldn't" and it was the "ahh tut" at the end of it. Heh.
PT: So it was just, just, almost like he was there?
Sue: Yeah.

Sue also hears Alan's voice when she is trying to deal with a problem. It draws her attention to aspects of the situation that she is not handling well, and this appears to trigger a conflict in her own mind. If she agrees with what he is saying she may have to modify what she is doing, something she is reluctant to do.

Sue: Other times when I'm getting angry with, I know that he's, he's saying "look this is not right, you're not doing this" erm I would try and qualify it to myself but then sometimes I think "well, I don't know, he's right" and then I find I'm drawn in then to something that I'm not prepared to take on.

Alan's past disapproval and criticism is experienced most vividly in regard to Sue's present struggle bringing up her children as a single parent:

Sue: And I say, well wait a minute, you know I'm the mother now you've fucked off. You're not part of this.
IL: That's interesting, so he's not stuck seven years ago, so he's
Sue: *He's moved with us yes*. I often, I try and qualify it sometimes, thinking OK, he's my conscience, you know, I'm like, I'm bringing up two teenagers on my own, it's very difficult, I want a balance. There is no balance and I used to try and qualify it by saying "I've invented him, I've brought him into my life". But I don't want him there, because he, he causes me a lot of hassle, a lot of problems, and a lot of preoccupation at times, and I don't want him there.

Again, the ambivalence of her relationship with Alan emerges in her relationship with his voice. After his death his presence in her life was a comfort, but now his words are negative. This passage indicates that Sue's experience of Alan is not bound to their shared distant past. His voice is not simply restricted to commenting on things that occurred between them when he was alive. His presence has lived on for her in such a way and with such power that he now comments critically on events that in his life he had no knowledge of. He does so in exactly the way in which he would have done were he actually witnessing the events unfold in the family. She recognises this and attempts to explain it by saying that he is part of her conscience. But she resents his presence and tries to handle it by saying that she is responsible for bringing his presence into being in her life now ("I've invented him, I've brought him into my life"). This suggests that for Sue, Alan's voice is embodied, her past in her present. In this sense we can regard Alan's voice as a quasi-present.

CONCLUSIONS

Sacks (1986) writes as follows in *The Man Who Mistook His Wife for a Hat* (pp. 18–19):

Of course, the brain *is* a machine and a computer—everything in classical neurology is correct. But our mental processes, which constitute our being and life, are not just abstract and mechanical, but personal as well—and, as such, involve not just classifying and categorising, but continual judging and feeling also.

Like Merleau-Ponty the philosopher, Sacks the neurologist recognises the limitations of accounting for experience narrowly in terms of either bodily or psychological processes. Alone, neither neurological nor psychological is capable of accounting for meaning. We have used Merleau-Ponty's ideas to augment our work, and to show that voices have meaning by exploring the situated and embodied features of voices. We are now using this approach with descriptions of the voices experienced by people who have a diagnosis of schizophrenia, and our early results indicate that they are every bit as meaningful. Most people who hear voices, whether in schizophrenia or as part of a bereavement reaction, struggle to make sense of the experience. Ultimately, whether or not we choose to understand voices and the other experiences of psychosis is an ethical decision. We should beware of accounting for voices only in terms of biology, psychology or culture. We should also beware of practices that identify experiences like voices as evidence of disorder, deterioration, and degeneration. A concern with meaning makes it possible for us to wonder at how the person integrates puzzling and distressing experiences within his or her life. We may then understand how some people cope with their experiences, and others do not. From this point on recovery becomes a possibility.

Manuscript accepted 17 January 2003

REFERENCES

Baker, M., Kale, R., & Menken, M. (2002). The wall between neurology and psychiatry: Advances in neuroscience indicate it's time to tear it down. *British Medical Journal, 324*, 1469–1470.

Blackman, L. (2001). *Hearing voices: Embodiment and experience.* London: Free Association Books.

Bracken, P. (1999). Phenomenology and psychiatry. *Current Opinion in Psychiatry, 12*, 593–596.

Bracken, P., & Thomas, P. (2000). Cognitive therapy, Cartesianism and the moral order. *European Journal of Psychotherapy, Counselling and Health, 2*, 325–344.

Bracken, P., & Thomas, P. (2001). Postpsychiatry: A new direction for mental health. *British Medical Journal, 322*, 724–727.

Bracken, P., & Thomas, P. (2002). Time to move beyond the mind-body split. *British Medical Journal, 325*, 1433–1434.

Csordas, T. (1994). Words from the Holy People: A case study in cultural phenomenology. In T. Csordas (Ed.), *Embodiment and experience: The existential ground of culture and self.* Cambridge, UK: Cambridge University Press.

Davies, P., Thomas, P., & Leudar, I. (1999). Dialogical engagement and verbal hallucinations: A single case study. *British Journal of Medical Psychology, 72*, 179–187.

Dreyfus, H. *Alternative philosophical conceptualizations of psychopathology.* On http://socrates.berkeley.edu/~hdreyfus/html/paper/_alternative.html

Frith, C. (1992). *The cognitive neuropsychology of schizophrenia.* Hove, UK: Psychology Press.

Harré, R. (1979). *Social being.* Oxford, UK: Blackwell.

Harré, R., & Gillett, G. (1994). *The discursive mind*. Sage: London.
Heidegger M. (1962). *Being and time* (J. Macquarrie & E. Robinson, Trans.). Oxford, UK: Blackwell.
Hoffman, R. E. (1986). Verbal hallucinations and language production processes in schizophrenia. *Behavioural and Brain Sciences*, *9*, 503–548.
Jaspers, K. (1963). *General psychopathology* (J. Hoenig & M. W. Hamilton, Trans.). Manchester, UK: Manchester University Press.
Langer, M. (1989). *Merleau-Ponty's phenomenology of perception: A guide and commentary*. Basingstoke, UK: Macmillan.
Merleau-Ponty, M. (1962). *Phenomenology of perception* (C. Smith, Trans.). London: Routledge & Kegan Paul.
Leudar, I. (2001). Voices in history. *Outlines*, *1*, 5–18.
Leudar, I., & Thomas, P. (2000). *Voices of reason, voices of insanity: Studies of verbal hallucinations*. London: Brunner-Routledge.
Leudar, I., Thomas, P., McNally, D., & Glinki, A. (1996). What can voices do with words? Pragmatics of verbal hallucinations. *Psychological Medicine*, *27*, 885–989.
Romme, M. A. J., & Escher, A. D. M. A. C. (1993). *The new approach: A Dutch experiment*. In M. A. J. Romme & A. D. M. A. C. Escher (Eds.), *Accepting voices* (pp. 11–27). London: MIND publications.
Sacks, O. (1986). *The man who mistook his wife for a hat*. London: Picador.

Psychological treatment for voices in psychosis

Til Wykes
Institute of Psychiatry, Kings College, London, UK

Hearing voices is often one of the most distressing aspects associated with a diagnosis of psychosis. These voices are often resistant to medication treatments. This review article discusses the development of complementary approaches to the treatment of voices—psychological and particularly cognitive treatments. It is clear that there are psychological rather than merely physical factors associated with the occurrence of, and distress caused by, voices. These factors can be engaged in the process of psychological therapy in order to reduce the distress that they cause and improve quality of life.

Psychological therapies have produced some improvements but very few have shown durable effects. Most psychological therapies have been individual with an emphasis on cognitive behavioural approaches. This paper describes the development of a new approach—group cognitive treatment—that might provide further success either as a single therapy for voices or as a complement to individual approaches. This type of therapy builds on the therapies and supports provided within the consumer movement as well as harnessing group and cognitive facilitators for change in beliefs. Some evidence is provided about the usefulness of such therapy in the health services. In addition, the evaluation of treatments for specific symptoms, particularly the appropriate outcome measures is discussed.

Apart from cognitive deficits, hearing voices is one of the earliest signs of likely psychosis and one of the main causes of distress to people with a diagnosis of schizophrenia. There is evidence that these voices can persist even after adequate levels of medication have been prescribed in 25–50% patients (Pantellis & Barnes, 1996) and these treatment-resistant voices are a major concern to both patients and their relatives. This paper is concerned with the developments of complementary psychological approaches to the treatment of voices, which have mainly been investigated in groups of people with treatment-resistant voices. Psychological treatment options are popular with both patients and their relatives and although this review is not a systematic meta-analysis it will draw together the evidence on the efficacy of the various treatments in order that a more measured approach to provision can be taken. Assessing the effects

---

Correspondence should be addressed to Professor Til Wykes, Department of Psychology, PO box 77, Institute of Psychiatry, De Crespigny Park, London SE5 8AF; e-mail:t.wykes@iop.kcl.ac.uk

of the therapy is not always a simple matter, as different outcomes will be valued by different groups. Health service professionals may emphasise the reduction in absolute symptoms on a scale, health service managers will emphasise the effects on use of psychiatric services, patients will want reductions in distress, and their relatives may wish to see the patient happier and having a better quality of life. The review will therefore also consider which outcomes should be measured in future studies and how new outcomes might inform both the theory behind, and future developments of, therapeutic approaches to voices.

What are voices and how many people hear them?

This review is taking a categorical rather than a dimensional approach to diagnosis and will concentrate on those people with a diagnosis of schizophrenia. There are a number of reasons for this, in my case, unusual stance and these would take much time in explaining. Therefore, the reader will have to accept that this is a pragmatic approach and that some but not all of my observations on the literature will also be relevant to people with other diagnoses. Because of this categorical approach I have turned to DSM-IV (American Psychological Association, 1994) for a description of auditory hallucinations. Voices in schizophrenia are described here as perceptions in the absence of a stimulus which are distinct from thoughts, whose content is variable but often pejorative and threatening, and which occur in the context of a clear sensorium. These criteria seem relatively clear-cut but evidence from studies of voices treatment and phenomenological data suggest problems with all of them. The most striking difficulty is the change in the perception of the voice over time. Sometimes the voices do appear to be actual people in the same room or a different place but occurring outside the head. Sometimes they are inside the head and possibly being transmitted there by an unseen force and on other occasions the person is unclear whether the voices are indeed his or her own thoughts or may switch between these explanations. Although perceptions may change over time (and be described as "changes in insight") they may indeed occur at the same time for different voices. The content of the voices also changes over time, with some people feeling that the voice is positive and helpful, or there may be changes in the content over very brief periods of time or between different voices at the same time. Finally, voices are most often heard when the person is alone and this is most likely to occur at night just before sleep, which may suggest an unclear sensorium. Many of these variations occur in the absence of evidence for changes in medication, either in prescription or adherence. The fact that there is evidence of changes in voices even when they are described as treatment-resistant shows that they are still malleable and that there is room for optimism in their treatment.

Not only is there evidence of variation in the phenomenology of voices as described by people with a diagnosis of schizophrenia but there is also evidence that "voices" are experienced by people in the general population who have never had contact with the psychiatric services. Even though Sidgewick, more than a century ago in the *Proceedings of the Society for Psychical Research*, had reported that hallucinations were common in normal populations, this information only achieved prominence after a television programme in the Netherlands. On this programme, a Professor of Social Psychiatry, Marius Romme, appeared with one of his patients and discussed alternative views of the experience of voices. Following the programme more than 500 people wrote in to report that they experienced voices and 35% of these had no psychiatric history.

The rate of hearing voices differs between different studies and is most obviously dependent on the type of question asked, with some studies producing figures for lifetime prevalence (e.g. Tien, 1991) whereas others produce a point prevalence (Johns, Nazroo, Bebbington, & Kuipers, 2002a). The lifetime prevalence figures vary widely between 10% and 39% and one recent study by Johns et al. (2002a) may provide some explanation for this variation. This study used data collected in a survey of over 8000 people in the Fourth National Survey of Ethnic Minorities conducted between 1993 and 1995. The survey explored the experiences of ethnic minorities living in England and Wales, and covered mental health, general health, and social variables. Caribbean, Indian, African, Asian, Pakistani, Bangladeshi, and Chinese ethnic minorities were represented in the sample as well as 2800 white respondents. The questions asked in the survey were ones that would provide the point prevalence, rather than the lifetime risk of hearing voices. In the white sample the rate was 4%, but this rate varied with ethnic group; the Caribbean sample's rate being 2.5 times higher and the rate for Asian respondents being half the rate for the white respondents. The differences between groups may explain the variation in rates between different studies carried out with different cultural groups.

Only 25% of the people experiencing auditory hallucinations in the Johns et al. (2002a) study sample fulfilled the criteria for psychosis, so variation is not dependent on the prevalence of psychosis in these groups. As well as differences across the general population there are also differences in experiences between individual diagnostic groups, and between people with a diagnosis of schizophrenia and the general population. The main ones to emerge seem to be the beliefs adopted as explanations for the voices and the distress experienced (Davies, Griffin, & Vice, 2001; Peters, Day, McKenna, & Orbach, 1999). Even within the group of people with a diagnosis of schizophrenia there seem to be differences between those who experience voices and those who do not. For instance, Delespaul, de Vires, & Van Os (2002) show that anxiety levels are raised concomitantly with the experience of an auditory hallucination. A further difference may be the attributions of power that patients give to voices and their actual content. Honig et al. (1998) found that the form of hallucinations was the same in different people who experienced auditory hallucinations but were from different diagnostic groups. However, the content, emotional quality, and locus of control differed for people with a diagnosis of schizophrenia. A similar result was found by Johns, Hemsley, & Kuipers (2002b) in a comparison with tinnitus. For further details of other cognitive differences that may underlie the experience of voices see David (2004) and Seal, Aleman, & McGuire (2004), this issue.

Why develop psychological treatment?

Some of the papers in this special issue describe brain imaging and cognitive changes associated with the experience of voices in the hope of building models to explain the phenomenon. However, it is clear from the information presented above that hearing voices is also influenced by social factors (shown by cultural differences), personal beliefs and attributions, previous experiences, such as trauma (e.g., Mueser, Rosenberg, Goodman, & Trumbetta, 2002), as well as the coping styles adopted following the experience of voices (Carter, Mackinnon, & Copolov, 1996). All these factors suggest that a treatment approach that is not biologically based may be helpful. Some of the early psychological approaches were also related to specific cognitive changes that were thought to underlie the abnormal perception. However, theory-driven studies have been rare and most have adopted a pragmatic approach with less attention paid to a detailed test of specific hypotheses.

Brief history of nondrug treatments for auditory hallucinations

Psychological treatments for auditory hallucinations have followed the general trends for treatments developed for other disorders, such as panic, anxiety, and depression. Initially, there was a concentration on behavioural therapies with the later introduction of therapy that depended on cognitive models. The most recent therapies have melded the two approaches to form cognitive behavioural therapy (CBT).

Early behavioural approaches concentrated on providing competing stimuli for the hallucination so that attention would be diverted from the voices. These methods were diverse and included simple thought-stopping techniques, such as pulling an elastic band on the wrist whenever a voice was heard, to higher levels of stimulation, including punishment. Apart from the ethical issues related to these therapeutic techniques the evidence for their efficacy was very sparse. Some controlled studies showed temporary improvements but these were rarely replicated and any improvements tended to disappear once the therapy had concluded. Slade (1990) in a review of intervention studies showed that the improvements following these techniques tended to be the equivalent of the improvements made from keeping a diary of hallucinatory activity. In other words, the self-monitoring which is part of the assessment of therapy is an intervention in itself and needs to be controlled for as part of any investigation of treatment effectiveness. This is also an issue for other forms of therapy, including pharmacotherapy for voices.

Auditory hallucinations are also associated with increases in anxiety and recent data suggest that this anxiety increases prior to the experience as well as being a result of the abnormal perception (Delespaul et al., 2002). These emotional changes were used much earlier by Slade (1976) to develop interventions specifically for the anxiety as part of a functional analysis of hallucination occurrence. In his patients, social anxiety seemed most relevant and when this was reduced there was also a reduction in the frequency of auditory hallucinations.

Later interventions more often depended on theoretical frameworks of brain function in schizophrenia. For instance, Green (1978) suggested that there is a problem of transferring information between one hemisphere and the other and that this deficit interferes with speech comprehension. Green also noticed that for those who had a right ear advantage (better comprehension when speech is presented to the right rather than left ear), wearing an ear plug in the left ear led to increased levels of speech comprehension compared to binaural listening. It was also noticed that there were reductions in the frequency of the hallucinations when these studies were carried out. The subsequent case study data from the introduction of ear plugs as therapy showed some dramatic effects on the frequency of hallucinations. A further controlled study by Done et al. (1986) also showed improvements. However, this study also provided evidence that the therapy did not work as suggested by the theory, because some patients returned with two ear plugs and others had switched the ear plug to the right ear as this seemed to be more effective. Again, on stopping use of the ear plug the voices returned to their usual frequency.

Other theories also suggest that there is a relationship between the monitoring of inner speech and the occurrence of voices (e.g., Frith, 1992). Some initial studies suggested a specific relationship with subvocal activity, which although unknown to the patients reflected the content of the hallucination. Green and Kinsbourne (1989, 1990) tested whether the suppression of such activity would reduce the frequency of hallucinations. In a controlled study, they compared an active condition (humming) with four other conditions that were designed to use different musculature, but would not necessarily use the same system as in subvocalisation. The results showed that only in the humming condition were hallucinations significantly reduced compared to baseline. Although the authors suggest that this effect was specific it might also be explained by the effect on the attentional resources of the patients as the humming condition could arguably be said to require more processing resources.

Another method of monitoring inner speech was developed by Richard Bentall. He approached the problem directly by developing a therapy whose aim was to try to get patients to accept that their hallucinations resulted from their own thoughts. Bentall's therapy was known as "focusing" (Bentall, Haddock,

& Slade, 1994). Patients were taught to monitor their own speech, for instance, to begin to concentrate on the physical attributes of the voices, and were then encouraged to attribute the voices to their own thoughts. In this small study, some patients did show improvements but a later randomised controlled trial showed that focusing therapy was as beneficial in reducing the frequency of hallucinations as simple distraction, so had no specific therapeutic effect (Haddock, Slade, Bentall, Reid, & Faragher, 1998).

These earlier therapies all targeted one outcome, namely a reduction in the frequency of hallucinations. It was argued that as hallucinations in people with schizophrenia were associated with distress and low self-esteem, the reductions in auditory hallucination frequency would reduce the negative consequences for the patient. But during the mid 1990s further studies of phenomenology found that the negative consequences of voices were not only dependent on their frequency but also on the associated beliefs about the voices. Birchwood and Chadwick (1997) and Chadwick and Birchwood (1994, 1995) suggest that the level of distress experienced was related to the perceived power and/or omnipotence of the voices rather than just their frequency. It has been suggested that omnipotence is also related to the likelihood of acting on command hallucinations (Cheung, Schweitzer, Crowley, & Tuckwell, 1997). This then led to a new target for treatment—changing the beliefs about voices. But before investigating these new therapies in more detail it is essential to investigate responses to voices more naturalistically. People who experience these abnormal perceptions do not do so in a vacuum and are not passive in their responses. It is by investigating their response too that an adequate and acceptable mode of treatment can be developed.

Consumer approaches to voices

The majority of studies of voices have concentrated on phenomenology, but there have also been more detailed studies of responses to voices, in order to ascertain if there are particular strategies which are universally beneficial. O'Sullivan (1994) reported that about 78% of the strategies in current use by his participants were those that they had devised themselves and that the only strategy suggested by their doctors had been "taking medication". It is therefore important to consider such strategies and whether they help or hinder recovery. Surveys of coping strategies have divided them into various categories depending on the theoretical orientation of the investigators at the time. One of the earliest studies was by Falloon and Talbot (1981) who reported on 40 patients who experienced voices at least every day. Their three categories of coping consisted of behavioural responses, a modification of sensory input, and cognitive techniques. Behavioural techniques consisted usually of increases in behaviour (e.g., walking, watching TV), changes to the sensory modality were relaxation techniques, and cognitive techniques consisted of distraction and emptying the mind of all thoughts. Falloon and Talbot concluded that successful coping appeared to result from the systematic application of widely used coping strategies and there were individual differences in both the number and type of strategies used and whether these were successful. Similar coping techniques have been identified in a number of studies (Carter et al., 1996; Nayani & David, 1996; O'Sullivan, 1994; Romme, Honig, Noorthhoorn, & Escher, 1992) although they tended to be grouped under different headings. Using multi-dimensional scaling Carter et al. (1996) identified three distinct dimensions of coping, with 69% of the sample showing some success using one or more of these strategies. Techniques in the largest cluster shared a number of characteristics: the patient plays an active role and there is a high preponderance of the use of speech or subvocal activity. In contrast to Falloon and Talbot, Carter and colleagues found relationships between efficacy and the specific use of some strategies. Following Green and Kinsbourne (1989), humming was a highly efficacious strategy although few people had tried it. Most studies of coping strategies have not taken into account any cultural issues and have tended to report on homogenous samples with western backgrounds. However, Wahass and Kent (1997) have reported on differences between the coping of patients from Saudi Arabia and Britain. In their survey the majority of Saudi Arabian patients used strategies associated with their religion whereas UK patients were more likely to use distraction or physiologically based approaches.

Although there is no current published evidence, clinical data from my own studies of voices (e.g., Wykes, Parr, & Landau, 1999) seem to show that coping strategies differ along a number of dimensions in addition to the descriptions given of the specific behaviours. For instance, strategies that are described, as "active" or "problem solving" often require more cognitive effort than "passive" strategies. Even some strategies described as distraction seem to differ in the amount of cognitive effort, with concentration on an alternative new activity taking up more resources than strategies that are repetitive and automatic (e.g., knitting). These levels of effort interact with the severity of the hallucinatory experience so that patients report that using music over headphones seems to be effective when the severity of the voices is low, but that it loses efficacy as voices become louder and more frequent. Activities that are most effective are often difficult to employ when the voices become intrusive and at these times only passive activities (such as sleeping and spending time alone) are possible. The majority of surveys are only cross-sectional and so never capture these sorts of relationships.

New cognitive approaches to therapy for voices and their evaluation

The recent developments of therapies for voices have depended on the notion that the effects of abnormal experiences, such as hallucinations, may be interpreted as resulting from the process of appraisal and subsequent beliefs about that abnormal experience. Unlike most of the previous therapies they pay close attention to the content of the voices and the target for therapy is the reduction in distress. The effectiveness of therapy has been associated with the development of more detailed psychological approaches to the measurement of the hallucinatory experience compared to previous scales. For example, the PSE (Wing, Cooper, & Satorius, 1974) and the BPRS-E (Ventura, Green, Shaner, & Liberman, 1993) are limited in their ability to reflect changes in these experiences. Three main measures exist which can be used as subtle measures of changes in experience. The first is the Mental Health Research Institute Unusual Perceptions Schedule (MUPS; Carter, Mackinnon, Howard, Zeegers, & Copolov, 1995), which is a lengthy schedule covering aspects of the experience, such as the number of voices, their volume, tone, location, as well as beliefs and coping strategies. This is rather long for an outcome assessment instrument and a much shorter self-report instrument containing similar information was developed by Gillian Haddock and colleagues and is called the Psychotic Symptom Rating Scales (PSYRATS; Haddock, McCarron, Tarrier, & Faragher, 1999). This scale is in two parts, one concentrating on auditory hallucinations and the other specifically on delusions. It is short and covers aspects of beliefs as well as the physical properties of the voices and the levels of distress experienced. It has a total score that may be used as a simple outcome measure for the evaluation of treatment. One further scale that is of use not necessarily as an outcome measure, but to test the mode of operation of therapy is the Beliefs about Voices Questionnaire (BAVQ-R). This questionnaire emphasises the importance of the beliefs about the omnipotence of the voice. In their study of 100 participants who hear voices, 86% endorsed the question: "My voice is very powerful" and three quarters also said that: "I cannot control my voices". In addition nearly four fifths thought that: "My voices seem to know everything about me" (Chadwick, Lees, & Birchwood, 2000). Often the evidence for this belief is that the voice seems to know what the person is thinking.

The use of these rating scales changes the focus of effectiveness, as the voices themselves may not reduce in frequency, but the characteristics of the voices may change making them less aversive and distressing. These voices, in other words, may have the same characteristics as those experienced by people in the nonpsychiatric population. The approaches vary but most of them provide therapy on a one-to-one basis. However, recent studies have emphasised group approaches to treatment, which also show some promise.

Coping strategy approaches

There are a number of reasons why coping strategy approaches have been adopted and these are summarised in Tarrier (2002). Apart from the obvious finding that people with schizophrenia make effortful attempts to overcome or cope with their persistent psychotic symptoms, coping strategies are seen as positive personal characteristics in the vulnerability-stress model of schizophrenia. An increase in these characteristics would increase resistance to psychotic decompensation. But the ways of increasing coping strategies have varied. Simple techniques try to increase coping strategies through a psycho-educational approach, whereas more sophisticated techniques try to understand the context in which the voices appear and use a behavioural analysis to devise an agreed corpus of coping strategies with the patient. These functional analyses have more recently incorporated cognitive mechanisms, as in the sorts of therapies devised to treat panic disorders. Usually, the simpler psycho-educational approaches are provided as part of a programme that includes other aspects of therapy and so it is hard to distinguish their specific effects.

Coping strategy enhancement (CSE) has, however, been described in detail and rigorously evaluated (Tarrier et al., 1990, 1993). This procedure identifies coping strategies which are already established in the patient's repertoire and through cognitive and behavioural methods develops further strategies in response to any psychotic symptom, including auditory hallucinations. In a small controlled trial that compared problem solving with CSE, the results were equivocal (i.e., both interventions produced positive effects so were amalgamated into one intervention). Later studies showed that this new therapy was more effective than supportive counselling and standard care in reducing overall symptoms. However, there was no specific effect on hallucinations, which the authors suggest are more difficult to change than delusions.

Changing beliefs

A therapy that has been successfully developed for changing beliefs is cognitive behaviour therapy (CBT). There are now more than 15 published studies of CBT, mainly for patients with resistant symptoms (e.g., Gould, Mueser, Bolton, Mays, & Goff, 2001; Pilling et al., 2002). Although these trials vary in their methodological rigour, the style of the CBT and the length of treatment, the most recent reviews suggest an improvement in general symptomatology with an effect size of about 0.65. But their success is limited and few studies show any improvements in hallucinations, particularly following the initial therapy window.

The majority of these cognitive therapies are one to one, with an emphasis on individual case formulation, and are relatively long term (i.e., about 20 sessions). The therapists are also highly trained in the majority of the studies. However, recent evidence from Turkington et al. (2002) suggests that CBT skills can be learned in a relatively short period of time by nursing staff. Even with the limitations of these one to one therapies in terms of translation into health care outcomes, for hallucinations there are few positive findings.

An alternative approach may be to provide CBT as part of a group. This would allow more people to be treated, although this form of therapy also requires high levels of therapeutic skills not only in cognitive therapy but also in facilitating groups. There is some evidence that CBT can be provided in groups. Morrison (2001) in a review of group CBT suggests that for depression and social anxiety, group treatment seems to provide as much improvement as individual therapy. Intensive group CBT (i.e., short treatments with longer sessions), produces slightly less improvement than longer therapies. However, there was an advantage in cost-effectiveness as more people could be treated over the same period of time with fewer therapists. Individual therapy does seem to provide the better therapeutic option for one disorder: Obsessive-compulsive disorder.

In general, group treatment is associated with some advantages and some disadvantages, as well as some specific issues relating directly to the provision of CBT for psychosis.

The disadvantages include:

- the differential rates of change between individuals, which means that some people can be left behind while others get bored with any repetition;
- the possibility that an individual can monopolise the proceedings or that confrontation can take place between attendees particularly when discussing different explanations of the same phenomenon;
- reluctance to discuss beliefs within the group because they are embarrassing or personal.

As noted above, these require high levels of skill by the group facilitator and groups do not require any less skill in terms of CBT than their one-to-one counterpart.

There are also some likely benefits to the provision of group CBT that might outweigh these potential disadvantages. People experiencing voices often report the loneliness that the voices produce. Not only does the experience sometimes rob the person of the concentration necessary to continue a conversation with others, the pejorative nature of the voices not only reduces self-esteem but can encourage social isolation by suggestions about the actions or intentions of others. Groups may be able to reduce these effects and combat the feelings of isolation that voice hearers report. They may enable people to:

- Share experiences, which facilitate testing and reframing of experiences (this is particularly important as, within the group, there will be a wide variety of explanations for the same abnormal perception);
- identify common factors that increase and decrease their experiences (such as finding out when the voices are more or less frequent);
- Share natural coping strategies to increase the coping repertoire (instead of the therapist having to make suggestions, the other members of the group can share their own effective strategies).

Groups also have a built-in social support, which can enable people to practice their social skills in a "safe" environment. Group treatment for voices is also appealing because the anomalous experiences reported by different people with voices are very similar to each other in form even if the explanations of their cause are different. These anomalous experiences are also relatively frequent and so it is easy to describe them. This is not true for delusions. The anomalous experiences associated with the delusion may have appeared a long time ago and only experiences associated with the maintenance of the delusion may be available. It is therefore difficult to envisage a group therapy in psychosis that could provide these sorts of homogenous experiences for anything other than hallucinations.

Apart from these issues, perhaps the most important reason for beginning a group for voice hearers is that people who hear voices report that talking about them is helpful. For instance, a young voice hearer, Michael, aged 16 years, reported on a TV programme in 2002 (UK Channel 4, *Inside My Head*, June 2002) that what brings the voices to a halt is talking to someone. Group therapy for voices is not new and has been part of some consumer organisations' provision for many years, such as the UK Hearing Voices Network. But provision within the health services has not been so forward looking and evaluations have been sparse.

Most published evaluations of group treatments for voices have shown beneficial effects but most are uncontrolled, in that they just investigated a cohort of patients at the beginning and the end of treatment (Chadwick et al., 2000; Gledhill, Lobban, & Selwood, 1998; Perlman & Hubbard, 2000; Trygstad et al., 2002). Previous work by Slade (1990) suggests that merely asking people to monitor their voices, irrespective of the specific treatment, is likely to decrease their occurrence. Therefore, studies that make comparisons with a waiting list period or, better still, a separate group that receive no treatment or an alternative treatment, are required to show clinical efficacy. However, uncontrolled studies do provide evidence of the feasibility and acceptability of this form of treatment. Most people in the studies reported that they were able to talk about their voices in the group after the first two or three sessions and there are no reports of problems in facilitating the groups. The majority of the patients improved either in terms of their distress, the frequency of their voices or some change in their beliefs about the voices; however, few statistical tests were carried out. For instance, Perlman and Hubbard (2000) reported that seven out of nine clients reported improved symptom control and Chadwick et al. (2000), in the largest of these studies, showed significant reductions in conviction of beliefs about the omnipotence of voices, and improved control.

These uncontrolled studies show the difficulty in trying to identify an outcome measure that can represent change in what is a variable experience. Some people may find that the voices occur infrequently but are very distressing when they do occur. Others report that the voices are not too distressing but distract the person from activities that they would like to carry out (e.g., watching television). The choice of an outcome measure that can reflect change with this variation is limited but not impossible. The hallucinations measure on the PSYRATS Scale (Haddock et al., 1999) does take all these dimensions into account and can therefore provide a more subtle measure of change. Wykes et al. (1999) used it in one of the few studies that had a controlled design (waiting list controls). They found significant improvements in voice frequency, severity, and insight over the treatment period compared to a waiting list period. Some of these improvements, but not all, were maintained at follow-up. A further study, using a randomised control design, has now completed recruitment and will be able to test more rigorously the clinical efficacy of group treatment.

ARE GROUPS FEASIBLE?

In order for therapies to be adopted in the health services they need to be acceptable to patients. The skills should be transferable to a variety of health care professionals in the health services. Both uncontrolled and controlled studies suggest that people who use the voices groups are not only satisfied with them but feel that they have gained benefit from their attendance (even if this has not been tested statistically). In our current randomised control trial (RCT), 79% of patients attended for at least five of the seven sessions, a high level compared to drop outs or noncompliance with other therapies.

In a small, unpublished study the transfer of the skills necessary to run the group was tested using nurses who were offered 8 hours of training (4 of these hours being spent in groups themselves). Rating scales of CBT skills were used, as well as ratings of the use of the protocol (Ehntholt, 2000). The results showed that the skills of the nurses were equivalent to those of the experienced therapists (85% vs. 83%). In addition, the novices actually tended to stick to the protocol more often than the experts (78 % vs. 96%). This evidence suggests that the skills can be transferred, although evidence on the effectiveness of the skill transfer on the voice hearers will only be available at the end of the current RCT.

Psychological treatments are expected to provide a relatively brief input for long lasting effects. This is an expectation never expressed of a medication in psychiatry. Indeed, for a chronic condition, such as schizophrenia, the fact that the symptoms reassert themselves after the removal of medication (a relapse) seems to be evidence that the medication works, whereas the same state of affairs in psychological treatments seems to imply that the psychological treatment has failed. A change in the way that the efficacy of psychological treatment is assessed is necessary, particularly for the symptom of voices in a treatment-resistant group (i.e., a group where the stimulus for a voice occurs frequently). In other words, if there is an improvement in voices following treatment then this is evidence of efficacy even if this improvement disappears during follow-up. A loss of effects over the follow-up period just suggests that maintenance therapy should be considered. For instance, treatment in a closed group does produce initial change but consideration should be given for repeated dosing at intervals following this intensive period of input.

Why would group CBT work?

There are a variety of benefits from group treatment that may affect the operation of the mechanisms for the maintenance of hallucinations, some of which differ from those of individual treatment. Fowler, Garety, & Kuipers (1998) set out four key factors that are important for successful CBT. These are: successful engagement, collaborative discussion of a shared formulation of the client's beliefs, cognitive restructuring of delusional interpretations, and work on negative evaluations of the self and others. Group CBT for voices seems to engage clients quickly as voice hearers realise that their own experiences are not idiosyncratic and most clients begin to discuss their experiences at the first group. Many people are surprised that the experiences related by others are so similar and they report that they find talking about their voices in such a group easier than talking in any other context, even to other involved health professionals. This enabling process also helps people to begin to discuss specific beliefs about the voices.

Although individuals do not discuss a shared formulation with the therapist, particularly the more distal factors that may have an effect, the group does allow individuals to build up a shared group formulation that encompasses not only factors that affect the occurrence of hallucinations, but also those that may decrease their frequency or the distress that they cause. This formulation is shared amongst the group and individuals can emphasise some factors rather than others in their own personal view. The groups also seem to enable the discussion and testing of different beliefs as different explanations are given by individuals for the same anomalous experience. Finally, the group also offers the experience of positive evaluations by others. The protocol developed by Wykes et al. (1999) emphasises the importance of increasing self-esteem and one session is also set aside to deal with this specific issue. Groups may be more enabling of these positive evaluations by others because they can first be offered within the group itself, whereas this opportunity is not available in individual CBT.

All the key CBT factors can be provided within a group format but groups may provide additional therapeutic opportunities. They may help to reduce anxiety through the presentation of a normative view of hallucinations (i.e., that many people have similar experiences). This reduction in anxiety is a factor identified by Delespaul et al. (2002) as an immediate precursor to hallucinatory experiences and was also suggested many years ago by Slade (1976) as an important part of the functional analysis of voices. Therefore, a reduction in anxiety may have a direct effect on the actual frequency of the voices.

Groups also provide a forum for the practice of social skills, which may reduce social isolation and increase confidence for further social interaction. From my own clinical experience it has not been uncommon for individuals to form supportive relationships within the group that continue after the group has ceased. The increase in social interaction may have two main effects. The first is a direct effect on the frequency of voices, as many individuals report that voices are reduced when they are involved in meaningful social interaction. The second possible effective route is to allow more opportunities to test out beliefs that help to maintain the voices and provide positive experiences of self-worth that may have an indirect effect on the attributions that lead to pejorative interpretations of abnormal perceptions.

Coping skills to deal with the distress of voices, to prevent voices from occurring, and to increase socially appropriate behaviours are also the focus of the group. Natural coping strategies (i.e., those developed by group members through experience) tend to have more approbation than those suggested by therapists. The usefulness of strategies can also be tested in different situations and by different people so that a range of responses can be discussed. This is helpful because a map of therapeutic efficacy can then be drawn up allowing clients to acknowledge that not every strategy works every time and for every person. This should encourage the use of a variety of strategies that has been shown to be helpful in previous studies (Carter et al., 1996; Falloon & Talbot, 1981).

Groups do have a direct effect on beliefs about the voices. Both Wykes et al. (1999) and Chadwick et al. (2000) report that beliefs about the powerfulness of voices were affected. In the Wykes study, it was possible to show that changes in beliefs about voices led directly to improvements in levels of distress. Group CBT for voices therefore can add to the therapeutic effects of individual CBT. Groups may not be suitable for everyone and individual CBT must also be available for those whose beliefs are too disturbing to discuss, except in a more supportive individual relationship. Individual CBT could also be complementary to group work where the client has been introduced to the new ways of thinking about their beliefs but needs some further work, particularly on possible distal factors affecting their current experience.

CONCLUSIONS

There is ample evidence that factors other than biology have an effect on the experience of auditory hallucinations. As many people with psychosis also suffer from hallucinations despite the prescription of adequate antipsychotic medication, the development of alternative treatments (e.g., psychological treatment) seems obvious. Many psychological treatments for hallucinations have been shown to be helpful although few of the effects are long lived. The latest individual CBT treatments have proved to be beneficial to overall symptom levels but few have shown specific effects on hallucinations. Group CBT has shown some promise. However, in order to test these interactions further there must be an agreement on what are the appropriate outcome measures to test. The PYRATS scale, which takes into account a number of different variables to form its total score, does seem appropriate as a proximal measure of the specific effect of treatment. However, the mechanism of action of group treatment is still to be determined and therefore factors, such as levels of coping strategies, the influence of social behaviour and self-esteem also need to be measured in any future trial, as well as effects on the specific belief systems. Although service providers may wish to see the effects of treatments on the use of services, it seems more appropriate, when identifying the effects of treatments for voices, to concentrate specifically on the direct effects on the voices and quality of life (outcomes emphasised by service users and their relatives) as it is unlikely that this specific treatment alone will have effects on hospital bed use in the near future.

Manuscript accepted 10 January 2003

REFERENCES

American Psychological Association (1994). *Diagnostic and statistical manual for the mental disorders* (4th ed.). Author: Washington, DC.

Bentall, R. P., Haddock, G., & Slade, P. D. (1994). Cognitive behaviour therapy for persistent auditory hallucinations: From theory to therapy. *Behaviour Therapy, 25,* 51–66.

Birchwood, M., & Chadwick, P. (1997). The omnipotence of voices: Testing the validity of a cognitive model. *Psychological Medicine, 27,* 1345–1353.

Carter, D. M., Mackinnon, A., & Copolov, D. (1996). Patients' strategies for coping with auditory hallucinations. *Journal of Nervous & Mental Disease, 184,* 159–164.

Carter, D. M., Mackinnon, A., Howard, S., Zeegers, T., & Copolov, D. (1995). The development and reliability of the Mental Health Research Institute Unusual Perceptions Schedule (MUPS): An instrument to record auditory hallucinatory experience. *Schizophrenia Research, 16,* 157–165.

Chadwick, P., & Birchwood, M. (1994). The omnipotence of voices. A cognitive approach to auditory hallucinations. *British Journal of Psychiatry, 164,* 190–201.

Chadwick, P., & Birchwood, M. (1995). The omnipotence of voices: II. The Beliefs About Voices Questionnaire (BAVQ). *British Journal of Psychiatry, 166,* 773–776.

Chadwick, P., Lees, S., & Birchwood, M. (2000). The revised Beliefs About Voices Questionnaire (BAVQ-R). *British Journal of Psychiatry, 177,* 229–232.

Cheung, P., Schweitzer, I., Crowley, K., & Tuckwell, V. (1997). Violence in schizophrenia: Role of hallucinations and delusions. *Schizophrenia Research, 26,* 181–190.

David, A. S. (2004). The cognitive neuropsychiatry of auditory verbal hallucinations: An overview. *Cognitive Neuropsychiatry, 9*(1/2), 107–123.

Davies, M. F., Griffin, M., & Vice, S. (2001). Affective reactions to auditory hallucinations in psychotic, evangelical and control groups. *British Journal of Clinical Psychology, 40,* 361–370.

Delespaul, P., de Vires, M., & van Os, J. (2002). Determinants of occurrence and recovery from hallucinations in daily life. *Social Psychiatry and Psychiatric Epidemiology, 37,* 97–104.

Done, D. J., Frith, C. D., & Owens, D. C. (1986). Reducing persistent auditory hallucinations by wearing an ear-plug. *British Journal of Clinical Psychology, 25,* 151–152.

Ehntholt, K. (2001). *Evaluation of a CBT group treatment for in-patients with auditory hallucinations: A pilot study.* D.Clin. Psych. Thesis, Kings College, London.

Falloon, I. R., & Talbot, R. E. (1981). Persistent auditory hallucinations: Coping mechanisms and implications for management. *Psychological Medicine, 11,* 329–339.

Fowler, D., Garety, P., & Kuipers, E. (1998). Understanding the inexplicable: An individually formulated cognitive approach to delusional beliefs. In C. Perris & P. D. McGorry (Eds.), *Cognitive psychotherapy of psychotic and personality disorders: Handbook of theory and practice* (pp. 129–146). Chichester, UK: John Wiley.

Frith, C. D. (1992). *The cognitive neuropsychology of schizophrenia.* Hove, UK: Psychology Press.

Gledhill, A., Lobban, F., & Sellwood, W. (1998). Group CBT for people with schizophrenia: A preliminary evaluation. *Behavioural and Cognitive Psychotherapy, 26,* 63–75.

Gould, R. A., Mueser, K. T., Bolton, E., Mays, V., & Goff, D. (2001). Cognitive therapy for psychosis in schizophrenia: An effect size analysis. *Schizophrenia Research, 48,* 335–342.

Green, M. F., & Kinsbourne, M. (1989). Auditory hallucinations in schizophrenia: Does humming help? *Biological Psychiatry, 25,* 633–635.

Green, M. F., & Kinsbourne, M. (1990). Subvocal activity and auditory hallucinations: Clues for behavioural treatments? *Schizophrenia Bulletin, 16,* 617–625.

Green, P. (1978). Inter-hemispheric transfer in schizophrenia: Recent developments. *Behavioural Psychotherapy, 6,* 105–110.

Haddock, G., McCarron, J., Tarrier, N., & Faragher, E. B. (1999). Scales to measure dimensions of hallucinations and delusions: The psychotic symptom rating scales (PSYRATS). *Psychological Medicine, 291,* 879–889.

Haddock, G., Slade, P. D., Bentall, R. P., Reid, D., & Faragher, E. B. (1998). A comparison of the long-term effectiveness of distraction and focusing in the treatment of auditory hallucinations. *British Journal of Medical Psychology, 71,* 339–349.

Honig, A., Romme, M., Ensink, B., Escher, S., Penning, M., & de Vires, M. (1998). Auditory hallucinations: A comparison between patients and non-patients. *Journal of Nervous & Mental Disease, 186,* 646–651.

Johns, L., Hemsley, D., & Kuipers, E. (2002b). A comparison of auditory hallucinations in psychiatric and non-psychiatric group. *British Journal of Clinical Psychology, 41,* 81–86.

Johns, L. C., Nazroo, J. Y., Bebbington, P., & Kuipers, E. (2002a). Occurrence of hallucinatory experiences in a community sample and ethnic variations. *British Journal of Psychiatry, 180,* 174–178.

Morrison, N. (2001). Group Cognitive Therapy: Treatment of choice or sub-optimal option? *Behavioural and Cognitive Psychotherapy, 29,* 311–332.

Mueser, K. T., Rosenberg, S. D., Goodman, L. A., & Trumbetta, S. L. (2002). Trauma, PTSD, and the course of severe mental illness: An interactive model. *Schizophrenia Research, 53,* 123–143.

Nayani, T. H., & David, A. S. (1996). The auditory hallucination: A phenomenological survey. *Psychological Medicine, 26,* 177–189.

O'Sullivan, K. (1994). Dimensions of coping with auditory hallucinations. *Journal of Mental Health, 3,* 351–361.

Pantelis, C., & Barnes, T. R. E. (1996). Drug strategies and treatment-resistant schizophrenia. *Australian & New Zealand Journal of Psychiatry, 30,* 20–37.

Pearlman, L. M., & Hubbard, B. A. (2000). A self-control skills group for persistent auditory hallucinations. *Cognitive and Behavioural Practice, 7,* 17–21.

Peters, E., Day, S., McKenna, J., & Orbach, G. (1999). Delusional ideation in religious and psychotic populations. *British Journal of Clinical Psychology, 38,* 83–96.

Pilling, S., Bebbington, P., Kuipers, E., Garety, P., Geddes, J., Orbach, G., & Morgan, C. (2002). Psychological treatments in schizophrenia: I. Meta-analysis of family interventions and cognitive behaviour therapy. *Psychological Medicine, 32,* 763–782.

Romme, M. A., Honig, A., Noorthhoorn, E. O., & Escher, A. D. (1992). Coping with hearing voices: An emancipatory approach. *British Journal of Psychiatry, 161*, 99–103.

Seal, M. L., Aleman, A., & McGuire, P. K. (2004). Compelling imagery, unanticipated speech and deceptive memory: Neurocognitive models of auditory verbal hallucinations in schizophrenia. *Cognitive Neuropsychiatry, 9*(1/2), 43–72.

Slade, P. D. (1976). An investigation of psychological factors involved in the predisposition to auditory hallucinations. *Psychological Medicine, 6*, 123–132. London: Routledge.

Slade, P. D. (1990). The behavioural and cognitive treatment of psychotic symptoms. In R. P. Bentall (Ed.), *Reconstructing schizophrenia* (pp. 234–253).

Tarrier, N. (2002). The use of coping strategies and self-regulation in the treatment of psychosis. In A. P. Morrison (Ed.), *A casebook of cognitive therapy for psychosis* (pp. 79–107). Hove, UK: Brunner-Routledge.

Tarrier, N., Beckett, R., Harwood, S., Baker, A., et al. (1993). A trial of two cognitive-behavioural methods of treating drug-resistant residual psychotic symptoms in schizophrenic patients: I. Outcome. *British Journal of Psychiatry, 162*, 524–532.

Tarrier, N., Harwood, S., Yusopoff, L., Beckett, R., et al. (1990). Coping Strategy Enhancement (CSE): A method of treating residual schizophrenic symptoms. *Behavioural Psychotherapy, 18*, 283–293.

Tien, A. Y. (1991). Distributions of hallucinations in the population. *Social Psychiatry and Psychiatric Epidemiology, 26*, 287–292.

Trygstad, L., Buccheri, R., Dowling, G., Zind, R., White, K., Griffin, J., Henderson, S., Suciu, L., Hippe, S., Kass, M., Covert, C., & Herbert, P. (2002). Behavioural management of persistent auditory hallucinations in schizophrenia: Outcomes from a 10-week course. *Journal of the American Psychiatric Nurses Association, 8*, 84–91.

Turkington, D., Kingdon, D., Turner, T., & the Insight Group (2002). Effectiveness of a brief cognitive behavioural therapy intervention in the treatment of schizophrenia. *British Journal of Psychiatry, 180*, 523–528.

Ventura, J., Green, M., Shaner, A., & Liberman, R. (1993). Training and quality assurance in the Brief Psychiatric Rating Scale: "The drift busters". *International Journal of Methods in Psychiatric Research, 3*, 221–244.

Wahass, S., & Kent, G. (1997). Coping with auditory hallucinations: A cross-cultural comparison between Western (British) and non-Western (Saudi Arabian) patients. *Journal of Nervous & Mental Disease, 185*, 664–668.

Wing, J. K., Cooper, J., & Satorius, N. (1974). *The present state examination.* Cambridge, UK: Cambridge University Press.

Wykes, T., Parr, A., & Landau, S. (1999). Group treatment of auditory hallucinations: Exploratory study of effectiveness. *British Journal of Psychiatry, 175*, 180–185.

Compelling imagery, unanticipated speech and deceptive memory: Neurocognitive models of auditory verbal hallucinations in schizophrenia

Marc L. Seal, Andre Aleman, and Philip K. McGuire
Institute of Psychiatry, UK

Introduction. The application of neurocognitive models to study schizophrenia has been influential in understanding the nature of this complex and heterogeneous disorder. However, a comprehensive and empirically validated account of auditory hallucinations remains elusive. The aim of this review was to critically assess the current evidence for specific neurocognitive deficits associated with auditory verbal hallucinations (AVHs) in schizophrenia.
Methods. A systematic literature search was conducted of research involving three influential cognitive models of auditory hallucinations: those implicating dysfunction in auditory imagery, verbal self-monitoring, and episodic memory.
Results. The findings of the review suggested that AVHs have been associated with impaired verbal self-monitoring, impaired memory for self-generated speech, heightened influence of top-down processing on perception, and an externalising response bias.
Conclusions. On the basis of the findings of the review a multidimensional model of AVHs is proposed incorporating the identified cognitive deficits and biases.

The experience of auditory verbal hallucinations (AVHs) or hearing voices is complex and highly personal (Carter, Mackinnon, Howard, Zeegers, & Copolov, 1995; Nayani & David, 1996; Stephane, Thuras, Nasrallah, & Georgopoulos, 2003). This experience occurs in various forms in a range of neurological and neuropsychiatric conditions as well as the general population. Amongst individuals with mental illness, these experiences are typically unwanted, intrusive, and distressing and often persist despite intensive and prolonged psychopharmacological treatment (Rector & Beck, 2002; Shergill, Murray, & McGuire,

1998). However, despite over a hundred years of psychological investigation, the cognitive mechanisms that transform self-generated mental events into the experience of perceived speech remain unclear Johns & Van Os (2001). Consequently, recent reviews have emphasised the benefits of employing a multidimensional approach to understanding the cognitive processes involved in psychosis. This approach highlights the social and psychological aspects of the experience and emphasises the importance of *cognitive biases* in the generation and maintenance of AVHs (see Beck & Rector, 2003; Garety, Kuipers, Fowler, Freeman, & Bebbington, 2001). These biases are believed to represent maladaptive sets of thinking that have been learnt and, thus, can be modified through therapeutic intervention. Typically, these models describe the evaluation and interpretation of the anomalous perception by the individual. While the nature of the cognitive biases associated with AVHs is becoming increasingly well understood, an account of possible coexisting neurocognitive *deficits* remains elusive. This is not in itself surprising as investigations of neuropsychological signatures of the major syndromes in schizophrenia have failed to find a reliable cognitive marker associated with positive symptoms (Baxter & Liddle, 1998; Zalewski, Johnson-Selfridge, Ohringer, Zarella, & Seltzer, 1998). Nevertheless, the application of neurocognitive models to study abnormal cognition in schizophrenia has been influential in understanding the nature of this complex and heterogeneous disorder (Halligan & David, 2001; Pantelis & Maruff, 2002). These models have been fruitful in increasing understanding of dysfunction in a range of cognitive processes and related brain networks in schizophrenia: working memory (Goldman-Rakic, 1994); semantic processing (Spitzer, 1997); intentional movements (Danckert, Rossetti, d'Amalo, Dalery, & Saoud, 2002; Daprati et al., 1997; Frith, Blakemore, & Wolpert, 2000); and theory of mind (Langdon & Coltheart, 1999).

The aim of this paper is to review the current evidence for a neurocognitive deficit associated with the occurrence of auditory verbal hallucinations in schizophrenia. The empirical evidence for the most influential neurocognitive models will be critically discussed and an attempt made to integrate these findings into a working explanatory model of AVHs.

METHODOLOGY

This review will focus on research conducted on three influential cognitive models of auditory hallucinations: those implicating dysfunction in auditory imagery, verbal self-monitoring, and episodic memory. Each of these approaches is based on established models of cognitive functioning so that it is possible to extrapolate from observed behaviour and cognitive deficits in participants with schizophrenia to the brain networks known to be responsible for these processes (Halligan & David, 2001). While other elegant and appealing cognitive models of auditory hallucinations have also been proposed, particularly in the form of disruption of language processes (Hoffman, 1986, 1999) these models have not generated as much interest or investigation. The evidence supporting the role of subvocal speech in the generation of auditory verbal hallucinations has recently been comprehensively reviewed elsewhere (Stephane, Barton, & Boutros, 2001) and will also not be discussed here. A systematic literature search, using Medline (1966–2002), was conducted, focusing on investigations that specifically tested these models of auditory hallucinations in schizophrenia. The scope of the search was limited to papers published in English.

Auditory imagery

Abnormal auditory verbal imagery is one of the earliest explanations for auditory hallucinations and has seen a resurgence of interest in more recent times. Nearly a century ago Galton (1907/1943) conducted a survey of the Fellows of the Royal Society with the aim of assessing individual differences in the vividness of mental imagery. He identified marked individual differences in the subjective vividness of mental imagery and made the observation that "the number of great men who have been once, twice, or more frequently, subject to hallucinations is considerable" (p.126). It was subsequently postulated that individuals prone to hallucinations experienced particularly vivid and lifelike mental imagery. This experience was theorised to be so convincing that the hallucinating individual would be led to believe that they actually heard a voice speaking; *the vivid imagery* explanation of AVHs.

Selected investigations of the relationship between aberrant auditory imagery and auditory hallucinations in schizophrenia are presented in Table 1. Inspection of the table will reveal that the only study to identify a relationship between vividness of auditory mental imagery and predisposition to auditory hallucinations is the oft-cited Mintz and Alpert (1972) "White Christmas" investigation. Early investigations comparing the phenomenology of reported hallucinations with predominant mental imagery in schizophrenia found no clear relationship between imagery vividness and hallucinations (Coren, 1938; Roman & Landis, 1945). On the contrary, Seitz and Molholm (1947) found that hallucinating subjects actually had *lower* ratings on auditory imagery than other schizophrenia subjects, with the remaining studies reporting equivalent or reduced rates of auditory imagery in hallucinating subjects. These findings led to the contrasting hypothesis that hallucinations in schizophrenia may be the result of individuals possessing *less* vivid auditory imagery than other individuals with schizophrenia (Starker & Jolin, 1982). It was postulated that, if visual imagery was normally the preferred imagery modality of the hallucinating individual then the experience of bizarre imagery in the nonpreferred auditory modality might be confusing and more likely to be misinterpreted as perception (Slade, 1976); the *nonpreferred modality* explanation of AVHs. While there is more empirical

TABLE 1
Mental imagery investigations of auditory hallucinations in schizophrenia

Study	Subjects	Paradigm	Findings	Relationship with symptoms
Coren (1938)	19 SZ 19 CN (all subjects male)	Structured interview measuring the experience of hallucinations and mental imagery		No relationship between hallucinations modality and principal imagery modality in SZ subjects
Roman & Landis (1945)	20 dementia praecox	Instrument measuring the experince of hallucinations and mental imagery	All subjects rated the experience of hallucinations as qualitatively different from mental imagery	No clear relationship between imagery and hallucinations. Individuals prone to auditory and visual hallucinations were predominantly auditory in their mental imagery
Seitz & Molholm (1947)	20 trait Hal 20 trait NH (all Dx SZ)	Test of concrete imagery	SZ and control subjects had the same rating for imagery evoked by a standard set of phrases	Hallucinating subjects had lower ratings on measures of auditory imagery than other SZ and control subjects
Mintz & Alpert (1972)	20 Hal 20 NH (all Dx SZ) 20 general medical inpatients	Rated vividness of auditory imagery ("White Christmas" paradigm)		Hallucinating subjects tended to report higher rates of imagery vividness
Slade (1976)	8 trait Hal 8 trait NH (majority Dx SZ) 16 CN	Battery of psychological instruments measuring vividness of mental imagery, imagery control, and the verbal transformation effect	SZ subjects reported higher mental imagery than controls	No differences between hallucinators and non-hallucinators
Brett & Starker (1977)	20 Hal 20 NH (all male & Dx SZ) 20 general medical inpatients (all male)	Rated vividness of auditory imagery and controllability of auditory imagery	No difference between groups with respect to vividness and controllability of auditory imagery	Hallucinators reported less vivid imagery for items of interpersonal content

Study	Sample	Method	Results	Conclusion
Starker & Jolin (1982)	99 psychiatric inpatients (majority Dx SZ & all male) includes: 36 currently hallucinating 22 previously hallucinating	Rated vividness of auditory imagery and controllability of auditory imagery	No difference between groups with respect to vividness and controllability of auditory imagery	No differences between hallucinators and nonhallucinators
Heilbrun et al. (1983)	16 trait Hal 14 trait NH (majority Dx SZ)	Rated vividness of auditory imagery and preferred imagery modality		Hallucinating subjects showed less preference for auditory mental imagery but no difference in rate of imagery vividness
Chandiramani & Varma (1987)	20 state Hal 20 trait NH (all Dx SZ) 20 CN	Rated vividness of auditory imagery and perceived control over imagery	No differences were observed between groups with respect to the reported vividness or control of mental imagery	Results suggest that hallucinations are not related to vividness of volitional mental imagery
Böcker et al. (2000)	13 trait Hal 19 state NH (all Dx SZ) 14 CN	Subjects completed a measure of imagery vividness involving an interaction between imagery and perception		Hallucinating subjects possessed equivalent auditory imagery but less vivid visual images than nonhallucinating subjects
Evans et al. (2000)	12 trait Hal 7 trait NH (all Dx SZ)	Utilised a battery of 5 established tasks indirectly measuring auditory imagery	There was no consistent difference between groups in task performance	
Aleman et al. (2002)	Case study design 1 continuous Hal 5 state NH (all Dx SZ)	4 established tasks of mental imagery and perception		Continuous hallucinating individual showed a different pattern of imagery/perception performance in the auditory modality but not the visual modality
Aleman et al. (in press)	12 State Hal (all Dx SZ)	Imagery tasks Imagery-perception gain task		No relation between imagery measures and hallucination ratings but there was a significant correlation between severity of hallucination and the relative influence of imagery on perception

SZ = schizophrenia group; CN = control group; Dx = diagnosed with schizophrenia; Hal = hallucinating group; NH = nonhallucinating group; n/r = not reported.

support for the "nonpreferred modality" explanation of AVHs these findings are limited by their reliance on subjective self-report measures. It does not necessarily follow that our impression of the relative vibrancy of our mental imagery will necessarily reflect genuine individual differences. Aleman, Nieuwenstein, Bocker, & de Haan (2000) observed that normal subjects with a disposition to hallucinatory experiences, as measured by the Launay-Slade Hallucinations Scale (LSHS), rated their mental imagery as more vivid than others on self-report scales but demonstrated lower mental imagery on experimental measures of imagery.

More recent investigations (Aleman de Haan, Bocker, Hijman, & Kahn, 2002; Aleman, Bocker, Hijman, de Haan, & Kahn, in press; Böcker, Hijman, Kahn, & de Haan, 2000; Evans, McGuire, & David, 2000) have incorporated more objective means of assessing mental imagery ability. These tasks attempt to measure imagery ability indirectly via the completion of simple cognitive tasks. For example, the meaningful letter strings task requires subjects to covertly read strings of letters or numbers that can only be recognised as a word if subjects can successfully imagine saying them aloud (e.g., M-T = "empty"). Despite employing relatively sophisticated techniques for measuring auditory imagery these investigations have provided equivocal results with respect to group differences in vividness of auditory imagery (see Table 1). While there was no evidence of overall perception or imagery deficits in hallucinating subjects, they appeared to demonstrate an abnormal balance between imagery and perception within sensory modalities (Aleman et al., in press; Böcker et al., 2000). That is, hallucinating individuals showed a greater relative influence of top-down cognitive processes on "perception" of an auditory stimulus. The influence of top-down processes on auditory perception in hallucinating subjects has previously been investigated using auditory signal detection tasks (Bentall & Slade, 1985; Böcker et al., 2000; Li, Chen, Yang, Chen, & Tsay, 2002). While these investigations have provided consistent findings with respect to the ability of schizophrenic subjects to detect auditory stimuli as well as control subjects (perceptual sensitivity), there are inconsistent findings with respect to the extent and nature of any deficits observed in hallucinating subjects. Nevertheless, there is limited evidence that hallucinating subjects demonstrate an auditory response bias, that is, they show a tendency to incorrectly report that they heard a noise (tones or speech) against a backdrop of white noise. So far, only the role of imagining stimuli on perception has been examined. Two recent theoretical models of auditory hallucinations have proposed possible neuroanatomical circuits for this process (Behrendt, 2003; Grossberg, 2000) that emphasise the role of previous learning on interpretation of ambiguous auditory perceptions and imagery. In order to further understand the influence of top-down processes on auditory perception in hallucinating subjects more sophisticated cognitive paradigms are required, specifically examining the role that learning and expectations have on perception (see Frith & Dolan, 1997).

In summary, there is no evidence that either abnormally vivid or reduced auditory imagery is related to the presence of auditory hallucinations in schizophrenia. This conclusion is consistent with investigations in the general population which have found no relationship between disposition to hallucinatory experiences and aberrant auditory or visual imagery (Aleman, Nieuwenstein, Bocker, & de Haan, 2000; Aleman, Bocker, & de Haan, 2001; Merckelbach & Van de Ven, 2001). Further, the vividness of mental imagery does not necessarily determine how this experience is appraised which would seem to represent a key aspect of the hallucinatory experience (see Bentall, 1990).

Verbal self-monitoring

A second principal area of investigation into the origin of AVHs involves dysfunction in verbal self-monitoring. In general, these paradigms involve assessing an individual's ability to identify their own speech in contrast to another's speech. The theoretical background for this model is based on the proposal that auditory hallucinations, like other positive symptoms in schizophrenia, can be conceptualised as resulting from a breakdown in the systems monitoring our intention to make an action. To distinguish between self-generated and externally generated actions we rely on a "feed forward" signal of our intentions to an internal monitor (for a review see Blakemore, Wolpert, & Frith, 2002). If information about our goals or plans fails to reach the internal monitor, then the resulting actions of those willed intentions can be experienced as unintended. Consequently, Frith (1992) theorises inner speech can be misinterpreted as alien or another's voice if the sense of intention does not accompany the experience of "hearing" it.

Six studies have attempted to measure verbal self-monitoring in schizophrenia with particular reference to auditory hallucinations (see Table 2). Research on self-monitoring of language production in schizophrenia by Hoffman (1999) and Leudar, Thomas, and Johnston (1992, 1994), which has shown that schizophrenic subjects were impaired with respect to monitoring speech production, has not been included as the tasks did not require subjects to make some form of on-line assessment of agency (i.e., self vs. other).

Morrison and Haddock (1997), and Morrison, Wells, and Nothard (1998) required schizophrenic subjects to generate words in response to experimentally provided cues and then to immediately rate their responses with respect to phenomenological aspects of self-monitoring. Dimensions measured included; "internality" (how much was the word that came to mind your own?), "control" (how much control did you have over the word that came to mind?), "involuntariness" (how involuntary was your thought?), and "wantedness" (how much did you want to think of that word rather than another one?). In both studies, hallucinating subjects tended to provide lower internality, control, and wantedness ratings than control groups. These findings were interpreted as

TABLE 2
Verbal self-monitoring investigations of auditory hallucinations in schizophrenia

Study	Subject	Pradigm	Findings	Relationship with symptoms
Cahill et al. (1996)	21 SZ (mixed symptomatology)	On-line monitoring of own speech (distorted vs. non-distorted)	Only compared performance within a group of SZ subjects	A tendency of claim own distorted voice as "other" was correlated with severity of delusion but not hallucinations
Goldberg et al. (1997)	10 state Hal 5 trait NH (all Dx SZ) 19 CN	Delayed auditory feedback of own speech while reading	SZ subjects showed increased dysfluency in speech as a consequence of receiving delayed feedback of own speech	No difference in performance between hallucinating and nonhallucinating subjects
Morrison & Haddock (1997)	15 state Hal 15 trait NH (all Dx SZ) 15 CN	Word self-generation in response to a cue accompanied by immediate ratings of internality, control, and involuntariness	SZ subjects did not differ from controls with respect to rating of control over own statements	Hallucinating subjects demonstrate an external misattribution bias: they tend to misattribute their own speech to an external source
Baker & Morrison (1998)	15 state Hal 15 trait NH (all Dx SZ) 15 CN	Word self-generation in response to a cue accompanied by immediate ratings of internality, control, and wantedness	Hallucinating subjects showed lower levels of perceived internality, control and wantedness than other groups	Hallucinating subjects demonstrate higher external misattribution bias: they tend to misattribute their own speech to an external source

Johns & McGuire (1999)	10 state Hal 8 trait NH (all Dx SZ & with prominent delusions) 20 CN	On-line monitoring of own speech (distorted vs. nondistorted)	SZ subjects showed impaired recognition of own speech once it had been distorted	Hallucinating subjects demonstrate higher external misattribution bias: more likely to say that a distorted voice is another speaker
Johns et al. (2001)	10 state Hal 8 trait NH (all Dx SZ & with prominent delusions) 20 CN	On-line monitoring of own speech Self (distorted vs. nondistorted) Other (distorted vs. nondistorted)	SZ subjects made more errors than control subjects with feedback of their own voice (distorted and nondistorted) but not for the alien voice	Impaired verbal self-monitoring was evident in both hallucinating and nonhallucinating groups but hallucinating subjects more likely to misattribute their own distorted voice to another speaker

SZ = schizophrenia group; CN = control group; Dx = diagnosed with schizophrenia; Hal = hallucinating group; NH = nonhallucinating group; n/r = not reported.

reflecting an external attribution bias in hallucinators (Baker & Morrison, 1998). The obvious methodological complication with this approach to assessing verbal self-monitoring is the reliance on self-report to describe complex cognitive states. It is also not clear if subject responses represented the degree to which individuals were monitoring their verbal responses or a general bias in reporting experiences.

The remaining investigations utilised more objective measures of verbal self-monitoring, requiring subjects to make a decision about the origin of perceived speech (self vs. other) while they were talking. Attempts to artificially create an experience of uncertainty in a speaker when hearing their own voice have involved distorting the pitch of the subject's speech (Cahill, Silbersweig, & Frith, 1996; Johns & McGuire, 1999), introducing a lag between speaking and perception (Goldberg, Gold, Coppola, & Weinberger, 1997) and mixing another person's speech in with their own responses (Johns et al., 2001). Overall, the findings from these studies have been mixed. The most success in discriminating hallucinating from nonhallucinating groups emerged when subjects were permitted to respond "Self", "Unsure", or "Other", thus making it possible to determine if subjects would have a particular response bias when uncertain of the origin of a word (Johns et al., 2001). As a group, schizophrenic subjects made more errors than volunteers when attempting to identify their own voice (distorted or nondistorted). However, hallucinating subjects demonstrated a tendency to positively misattribute their own distorted speech to an external speaker. These behavioural findings have been replicated in ongoing functional neuroimaging investigations of verbal self-monitoring (Fu et al., 2001), which have replicated this finding and identified cortical correlates of this behaviour in hallucinating subjects.

The extent to which defective self-monitoring alone can account for the presence of AVHs still needs to be determined but recent research by our group (Allen et al., 2003) suggests that additional cognitive processes are also involved. Hallucinating and nonhallucinating schizophrenic and healthy control subjects participated in making recordings of their voice and after a delay were asked to identify the source (self or other) of prerecorded speech (distorted or nondistorted), which they were hearing through headphones. As subjects were simply required to indicate when they recognised their own voice and not concurrently generate speech, overt verbal self-monitoring of speech was not specifically assessed. Despite this, hallucinating subjects were more likely to claim that their own recorded speech was spoken by the other voice. This finding suggests that abnormal verbal self-monitoring in itself cannot account for the response bias observed in hallucinating subjects.

Of the three areas of research included in this review the verbal self-monitoring model of AVHs has been the most investigated using functional neuroimaging. A series of studies in schizophrenia have shown that hallucinating subjects demonstrate an atypical pattern of temporal, parahippocampal, and cerebellar cortical activation when completing tasks requiring them to monitor their own inner speech (Fu et al., 2001; McGuire et al., 1995; Picchioni et al., 2002; Shergill, Bullmore, Simmons, Murray, & McGuire, 2000a; Shergill et al., 2003). These observations are consistent with recent electrophysiological investigations of speech in schizophrenia (Ford et al., 2001, 2002) which have identified evidence of impaired connectivity between frontal and temporal regions, suggesting reduced corollary discharge functioning for inner speech and talking in schizophrenia.

Episodic memory processes

The final area of neuropsychological investigation of AVHs included in this review involves investigation of dysfunction in the processes involved in the storing and retrieving of memories. Episodic memories are stored as a pattern containing distinct features of that experience. This memory trace includes within it sensory or perceptual information, semantic or conceptual information, as well as records of our emotional response, motor actions, and concurrent cognitive processes (for a review see Schacter, Norman, & Koutstaal, 1998). Disturbances in the reconstruction of these memory fragments may result in fragmented retrieval of memories, potentially causing confusion about their origin: "Did they say that before or did I just imagine it?" Thus, auditory hallucinations have been conceptualised as the result of a breakdown in the processes monitoring the source of memories.

The most direct way to assess constructive memory is to manipulate the conditions or personal experiences under which information is encoded and then to examine the effect of these manipulations upon retrieval of that episode. The three major types of source memory paradigms involve: discrimination of items from two external sources (Listen-Listen), discrimination of items from two self-generated sources (Say-Imagine), and a combination of the external and self-generated source (Listen-Say). The typical source memory paradigm allows recognition memory processes to be partitioned into three key aspects of constructive memory: item memory, source memory, and response bias (Murnane & Bayen, 1998). These attributes represent identifiable dimensions of recognition memory and have been operationally defined in experimental studies of memory (Dodson, Prinzmetal, & Shimamura, 1998). Item memory refers to the memory processes involved in retrieving a memory of a specific item that was presented earlier (Corwin, 1994). Source memory is defined as that set of processes involved in remembering the contextual features of an episode (Johnson, Hashtroudi, & Lindsay, 1993). Thus, item memory is a measure of whether a memory for the item was retained (i.e., the content of a memory), while source memory is a measure of the context in which that memory was acquired. The concept of response bias refers to the tendency of an individual to claim that an item was presented from a specific source when they are actually unsure about its origin (Snodgrass & Corwin, 1988). While these three processes are related in healthy adults, they have been found to be dissociated in neuropsychological studies of individuals with different focal brain lesions (Johnson, 1997).

A review of the literature identified 16 relevant investigations of constructive memory in schizophrenia (see Table 3). Only studies that made an attempt to relate memory function to a particular symptom or syndrome were included (see Brébion, Smith, Gorman, & Amador, 1996). The series of investigations conducted by Harvey and colleagues (Harvey, 1985, Harvey, Earl-Boyer, & Levinson, 1988; Harvey & Spencer, 1990) has not been included as they were specifically measuring the impact of positive thought disorder on constructive memory performance. Although all the studies shown in Table 3 made inferences about constructive memory in schizophrenia, they involved a range of experimental paradigms, stimulus material, and participant groups. Perhaps not surprisingly under these circumstances, the results and related theoretical inferences regarding constructive memory are inconsistent, even contradictory.

Item memory. As evident from Table 3, just over half of the relevant studies reported item memory performance in conjunction with source memory. Of these, only two found no difference in item memory performance between their schizophrenia and control groups (Frith, Leary, Cahill, & Johnstone, 1991; Vinogradov et al., 1997). This result may be a consequence of the varying task demands of the particular paradigms employed, since these studies required subjects to learn relatively fewer items. Thus, the poorer item memory performance observed in the other studies could be accounted for by increased task difficulty, that in turn reducing encoding efficiency. Also of note is the observation that poor item-memory performance seemed to be independent of the nature of the source memory paradigm employed.

Source memory. The majority of studies employed a Listen-Say source memory paradigm, which requires participants to distinguish between memories of their own speech and memories of another person's speech. This represents an attempt to investigate the hypothesis that individuals with schizophrenia, particularly those with prominent positive symptoms, are unable to recognise the source of their own thoughts and subsequently misattribute these items to an external source (Bentall, 1990). The most consistent finding in this field is that hallucinating individuals are impaired at discriminating between memories of their own speech and memories of another's speech. This finding in not universal, however, as evidenced by the failure of Smith and Gudjonsson (1995) and Morrison and Haddock (1997) to find group differences using this paradigm. In addition, the group differences in source memory identified by Seal, Crowe, and Chung (1997) were accounted for by variation in estimated premorbid IQ and overall verbal memory function between hallucinating and nonhallucinating groups. An additional complication to the interpretation of findings from Listen-

Say tasks is that the design of these experiments does not make it clear whether the poor performance in schizophrenia is due to a general problem with source memory or is specific to identifying the source of externally generated or self-generated items. When differences in source memory for externally generated (Listen-Listen) and self-generated (Say-Imagine) items have been compared independently, using separate tasks, subjects with schizophrenia have performed poorly on both (Harvey, 1985; Harvey et al., 1988; Keefe, Arnold, Bayen, & Harvey, 1999; Keefe, Arnold, Bayen, McEvoy, & Wilson, 2002). This suggests that the source memory dysfunction observed in schizophrenia in general, may be generalised and is not specific to a particular encoding modality (self-generated vs. externally generated).

The most significant observation that emerges from inspection of Table 3 is, that as a whole, source memory deficits are invariably reported in conjunction with a corresponding deficit in item memory. Thus, it appears that hallucinating subjects are forgetting where they heard items simply because they never remembered the item in the first place. The two studies that do report source memory deficits without related item memory deficits were those mentioned earlier that involved fewer items and relatively undemanding paradigms (Frith et al., 1991; Vinogradov et al., 1997). Investigations using multinomial analysis techniques to examine item memory and source memory and response bias separately have consistently found that the best model to explain hallucinating subjects' performance involved impaired recognition of self-generated material rather than a source-memory deficit (Keefe et al., 1999, 2002).

Response bias. The source memory model of auditory hallucinations predicts that when hallucinating subjects fail to recognise the source of a word, they will demonstrate a tendency to misattribute words they have said or thought to an external speaker. There are, however, mixed findings with respect to the nature and strength of a response bias in schizophrenia, suggesting that this phenomenon may be dependent on the memory paradigm employed. When response biases are identified they are typically associated with the presence of prominent positive symptoms (Bentall, Baker, & Havers, 1991; Brébion et al., 2000; Franck et al., 2000; Seal et al., 1997).

In summary, despite the appeal of the source memory model of auditory hallucinations there is no clear evidence of a specific source memory deficit in schizophrenia for self-generated material. In contrast, there is growing evidence that the nature of memory deficit observed amongst those with prominent positive symptoms is not a problem with identifying the *source* of memories but with remembering what they said or imagined in the first place. There is little doubt that schizophrenia is associated with a significant impairment in episodic memory functioning (see Aleman et al., 1999; Weiss & Heckers, 2001), however, this finding appears to be specific to memories of self-generated material. This finding is consistent with Keefe's (1998) notion that positive symptoms in

TABLE 3
Constructive memory investigations of auditory hallucinations in schizophrenia

Study	Subjects	Paradigm	Overall group differences			Relationship with symptoms
			Item memory	Source memory	Response bias	
Frith et al. (1991)	283 SZ (mixed symptomatology) 35 CN	Listen-Say	No	SZ < CN	n/r	Source memory performance was related to the symptoms incongruity and flattening of affect, as well as duration of illness and low current IQ
Bentall et al. (1991)	22 state Hal 16 trait NH (majority Dx SZ) 22 CN	Listen-Say	n/r	SZ < CN SZ > CN		No overall difference in accuracy between clinical groups but hallucinators more often misattributed self-generated items in the high cognitive effort condition to the experimenter than other groups
Smith & Gudjonsson (1995)	17 trait Hal 15 trait NH (mixed Dx)	Listen-Say (after Bentall et al., 1991)	n/r	No	No	Results failed to replicate Bentall et al. (1991). No differences between groups with respect to overall source memory performance or type of errors made
Brébion et al. (1997)	36 SZ (mixed symptomatology) 31 CN	Listen-Picture-Say	SZ < CN	SZ < CN SZ > CN		Positive symptoms (PANSS) were positively correlated with tendency to claim that spoken items were presented as pictures

Morrison & Haddock (1997)	15 state Hal 15 trait NH (all Dx SZ) 15 CN	Listen-Say	n/r	No	No	No difference in performance observed
Seal et al. (1997)	10 trait Hal 11 trait NH (all Dx SZ) 15 CN	Listen-Say	SZ < CN	SZ < CN	SZ > CN	Hallucinating subjects show impaired source memory but after controlling for the influence of verbal IQ and verbal memory on task performance, no between-group differences found
Stirling et al. (1998)	27 SZ (mixed symptomatology) 19 CN	Listen-Say (after Frith et al., 1991)	SZ < CN	SZ < CN	n/r	Source memory and overall memory performance was related to total SANS score
Vinogradov et al. (1997)	26 SZ (mixed symptoomatology) 21 CN	Listen-Say	No	SZ < CN	SZ > CN	Source memory performance weakly related to negative symptoms as measured by the BPRS
Keefe et al. (1999)	18 First rank symptoms 10 no first rank symptoms (all Dx SZ)	Listen-Listen	SZ < CN	SZ < CN	No	Individuals with first rank symptoms poorer at distinguishing between items they had imagined saying and items they had imagined the experimenter saying
		Say-Imagine	SZ < CN	SZ < CN	No	
	19 CN	Listen-Listen	SZ < CN	No	SZ > CN	
		Imagine (Self) Imagine (Other)	SZ < CN	SZ < CN	No	Overall, results suggest that source memory deficits are characteristic of schizophrenia not just those with prominent positive symptoms

(Continued)

TABLE 3
(Continued)

Study	Subjects	Paradigm	Overall group differences				Relationship with symptoms
			Item memory	Source memory	Response bias		
Böcker et al. (2000)	13 trait Hal 19 state NH (all Dx SZ) 14 CN	Say-Imagine	n/r	No	No		Hallucinations associated with impaired source discrimination and a response bias to report imagined items as said
Brébion et al. (2000)	40 SZ (mixed symptomatology) 40 CN	Listen-Picture-Say	n/r	SZ < CN	SZ > CN		Hallucinations associated with a response bias to claim that novel items are familiar and to misattribute self-generated items to an external source.
Franck et al. (2000)	17 SZ (mixed symptomatology) 17 CN	Say-Imagine (same as Harvey, 1985)	SZ < CN	SZ < CN	n/r		Hallucinating subgroup ($n = 7$) significantly poorer at recognising words and more likely to claim that imagined words were spoken
Brébion et al. (2002)	40 SZ (mixed symptomatology) 40 CN	Listen-Picture-Say	SZ < CN	SZ < CN	No		Recognition and source memory performance not related to positive or negative symptomatology. However, positive symptoms, including hallucinations, associated with all possible forms of memory errors

Study	Subjects	Task			Results
Keefe et al. (2002)	18 first rank symptoms 11 no first rank symptoms (all Dx SZ) 19 CN	Listen-Picture-Say	SZ < CN	SZ < CN	No	Individuals with first rank symptoms significantly poorer at recognising items they had self-generated and said aloud in response to categories
Aleman et al. (in press)	22 state Hal 35 state/trait NH (all DX SZ) 20 CN	Listen-Say	n/r	SZ = CN	n/r	In a subgroup of hallucinating subjects ($n = 12$) source discrimination negatively correlated with severity of hallucinations
Keefe et al. (in press)	40 SZ (mixed symptomatology)	Listen-Picture-Say Repeated measures design				Individuals with first rank symptoms significantly poorer at recognising items they had self-generated and said aloud in response to categories

SZ = schizophrenia group; CN = control group; Dx = diagnosed with schizophrenia; Hal = hallucinating subjects, NH = nonhallucinating subjects; n/r = not reported.

Listen-Listen = task involves trying to remember words read aloud by 2 different external sources, typically a male and female voice.
Say-Imagine = task involves trying to remember words from 2 self-generated sources (read aloud by the subject and imagined being spoken aloud).
Listen-Picture-Say = task involves trying to remember words from 3 sources, words said by another person, read aloud by subject to describe a picture and words which subjects generated in response to a category.

schizophrenia are associated with an *autonoetic agnosia*, "a deficit in the ability to identify self-generated events" (p.142). It is not clear to what extent this specific recognition deficit for memories of self-generated material represents impoverished encoding or inefficient retrieval strategies or a combination of both. Poor recognition memory performance in schizophrenia has been consistently related to reduced cognitive processing speed, which suggests that these individuals may not be efficiently encoding material (Brébion, Amador, Smith, & Gorman, 1998; Brébion et al., 2000).

There are obvious similarities with respect to the nature of this memory deficit for self-generated speech and the self-monitoring deficit described earlier. It is possible that the memory deficit represents a pre-existing failure to attend to, and efficiently encode, speech. While further research is required there is some support for the notion that they may involve common neurocognitive resources. A recent investigation incorporating measures of both self-monitoring and memory (Böcker et al., 2000) identified a consistent relationship between poor self-monitoring and memory performance in hallucinating subjects. It is acknowledged that Morrison and Haddock (1997) found impaired self-monitoring but intact source-monitoring in hallucinating subjects. However, as discussed earlier, the self-report measures they used to measure self-monitoring relied on subjective ratings. It is interesting to note that an often cited criticism of this approach to the investigation of auditory hallucinations (see Cahill, Silbersweig, & Frith, 1996) is that source memory paradigms only assess discrimination of the source of memories of events rather than *immediate, on-line* discrimination of the source of speech (cf self-monitoring tasks). We propose that the memory deficit for self-generated verbal material could be a consequence of the noted impairment in self-monitoring of speech.

INTEGRATION AND CONCLUSION

The results of this review indicate that a deficit in either auditory imagery, self-monitoring or episodic memory is insufficient, in itself, to account for the generation of auditory verbal hallucinations. This conclusion is not surprising as it is unlikely that any unidimensional model of cognitive dysfunction could account for the diverse and striking experiences reported by hallucinating individuals. Nevertheless, there is evidence that AVHs are associated with:

1. impaired verbal self-monitoring and impaired memory for own speech;
2. an abnormal influence of top-down processing on perception; and
3. an externalising response bias in the form of a tendency to claim that unfamiliar or unrecognised material originated from an external source: "You said it not me".

We propose that the impairment in self-monitoring represents a form of neurocognitive deficit while the other impairments can be conceived of as representing forms of idiosyncratic cognitive bias (after Garety et al., 2001). We have speculated that the identified deficits in verbal self-monitoring and memory for own speech are associated and represent some form of autonoetic agnosia (after Keefe, 1998). It is possible that this deficit extends beyond verbal self-monitoring. There is a growing body of research that indicates that individuals with schizophrenia show impaired monitoring of imagined and performed motor movement (Danckert et al., 2002; Daprati et al., 1997; Malenka, Angel, Hampton, & Berger, 1982; Mlakar, Jensterle, & Frith, 1994). Further, Stirling, Hellewell, and Ndlovu (2001) and Stirling, Hellewell, and Quraishi (1998) observed that performance on a range of self-monitoring motor tests was related to the presence of positive symptoms including auditory hallucinations. In addition, there is evidence to suggest that individuals with hallucinations and/or passivity experiences are particularly impaired at monitoring self-produced sensations (Blakemore, Smith, Steel, Johnstone, & Frith, 2000). If the nature of the self-monitoring deficit is generalised to both verbal and motor actions then task complexity may also be a factor since Fourneret, Franck, Slachevsky, and Jeannerod (2001) found that performance on a simple performance self-monitoring task was not specifically related to positive symptoms.

How these deficits may interact with the identified biases to generate and maintain AVHs is currently unclear. These impairments may be related, expressions of a common underlying neuropathology, or represent independent cognitive abnormalities. There is some evidence of an interaction between impaired recognition of self-generated material and top-down influences in hallucinating subjects. Both Johns & McGuire (1999) and Allen et al. (2003) observed that the external misattribution of self-generated speech by subjects was more likely when its content had high emotion valence. The postulated relationship between these three types of impairments and AVHs could be further clarified by functional imaging investigations. Neuroimaging investigations of AVHs have implicated an extensive network of cortical and subcortical regions that normally mediate auditory perception and imagery, as well as other regions involved in monitoring behaviour and memory retrieval (see Copolov et al., 2003; Shergill, Brammer, Williams, Murray, & McGuire, 2000b; Weiss & Heckers, 2001). Given that these networks participate in multiple cognitive processes it is not surprising that it is difficult to neatly match the neuroimaging correlates of AVHs with existing cognitive models of AVHs. More informative are the results of the handful of "cognitive interference" studies of AVHs (see David et al., 1996; McGuire et al., 1995, Shergill et al., 2000a; Woodruff et al., 1997). These studies have attempted to identify the cortical regions and corresponding cognitive processes associated with AVHs by demonstrating dysfunction in established neurocognitive networks of language, perception, and self-monitoring. Relative to control groups, hallucinating subjects have demonstrated reduced activation of cortical areas implicated in verbal self-monitoring (Fu et al., 2001; McGuire et al., 1996; Shergill et al., 2000a) and processing of external auditory stimuli (David et al., 1996; Woodruff et al., 1997; Allen et al., 2003).

It remains to be established to what extent these impairments produce AVHs or are merely epiphenomena. A related but distinct question is whether these impairments are specific to AVHs, positive psychotic symptoms or to schizophrenia in general. In schizophrenia the experience of AVHs typically occurs in conjunction with delusions, passivity experiences and thought insertion, and is consistently identified as being part of the reality distortion syndrome (Liddle, Friston, Frith, & Frackowiak, 1992). Data from studies of patients with prominent AVHs may thus also be related to the presence of delusions. Indeed, Cahill et al. (1996) found that self-monitoring deficits were more related to the severity of delusions than AVHs. A parsimonious explanation for their co-occurrence is that delusions and hallucinations reflect a common impairment in the appraisal of external stimuli: The former resulting from the misinterpretation of innocuous behaviour or events, and the latter from the misinterpretation of auditory perceptions (Fleminger, 1992). The relevance of impaired appraisal may explain why it is so unusual to find individuals with schizophrenia who experience AVHs but do not possess delusions.

PROPOSED NEUROCOGNITIVE MODEL OF AUDITORY VERBAL HALLUCINATIONS

> For perception to occur incoming sensations must be imbued with meaning on the basis of our past experience and prior knowledge.
>
> Frith and Dolan (1997)

On the basis of the findings of this review we have developed a working model of AVHs that attempts to explain how the identified cognitive impairments could contribute to the generation of this anomalous experience. As the primary cognitive deficit identified in the review involves impaired verbal self-monitoring we have drawn on the established framework of intentional motor control developed by Wolpert and colleagues (see Miall, Weir, Wolpert, & Stein, 1993; Wolpert, Gahramani, & Jordan, 1995). This framework describes a network of cognitive processes and feedback loops involved in sensory perception and motor actions that allow individuals to distinguish between the consequences of self-generated and externally generated actions (see Figure 1). Wolpert and colleagues propose that the motor network is a dynamic system that makes adjustments on the basis of a comparison between expected and actual sensory feedback. This is possible since, as well as initiating movement, the motor system, generates a predicted sensory consequence of the action, *an efference copy* of the action, that is then used to modulate the actual sensory

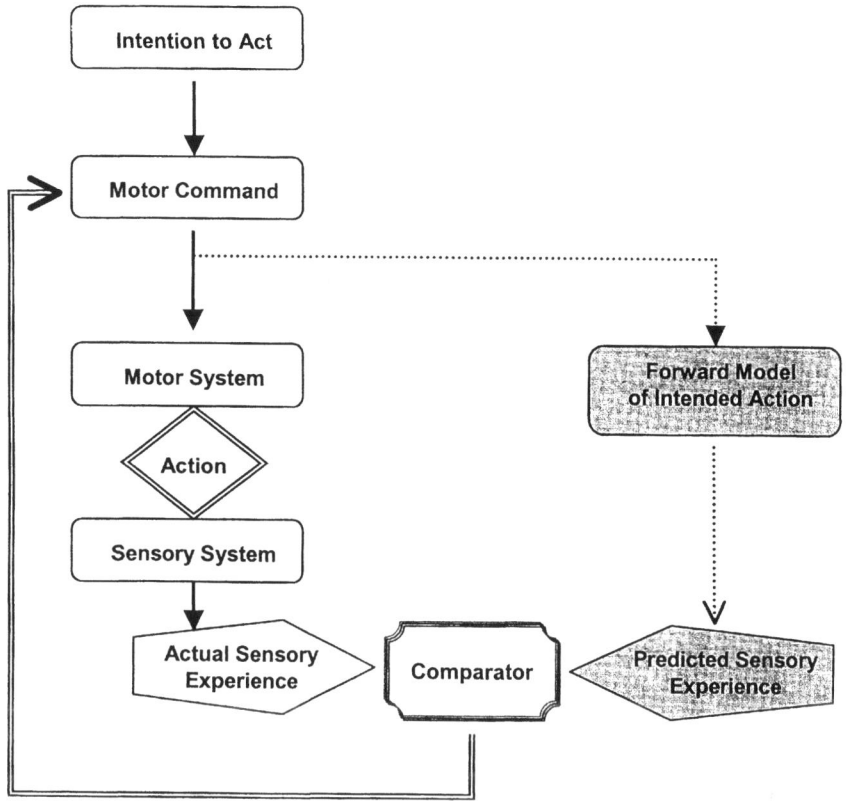

Figure 1. Forward model of motor control (adapted from Wolpert et al., 1995 and Blakemore et al., 2002).

feedback received (*re-afference*). This assessment takes place in the comparator, not a single structure but a parietal-cerebellar network (Blakemore & Frith, 2003). The implications of this match/mismatch are then fed back to the motor system so that the necessary adjustments to the motor commands can be made. Thus, it is possible for an individual to learn to walk, pronounce foreign words, and perfect their golf swing.

The extent of the match/mismatch between the predicted and actual sensory feedback of an action is the basis on which a perceived act is determined to be self-generated (for a review see Blakemore & Frith, 2003). The forward model of a self-generated action contains distinctive sensory and proprioceptive information that specifies that the subject is the agent of the perceived action. Investigations of motor self-monitoring suggest that individuals are largely unaware of the sensory information that is used to inform these judgements (Blakemore et al., 2002). Blakemore and colleagues (2000; Blakemore, Oatley,

& Frith, 2003; Frith, Reis, & Friston, 1998) have proposed that a breakdown in the forward modelling of the consequences of an action could lead to the situation where the relevant sensory information is inefficiently communicated to the comparator, resulting in abnormal sensory experiences observed in individuals with utilization behaviour or delusions of control.

We propose that the generation of AVHs, as opposed to the experience of AVHs, can be accounted for by disruptions to this network (see Figure 2). The notion that AVHs may be explained by a breakdown in the intentional motor model is not new (e.g., Frith et al., 1998), however, the current model represents an attempt to integrate findings from the broad range of empirical studies cited in this review and the literature on psychosocial factors involved in the generation and maintenance of AVHs.

Any neurocognitive model of AVHs needs to account for two key features of the experience: how self-generated thought is subsequently *misperceived* as speech, and the experience of *unintendedness* that characteristically accompanies this perception. The experience of unintendedness can be accounted for by failure of feed forward information to reach the comparator. If the forward modelling of the predicted sensory consequences of an action is distorted or absent then the experienced sensory information is not appropriately modulated

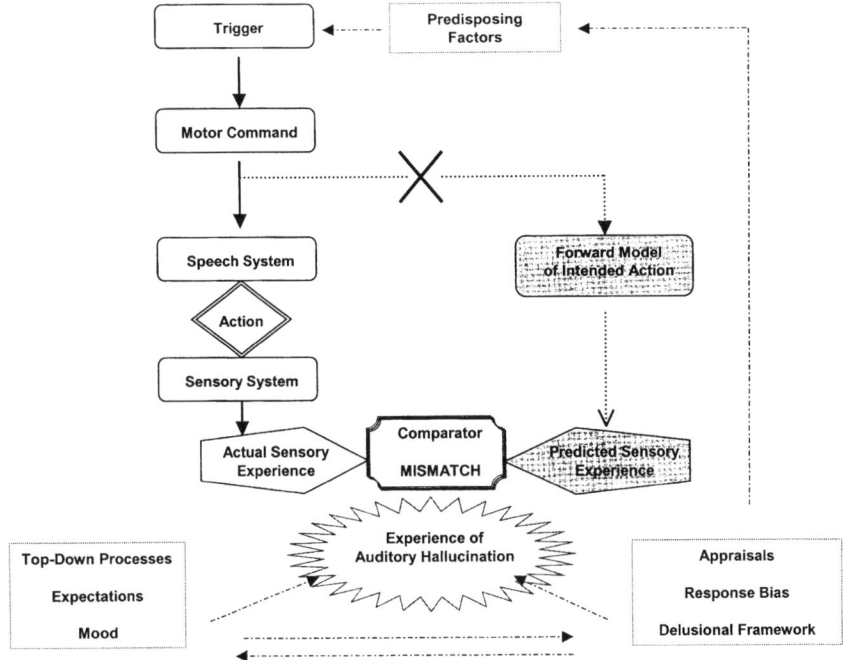

Figure 2. Proposed model of auditory verbal hallucinations.

in the comparator (represented by the dashed line in forward model circuit in Figure 2). Consequently, self-generated actions are perceived without the distinctive information informing the individual that they are self-generated. Whereas, the misperception of endogenous verbal material can be accounted for by the subsequent interpretation of the mismatch between the predicted sensory consequences of an action and the actual perceived sensory experience of that action. It is likely that the hallucinating individuals experience various states of ambiguity with respect to the origin of an action rather than two distinct states of awareness (self/other). As noted earlier, this process occurs at a preconscious level but can be moderated by *top-down* factors, such as previous experience, mood, and expectation. In this context, we are using top-down processes in the broadest sense to refer to the influence exerted by prior knowledge or experiences on sensory perceptions or imagery (Frith & Dolan, 1997). It is possible that hallucinating individuals are able to generate some information about potential actions, which is efficiently conveyed to the comparator, but the impact of this information may be sufficiently moderated by these top-down factors that it is ignored (Danckert, Saoud, & Maruff, 2003).

The nature of the primary material of auditory hallucinations still remains unclear: it may be in the form of inner speech, auditory verbal imagery, or reactivated episodic memories of speech. There is substantial evidence that the experience of AVHs is accompanied by subvocalisation and/or inner speech (Hoffman, 1999; McGuire et al., 1996). These observations have led some researchers (Stephane et al., 2001) to suggest that cortical areas responsible for language production must be implicated in the generation of auditory hallucinations. However, these findings are consistent with the generation of material in some verbal form and do not necessarily exclude other potential sources. Despite this assertion, the personal content and purely auditory form of AVHs seem more redolent of stimulus-independent thoughts than reactivated episodic memories.

It is proposed that once some trigger event brings about the generation of the AVHs motor commands are issued and inner speech is produced. In some individuals this may be accompanied by subvocalisation and, rarely, by overt vocalisation. The internal perception of the inner speech is then compared with the expected output in the comparator. Perception of speech is not simply a passive sensory process but a complex, interpretative process (for a review see Zatorre, Bouffard, Ahad, & Belin, 2002). To varying degrees, top-down cognitive processes influence how an individual determines the content, meaning, location, and affective tone of speech. We have loosely grouped together under the heading of top-down process: expectations and appraisals, response bias, and delusional framework. These factors have all been identified as increasing the probability that an individual will accept an ambiguous percept as the voice of another. The contribution of these factors is specific to the individual and reinforces the likelihood that this event will occur in the future (Garety et al.,

2001). Once experienced, the voice is subject to appraisal within the context of the individual's cognitive framework, which in a hallucinating individual is typically delusional.

Why AVHs in schizophrenia are so frequently abusive and distressing has not yet been established. However, investigations of thought suppression clearly demonstrate that attempts to suppress negative or critical thoughts typically result in the opposite effect (Wegner & Erber, 1992). Thus, an agitated or depressed individual will find their mind invaded by the very things they least want to think about. Further, individuals who are prone to AVHs are significantly more likely to misattribute self-generated speech to an external source when it has negative emotional content (Allen et al., 2003; Johns & McGuire, 1999). Overall, the above observations suggest that the unpleasant content of AVHs may be particularly common because it is more likely to arise spontaneously and, in turn, because it is more likely to be misinterpreted as alien in origin.

Also of relevance to the proposed model are the psychological and social factors that predispose individuals with schizophrenia to experience AVHs (Delespaul de Vries, & Van Os, 2002; Morrison et al., 2002). These factors need to be addressed by any model since the psychological response to environmental factors such as increased levels of stress, depressed mood and isolation have all been identified as contributing to the generation of AVHs (Garety et al., 2001). Other theories of AVHs (Beck & Rector, 2003) have emphasised the role or pre-existing distortions in reasoning and thinking. In addition to these psychosocial factors it is well established that AVHs can be triggered by a range of psychoactive substances, such as delta-9-tetrahydrocannabinol (THC), amphetamines, and phencyclidine (PCP) (McGuire et al., 1994). While further discussion of these factors is beyond the scope of this review a comprehensive account of how these different types of predisposing factors interact warrants further investigation. Another potentially fruitful avenue of investigation involves the naturalistic coping mechanisms employed by hallucinating subjects (Carter, Mackinnon, & Copolov, 1996). If these simple behaviours do actually reduce the frequency and severity of AVHs, then it is reasonable to assume that they provide information about the cognitive processes involved in maintenance of AVHs. For example, one of the behavioural techniques claimed by hallucinators to be very effective in abolishing AVHs is to read aloud or speak to another person (Carter et al., 1996; Shergill et al., 1998). This observation is consistent with the notion that AVHs involve the generation of inner speech, and rely on the same neural substrates as overt articulation.

In conclusion, we have proposed a speculative model of AVHs that conceptualises this experience as the consequence of a breakdown in the intentional motor network and the subsequent misinterpretation of this breakdown. We anticipate that the proposed model will provide a useful framework for further empirical investigation of AVHs in schizophrenia, and a range of disorders, and assist in clarifying the nature of this experience.

Manuscript accepted 7 May 2003

REFERENCES

Aleman, A., Bocker, K. B., & de Haan, E. H. (2001). Hallucinatory predisposition and vividness of auditory imagery: Self-report and behavioral indices. *Perceptual and Motor Skills 93*, 268–274.

Aleman, A., Bocker, K. B., Hijman, R., de Haan, E. H., & Kahn, R. S. (in press). Cognitive basis of hallucinations in schizophrenia: Role of top-down information processing. *Schizophrenia Research*.

Aleman, A., de Haan, E. H., Bocker, K. B., Hijman, R., & Kahn, R. S. (2002). Hallucinations in schizophrenia: Imbalance between imagery and perception? *Schizophrenia Research, 57*, 315–316.

Aleman, A., Hijman, R., de Haan, E. H., & Kahn, R. S. (1999). Memory impairment in schizophrenia: A meta-analysis. *American Journal of Psychiatry, 156*, 1358–1366.

Aleman, A., Nieuwenstein, M. R., Bocker, K. B., & de Haan, E. H. (2000). Mental imagery and perception in hallucination-prone individuals. *Journal of Nervous and Mental Disease, 188*, 830–836.

Allen, P., Johns, L. C., Fu, C., Broome, M. R., McGuire, P. K., & Vythelingum, N. (2003). Auditory hallucinations are not simply due to defective self-monitoring [Abstract]. *Schizophrenia Research, 60*, 164.

Baker, C. A., & Morrison, A. P. (1998). Cognitive processes in auditory hallucinations: Attributional biases and metacognition. *Psychological Medicine, 28*, 1199–1208.

Baxter, R. D., & Liddle, P. F. (1998). Neuropsychological deficits associated with schizophrenic syndromes. *Schizophrenia Research, 30*, 239–249.

Beck, A. T., & Rector, N. A. (2003). A cognitive model of hallucinations. *Cognitive Therapy and Research, 27*, 19–52.

Behrendt, R. P. (2003). Hallucinations: Synchronisation of thalamocortical gamma oscillations underconstrained by sensory input. *Consciousness and Cognition, 12*, 413–451.

Bentall, R. P. (1990). The illusion of reality: A review and integration of psychological research on hallucinations. *Psychological Bulletin, 107*, 82–95.

Bentall, R. P., Baker, G. A., & Havers, S. (1991). Reality monitoring and psychotic hallucinations. *British Journal of Clinical Psychology, 30*, 213–222.

Bentall, R. P., & Slade, P. D. (1985). Reality testing and auditory hallucinations: A signal detection analysis. *British Journal of Clinical Psychology, 24*, 159–169.

Blakemore, S. J., & Frith, C. D. (2003). Self-awareness and action. *Current Opinion in Neurobiology, 13*, 219–224.

Blakemore, S. J., Oakley, D. A., & Frith, C. D. (2003). Delusions of alien control in the normal brain. *Neuropsychologia, 41*, 1058–67.

Blakemore, S. J., Smith, J., Steel, R., Johnstone, C. E., & Frith, C. D. (2000). The perception of self-produced sensory stimuli in patients with auditory hallucinations and passivity experiences: Evidence for a breakdown in self-monitoring. *Psychological Medicine, 30*, 1131–1139.

Blakemore, S. J., Wolpert, D. M., & Frith, C. D. (2002). Abnormalities in the awareness of action. *Trends in Cognitive Sciences, 6*, 237–242.

Böcker, K. B., Hijman, R., Kahn, R. S., & de Haan, E. H. (2000). Perception, mental imagery and reality discrimination in hallucinating and non-hallucinating schizophrenic patients. *British Journal of Clinical Psychology, 39*, 397–406.

Brébion, G., Amador, X., David, A., Malaspina, D., Sharif, Z., & Gorman, J. M. (2000). Positive symptomatology and source-monitoring failure in schizophrenia: An analysis of symptom-specific effects. *Psychiatry Research 95*, 119–131.

Brébion, G., Amador, X., Smith, M. J., & Gorman, J. M. (1998). Memory impairment and schizophrenia: The role of processing speed. *Schizophrenia Research, 30*, 31–39.

Brébion, G., Gorman, J. M, Amador, X., Malaspina, D., & Sharif, Z. (2002). Source monitoring impairments in schizophrenia: Characterisation and associations with positive and negative symptomatology. *Psychiatry Research, 112*, 27–39.

Brébion, G., Smith, M. J., Gorman, J. M., & Amador, X. (1996). Reality monitoring failure in schizophrenia: The role of selective attention. *Schizophrenia Research, 22*, 173–180.

Brébion, G., Smith, M. J., Gorman, J. M., & Amador, X. (1997). Discrimination accuracy and decision biases in different types of reality monitoring in schizophrenia. *Journal of Nervous and Mental Disease, 185*, 247–253.

Brett, E. A., & Starker, S. (1977). Auditory imagery and hallucinations. *Journal of Nervous and Mental Disease, 164*, 394–400.

Cahill, C., Silbersweig, D., & Frith, C. (1996). Psychotic experiences induced in deluded patients using distorted auditory feedback. *Cognitive Neuropsychiatry, 1*, 201–211.

Carter, D. M., Mackinnon, A., & Copolov, D. L. (1996) Patients' strategies for coping with auditory hallucinations. *Journal of Nervous and Mental Disease, 184*, 159–164.

Carter, D. M., Mackinnon, A., Howard, S., Zeegers, T., & Copolov, D. L. (1995). The development and reliability of the Mental Health Research Institute Unusual Perceptions Schedule (MUPS): An instrument to record auditory hallucinatory experience. *Schizophrenia Research, 16*, 157–165.

Chandiramani, K., & Varma, V. K. (1987). Imagery in schizophrenic patients compared with normal controls. *British Journal of Medical Psychology, 60*, 335–41.

Copolov, D. L., Seal, M. L., Maruff, P., Ulusoy. R., Wong, M. T., Tochon-Danguy, H. J., & Egan, G. F. (2003). Cortical activation associated with the experience of auditory hallucinations and perception of human speech in schizophrenia: A PET correlation study. *Psychiatry Research, 122*, 139–152.

Coren, L. H. (1938). Imagery and its relation to schizophrenic symptoms. *Journal of Mental Science, 84*, 284–346.

Corwin, J. (1994). On measuring discrimination and response bias: Unequal numbers of targets and distractors and two classes of distractors. *Neuropsychology, 8*, 110–117.

Danckert, J., Rossetti, Y., d'Amato,T., Dalery, J., & Saoud, M. (2002). Exploring imagined movements in patients with schizophrenia. *Neuroreport, 13*, 605–609.

Danckert, J., Saoud, M., & Maruff, P. (2003). *Attention, motor control and motor imagery in schizophrenia: Implications for the role of the parietal cortex.* Manuscript submitted for publication.

Daprati, E., Franck, N., Georgieff, N., Proust, J., Pacherie, E., Dalery, J., & Jeannerod, M. (1997). Looking for the agent: An investigation into consciousness of action and self-consciousness in schizophrenic patients. *Cognition, 65*, 71–86.

David, A. S., Woodruff, P. W., Howard, R., Mellers, J. D., Brammer, M., Bullmore, E., Wright, I., Andrew, C., & Williams, S. C. (1996). Auditory hallucinations inhibit exogenous activation of auditory association cortex. *Neuroreport, 7*, 932–936.

Delespaul, P., deVries, M., & Van Os, J. (2002) Determinants of occurrence and recovery from hallucinations in daily life. *Social Psychiatry and Psychiatric Epidemiology, 37*, 97–104.

Dodson, C. S., Prinzmetal, W., & Shimamura, A. P. (1998). Using excel to estimate paramters from observed data: An example from source memory data. *Behavior Research Methods, Instruments, and Computers, 30*, 517–526.

Evans, C. L., McGuire, P. K., & David, A. S. (2000). Is auditory imagery defective in patients with auditory hallucinations? *Psychological Medicine, 30*, 137–148.

Fleminger, S. (1992). Preconscious perceptual processing. *British Journal of Psychiatry, 161*, 572–573.

Ford, J. M., Mathalon, D. H., Heinks, T., Kalba, S., Faustman, W. O., & Roth, W. T. (2001). Neurophysiological evidence of corollary discharge dysfunction in schizophrenia. *American Journal of Psychiatry, 158*, 2069–2071.

Ford, J. M., Mathalon, D. H., Whitfield, S., Faustman, W. O., & Roth, W. T. (2002). Reduced communication between frontal and temporal lobes during talking in schizophrenia. *Biological Psychiatry, 51*, 485–492.

Fourneret, P., Franck, N., Slachevsky, A., & Jeannerod, M. (2001). Self-monitoring in schizophrenia revisited. *Neuroreport, 12*, 1203–1208.

Franck, N., Rouby, P., Daprati, E., Dalery, J., Marie-Cardine, M., & Georgieff, N. (2000). Confusion between silent and overt reading in schizophrenia. *Schizophrenia Research, 41*, 357–364.

Frith, C. D. (1992). *The cognitive neuropsychology of schizophrenia*. Hove, UK: Psychology Press.

Frith, C. D., Blakemore, S. J., & Wolpert, D. M. (2000). Abnormalities in the awareness and control of action. *Philosophical Transactions of the Royal Society of London. Series B: Biological Sciences, 355*, 1771–1788.

Frith, C., & Dolan, R. J. (1997). Brain mechanisms associated with top-down processes in perception. *Philosophical Transactions of the Royal Society of London. Series B: Biological Sciences, 352*, 1221–1230.

Frith, C. D., Leary, J., Cahill, C., & Johnstone, E. C. (1991). Performance on psychological tests: Demographic and clinical correlates of the results of these tests. *British Journal of Psychiatry Supplement, 13, 159*, 26–29.

Frith, C. D., Rees, G., & Friston, K. (1998). Psychosis and the experience of self: Brain systems underlying self-monitoring. *Annals of the New York Academy of Sciences, 15*, 170–178.

Fu, C. H. Y., Vythelingum, N., Andrew, C., Brammer, M. J., Amaro, E., Williams, S. C. R., & McGuire, P. K. (2001). Alien voices ... who said that? Neural correlates of impaired verbal self-monitoring in schizophrenia [Abstract]. *NeuroImage, 13*, 1052.

Galton, F. (1943). *Inquiries into human faculty and its development* (2nd ed.). London: Dent & Sons.

Garety, P. A., Kuipers, E., Fowler, D., Freeman, D., & Bebbington, P. E. (2001). A cognitive model of the positive symptoms of psychosis. *Psychological Medicine, 31*, 189–195.

Goldberg, T. E., Gold, J. M., Coppola, R., & Weinberger, D. R. (1997). Unnatural practices, unspeakable actions: A study of delayed auditory feedback in schizophrenia. *American Journal of Psychiatry, 154*, 858–860.

Goldman-Rakic, P. S. (1994). Working memory dysfunction in schizophrenia. *Journal of Neuropsychiatry and Clinical Neurosciences, 6*, 348–357.

Grossberg, S. (2000). How hallucinations may arise from brain mechanisms of learning, attention, and volition. *Journal of the International Neuropsychological Society, 6*, 583–592.

Halligan, P. W., & David, A. S. (2001). Cognitive neuropsychiatry: Towards a scientific psychopathology. *Nature Reviews Neuroscience, 2*, 209–215.

Harvey, P. D. (1985). Reality monitoring in mania and schizophrenia: The association of thought disorder and performance. *Journal of Nervous and Mental Disease, 173*, 67–73.

Harvey, P. D., Earle-Boyer, E. A., & Levinson, J. C. (1988). Cognitive deficits and thought disorder: A retest study. *Schizophrenia Bulletin, 14*, 57–66.

Harvey, P. D., & Serper, M. R. (1990). Linguistic and cognitive failures in schizophrenia: A multivariate analysis. *Journal of Nervous and Mental Disease, 178*, 487–493.

Heilbrun, A. B., Blum, N., & Haas, M. (1983). Cognitive vulnerability to auditory hallucination. Preferred imagery mode and spatial location of sounds. *British Journal of Psychiatry, 143*, 294–299.

Hoffman, R. E. (1986). Verbal hallucinations and language production processes in schizophrenia. *Behavioural and Brain Sciences, 9*, 503–517.

Hoffman, R. E. (1999). New methods for studying hallucinated 'voices' in schizophrenia. *Acta Psychiatrica Scandinavica, Supplementum, 395*, 89–94.

Johns, L. C., & McGuire, P. K. (1999). Verbal self-monitoring and auditory hallucinations in schizophrenia. *Lancet, 353*, 469–470.

Johns, L. C., Rossell, S., Frith, C., Ahmad, F., Hemsley, D., Kuipers, E., & McGuire, P. K. (2001). Verbal self-monitoring and auditory verbal hallucinations in patients with schizophrenia. *Psychological Medicine, 31*, 705–715.

Johns, L. C., & Van Os, J. (2001). The continuity of psychotic experiences in the general population. *Clinical Psychology Review, 21*, 1125–1141.

Johnson, M. K. (1997). Source monitoring and memory distortion. *Philosophical Transactions of the Royal Society of London: Series B, 352*, 1733–1745.

Johnson, M. K., Hashtroudi, S., & Lindsay, D. S. (1993). Source monitoring. *Psychological Bulletin, 114*, 3–28.

Keefe, R. S. E. (1998). The neurobiology of disturbances of the self: Autonoetic agnosia in schizophrenia. In X. F. Amador & A. S. David (Eds.), *Insight and psychosis* (pp.142–173). Oxford, UK: Oxford University Press.

Keefe, R. S. E., Arnold, M. C., Bayen, U. J., & Harvey, P. D. (1999). Source monitoring deficits in patients with schizophrenia: A multinomial modelling analysis. *Psychological Medicine, 29*, 903–914.

Keefe, R. S., Arnold, M. C., Bayen, U. J., McEvoy, J. P., & Wilson, W. H. (2002). Source-monitoring deficits for self-generated stimuli in schizophrenia: Multinomial modeling of data from three sources. *Schizophrenia Research, 57*, 51–67.

Keefe, R. S., McEvoy, J. P., Vaughan, A., & Poe, M. P. (in press). Source monitoring improvement in patients with schizophrenia receiving antipsychotic medications. *Psychopharmacology*.

Langdon, R., & Coltheart, M. (1999). Mentalising, schizotypy, and schizophrenia. *Cognition, 71*, 43–71.

Leudar, I., & Thomas, P., & Johnston, M. (1992). Self-repair in dialogues of schizophrenics: Effects of hallucinations and negative symptoms. *Brain and Language, 43*, 487–511.

Leudar, I., Thomas, P., & Johnston, M. (1994). Self-monitoring in speech production: Effects of verbal hallucinations and negative symptoms. *Psychological Medicine, 24*, 749–761.

Li, C. S., Chen, M. C., Yang, Y. Y., Chen, M. C., & Tsay, P. K. (2002). Altered performance of schizophrenia patients in an auditory detection and discrimination task: Exploring the 'self-monitoring' model of hallucination. *Schizophrenia Research, 55*, 115–128.

Liddle, P. F., Friston, K. J., Frith, C. D., & Frackowiak, R. S. (1992). Cerebral blood flow and mental processes in schizophrenia. *Journal of the Royal Society of Medicine, 85*, 224–227.

Malenka, R. C., Angel, R. W., Hampton, B., & Berger, P. A. (1982). Impaired central error-correcting behavior in schizophrenia. *Archives of General Psychiatry, 39*, 101–107.

Maruff, P., Wilson, P., & Currie, J. (2003). Abnormalities of motor imagery associated with somatic passivity phenomena in schizophrenia. *Schizophrenia Research, 60*, 229–238.

McGuire, P. K., Jones, P., Harvey, I., Bebbington, P., Toone, B., Lewis, S., & Murray, R. M. (1994). Cannabis and acute psychosis. *Schizophrenia Research, 13*, 161–167.

McGuire, P. K., Silbersweig, D. A., Wright, I., Murray, R. M., David, A. S., Frackowiak, R. S., & Frith, C. D. (1995). Abnormal monitoring of inner speech: A physiological basis for auditory hallucinations. *Lancet, 346*, 596–600.

McGuire, P. K., Silbersweig, D. A., Wright, I., Murray, R. M., Frackowiak, R. S., & Frith, C. D. (1996). The neural correlates of inner speech and auditory verbal imagery in schizophrenia: Relationship to auditory verbal hallucinations. *British Journal of Psychiatry, 169*, 148–159.

Merckelbach, H., & Van de Ven, V. (2001). Another White Christmas: Fantasy proneness and reports of 'hallucinatory experiences' in undergraduate students. *Journal of Behaviour Therapy and Experimental Psychiatry, 32*, 137–144.

Miall, R. C., Weir, D. J., Wolpert, D. M., & Stein, J. F. (1993). Is the cerebellum a Smith predictor? *Journal of Motor Behaviour, 25*, 203–216.

Mintz, S., & Alpert, M. (1972). Imagery vividness, reality testing, and schizophrenic hallucinations. *Journal of Abnormal Psychology, 79*, 310–316.

Mlakar, J., Jensterle, J., & Frith, C. D. (1994). Central monitoring deficiency and schizophrenic symptoms. *Psychological Medicine, 24*, 557–564.

Morrison, A. P., & Haddock, G. (1997). Cognitive factors in source monitoring and auditory hallucinations. *Psychological Medicine, 27*, 669–679.

Morrison, A. P., Wells, A., & Nothard, S. (2002). Cognitive and emotional predictors of predisposition to hallucinations in non-patients. *British Journal of Clinical Psychology, 41*, 259–270.

Murnane, K., & Bayen, U. J. (1998). Measuring memory for source: Some theoretical assumptions and technical limitations. *Memory and Cognition, 26*, 674–677.

Nayani, T. H., & David, A. S. (1996a). The auditory hallucination: A phenomenological survey. *Psychological Medicine, 26*, 177–189.

Nayani, T., & David, A. (1996b). The neuropsychology and neurophenomenology of auditory hallucinations. In C. Pantelis, H. E. Nelson, & T. R. E. Barnes (Eds.), *Schizophrenia: A neuropsychological perspective* (pp.345–372). Chichester: Wiley.

Pantelis, C., & Maruff, P. (2002). The cognitive neuropsychiatric approach to investigating the neurobiology of schizophrenia and other disorders. *Journal of Psychosomatic Research, 53*, 655–664.

Picchioni, M. M., Chitnis, X. A., Fu, C. H. Y., Vythelingum, N., Andrew, C., Toulopoulou, T., Williams, S. C. R., Murray, R. M., & McGuire, P. K. (2002). Imaging verbal self monitoring in monozygotic twins discordant for schizophrenia [Abstract]. *Schizophrenia Research, 53*, (Suppl.), 23.

Rector, N. A., & Beck A. T. (2002). Cognitive therapy for schizophrenia: From conceptualization to intervention. *Canadian Journal of Psychiatry, 47*, 39–48.

Roman, R., & Landis, C. (1945). Hallucinations and mental imagery. *Journal of Nervous and Mental Disease, 102*, 327–331.

Schacter, D. L., Norman, K. A., & Koutstaal, W. (1998). The cognitive neuroscience of constructive memory. *Annual Review of Psychology, 49*, 289–318.

Seal, M. L., Crowe, S. F., & Cheung, P. (1997). Deficits in source monitoring in subjects with auditory hallucinations may be due to differences in verbal intelligence and verbal memory. *Cognitive Neuropsychiatry, 2*, 273–290.

Seitz, P. F., & Molholm, H. B. (1947). Relation of mental imagery to hallucinations. *Archives of Neurology and Psychiatry, 57*, 469–480.

Shergill, S. S., Brammer, M. J., Fukuda, R., Williams, S. C. R., Murray, R. M., & McGuire, P. K. (2003). Engagement of brain areas implicated in processing inner speech in people with auditory hallucinations. *British Journal of Psychiatry, 182*, 525–531.

Shergill, S. S., Bullmore, E., Simmons, A., Murray, R., & McGuire, P. K. (2000a). Functional anatomy of auditory verbal imagery in schizophrenic patients with auditory hallucinations. *American Journal of Psychiatry, 157*, 1691–1693.

Shergill, S. S., Brammer, M. J., Williams, S. C., Murray, R. M., & McGuire, P. K. (2000b). Mapping auditory hallucinations in schizophrenia using functional magnetic resonance imaging. *Archives of General Psychiatry, 57*, 1033–1038.

Shergill, S. S., Murray, R. M., & McGuire, P. K. (1998). Auditory hallucinations: A review of psychological treatments. *Schizophrenia Research, 32*, 137–50.

Slade, P. D. (1976). An investigation of psychological factors involved in the predisposition to auditory hallucinations. *Psychological Medicine, 6*, 123–132.

Smith, P., & Gudjonsson, G. (1995). The relationship of mental disorder to suggestibility and confabulation among forensic inpatients. *Journal of Forensic Psychiatry, 6*, 499–515.

Snodgrass, J. G., & Corwin, J. (1988). Pragmatics of measuring recognition memory: Application to dementia and amnesia. *Journal of Experimental Psychology. General, 117*, 34–50.

Spitzer, M. (1997). A cognitive neuroscience view of schizophrenic thought disorder. *Schizophrenia Bulletin, 23,* 29–50.

Starker, S., & Jolin, A. (1982). Imagery and hallucination in schizophrenic patients. *Journal of Nervous and Mental Disease, 170,* 448–451.

Stephane, M., Barton, S., & Boutros, N. N. (2001). Auditory verbal hallucinations and dysfunction of the neural substrates of speech. *Schizophrenia Research, 50,* 61–78.

Stephane, M., Thuras, P., Nasrallah, H., & Georgopoulos, A. P. (2003). The internal structure of the phenomenology of auditory verbal hallucinations. *Schizophrenia Research, 61,* 185–193.

Stirling, J. D., Hellewell, J. S., & Ndlovu, D. (2001). Self-monitoring dysfunction and the positive symptoms of schizophrenia. *Psychopathology, 34,* 198–202.

Stirling, J. D., Hellewell, J. S., & Quraishi, N. (1998). Self-monitoring dysfunction and the schizophrenic symptoms of alien control. *Psychological Medicine, 28,* 675–683.

Vinogradov, S., Willis-Shore, J., Poole, J. H., Marten, E., Ober, B. A., & Shenaut, G. K. (1997). Clinical and neurocognitive aspects of source monitoring errors in schizophrenia. *American Journal of Psychiatry, 46,* 83–27.

Wegner, D. M., & Erber, R. (1992). The hyperaccessibility of suppressed thoughts. *Journal of Personality and Social Psychology, 65,* 1093–1104.

Weiss, A. P., & Heckers, S. (2001). Neuroimaging of declarative memory in schizophrenia. *Scandinavian Journal of Psychology, 42,* 239–250.

Wolpert, D. M., Ghahramani, Z., & Jordan, M. I. (1995). An internal model for sensorimotor integration. *Science, 269,* 1880–1882.

Woodruff, P. W., Wright, I. C., Bullmore, E. T., Brammer, M., Howard, R. J., Williams, S. C., Shapleske, J., Rossell, S., David, A. S., McGuire, P. K., & Murray, R. M. (1997). Auditory hallucinations and the temporal cortical response to speech in schizophrenia: A functional magnetic resonance imaging study. *American Journal of Psychiatry, 154,* 1676–1682.

Zalewski, C., Johnson-Selfridge, M. T., Ohriner, S., Zarrella, K., & Seltzer, J. C. (1998). A review of neuropsychological differences between paranoid and nonparanoid schizophrenia patients. *Schizophrenia Bulletin, 24,* 127–145.

Zatorre, R. J., Bouffard, M., Ahad, P., & Belin, P. (2002). Where is 'where' in the human auditory cortex? *Nature Neuroscience, 5,* 905–909.

Auditory hallucinations: Insights and questions from neuroimaging

P. W. R. Woodruff
University of Sheffield, UK

Introduction. The human brain has the capacity to hallucinate but rarely, except in severe neuropsychiatric conditions such as schizophrenia, do they naturally predominate. The neural basis of auditory verbal hallucinations (AVHs) has been investigated using structural and functional neuroimaging techniques. So far, no studies have defined a model that explains why auditory hallucinations are *perceived* in the absence of an external stimulus.

Methods. A selective literature review was undertaken specifically to focus on: (1) clinical phenomenology; (2) putative brain systems involved in the pathogenesis of auditory hallucinations as suggested by neuroimaging studies; (3) contributions and weaknesses of the neuroimaging findings in potentially bridging the gap between the neuroscience and phenomenology. Throughout, an attempt was made to ask questions as much as to answer them.

Results. Functional domains implicated in the genesis of auditory verbal hallucinations include: (1) hearing and language; (2) "sense of reality", including externality of voices; (3) attention and salience; (4) emotional response; (5) memory; (6) volition and self-monitoring; (7) impulse control. Each of these domains can be mapped onto neural "systems" that comprise components that overlap with brain regions known to activate during the experience of auditory hallucinations

Conclusions. In the next phase of neuroimaging research into the pathogenesis of auditory hallucinations we need to examine component processes that lead to the patient's *perception* of them as *real.*

The aim of this paper is to discuss themes relevant to our understanding of auditory hallucinations with particular reference to insights from neuroimaging work. Specifically, I will address: (1) the link between clinical phenomenology of auditory hallucinations and auditory processing in neuropsychiatric disorder,

---

Correspondence should be addressed to Professor P.W.R. Woodruff, Sheffield Cognition and Neuroimaging Laboratory, University of Sheffield, Sheffield S5 7JT, UK.

I gratefully acknowledge help from Kathryn Pursall in the preparation of the manuscript, and to Dr Michael Hunter for helpful scientific discussion. I express my thanks to Dr Sean Spence, Jean Woodhead, and Beverley Nesbitt for organising the Sheffield 2 Psychopathology Symposium, which helped stimulate the debate.

particularly schizophrenia; and (2) putative brain systems involved in the pathogenesis of auditory hallucinations as suggested by neuroimaging studies. It is intended that further testable hypotheses will derive from this discussion.

The premise is that auditory hallucinations are auditory *perceptions* in the absence of an external stimulus. Hence, whatever their mental origin, they must involve the neural apparatus responsible for auditory perception (i.e., the primary and secondary auditory cortex). Auditory hallucinations are a prominent feature of psychosis. But they do occur in other conditions. Many otherwise healthy people complain of this symptom, particularly on falling asleep or on waking. Hence, the brain has the *capacity* and *potential* to experience these phenomena under certain conditions. However, in schizophrenia, the frequency and intensity of auditory hallucinations are such as to intrude upon and dominate lives. One could ask, why don't we normally hallucinate? Presumably, whatever process the normal brain exercises whilst awake eliminates the possibility of auditory hallucinations; be it the exercise of attention, or some other feature of wakefulness.

On the basis that our experiences and emotions are mediated by the brain, without which we would cease to experience anything meaningful, I am working on the assumption that abnormal experiences, such as auditory hallucinations, are mediated by brain mechanisms. I will therefore also focus on the brain and a particular means of examining the structure and function of the living human brain: Neuroimaging.

I intend to start with the clinical phenomenology, and move to neuroimaging studies that have examined putative brain mechanisms underlying auditory hallucinations in schizophrenia. The challenge is to derive models that explain the phenomenology rather than fitting the models to a phenomenology that does not pertain to the condition.

Clinical phenomenology and auditory processing in schizophrenia

Nayani and David's (1996) phenomenological survey of 100 psychotic patients who experienced auditory hallucinations revealed a number of key clinical features. This sample consisted of 100 individuals drawn from a psychiatry patient population. Most were young male patients with schizophrenia, socially isolated, unmarried and unemployed. The duration of auditory hallucinations was 11.4 ± 9.4 years and the onset, on average, preceded the diagnosis.

I have divided the phenomenology described in Nayani and David's paper into seven functional domains, which could be related to functional networks amenable to study using neuroimaging (Table 1).

Hearing and language. Auditory hallucinations convey meaning via words and language, and are thus likely to involve the *language* system in those who

TABLE 1
Component cortical regions expected to activate during auditory verbal hallucinations

Functional domain	Predicted cortical regions activated during auditory hallucinations
Auditory and language function	Temporal cortex: Heschl's gyrus (primary auditory cortex), superior temporal gyrus; Broca's area; MTG
"Sense of reality" (similarity to external voices; awareness of spatial location, "externality")	Planum temporale
Attentional mechanisms (salience)	Anterior and posterior cingulate; thalamus (direction to cortical awareness)
Emotional response	Amygdala; insula (relay to limbic regions); parahippocampal gyrus
Memory (linguistic, emotional)	Hippocampus, amygdala
Volition and self-monitoring	Supplementary motor association cortex, anterior cingulate, prefrontal cortex, ventral striatum, parahippocampus
Impulse control	Orbitofrontal gyrus

experience them. For instance, in Nayani and David's paper, the voices were heard frequently and for long periods, most or all of the time (in 52%), and over 1 hour duration (in 42%). The form of the voice was of normal conversational volume (in 73%). There were different types of voice but most commonly these were commands.

Spatial location and "sense of reality". An intriguing aspect of auditory hallucinations is their spatial attribute, which can be external (in 49%), internal (in 38%) or both external and internal to the subject (in 12%). Presumably, this attribute is perceived as part of the "impression" of the overall feature of the voices. Its central importance phenomenologically is, I would argue, its direct association with the *sense of reality* with which auditory hallucinations are experienced. The sense of reality with which auditory hallucinations are perceived is a *key feature* of psychosis that needs to be explored further.

Attention and salience. A number of clinical observations imply that attention influences the salience of the experience of auditory hallucinations. For instance, auditory hallucinations tend to be worse in the morning or evening, and when those suffering from them are on their own (in 80% of cases) and therefore more likely to be focusing their attention on them (Nayani & David, 1996). That sufferers from auditory hallucinations can exercise a degree of control, by concentrating on the voice and thereby modulating their salience (in 38%), or even stopping them completely (in 21%), is testament to the ability of attention to modulate (top-down) these perceptual experiences. Presumably, distraction techniques operate through similar mechanisms by diverting attentional resources away from the unwanted auditory hallucinations. Hence, auditory hallucinations are symptoms that can be modified via *attentional* systems that may facilitate coping.

We know, from previous electrophysiological and neuroimaging studies, that attention to a stimulus enhances the activation in those brain regions that subserve the perception of that stimulus (Woldorf et al., 1993; Woodruff et al., 1996). It is likely therefore, that attention to auditory hallucinations, will not only increase the subject's awareness of them, but also activity within cerebral cortex responsible for their perception. It is tempting to suppose that the two processes are causally related.

Emotional response to auditory hallucinations. In Nayani and David's survey, around half of the individuals suffering from auditory hallucinations experienced them as distressing and anxiety-provoking or associated with feeling sad. Fear and anger were less common, but equally distressing in those who suffered from them. Hence, emotional networks, such as the limbic system and insula, are likely to be invoked by auditory hallucinations. We might also expect activation during auditory hallucinations of regions within the temporal cortex closely connected to limbic regions, such as the middle temporal cortex (MTG). We know, for example, from our own work that the MTG normally activates during tasks involving empathy (Farrow et al., 2001).

Memory. The strong emotional response associated with auditory hallucinations is likely to involve emotional memory. One of the most robust structural abnormalities described in populations of patients with schizophrenia is reduced amygdala/hippocampal volume bilaterally (see Wright et al., 2000). However, the functional significance of this finding remains incompletely explained. Also, working memory deficits in schizophrenia are well described and the role of (mainly left) dorsolateral prefrontal cortex (DLPFC) in the successful performance of executive tasks has led investigators to suggest lack of function in the prefrontal cortex may be responsible for the observed "hypofrontal" activation in many neuroimaging studies in schizophrenia (Weinberger, Aloia, Goldberg, & Berman, 1994).

However, the possible role of linguistic and emotional memory in the evolution of auditory hallucinations needs investigation (see later).

Volition and self-monitoring. Auditory hallucinations are generally unwanted, unwilled, outside volitional control, implicating mechanisms of *volition and self-monitoring* of mental events. In developing Frith's ideas on self-monitoring, McGuire and others have argued that inner speech generates the linguistic signals which are perceived as "alien" auditory verbal hallucinations because a failure of the person to successfully "monitor" their own inner speech (Frith, 1987; McGuire et al., 1996).

Impulse control. Auditory hallucinations that command the person experiencing them to harm themselves, accompanied by the urge to act upon them, are likely to invoke *impulse control* systems. In those at high risk of suicide (10% lifetime risk in schizophrenia) impulse control is a key protective factor (Oquendo & Mann, 2000). One would predict therefore that those in whom auditory hallucinations are predominantly of a commanding nature would activate those brain regions associated with impulse control.

Brain regions activated by auditory hallucinations

Table 1 lists some of the component regions within each of the seven domains we might expect to be activated or modulated in some way during auditory hallucinations. Figure 1 summarises, schematically, the brain systems that may be involved in the experience of, and response to, auditory hallucinations and their putative interactions.

Table 2 lists, from a sample of ten studies, brain areas actually activated within the prime functional domains that we would predict to be involved from the phenomenology (described above; see also David 1999; Weiss & Heckers, 1999). For instance, the study by Shergill, Brammer, Williams, Murray, & McGuire (2000) shows activation during auditory hallucinations in a repre-

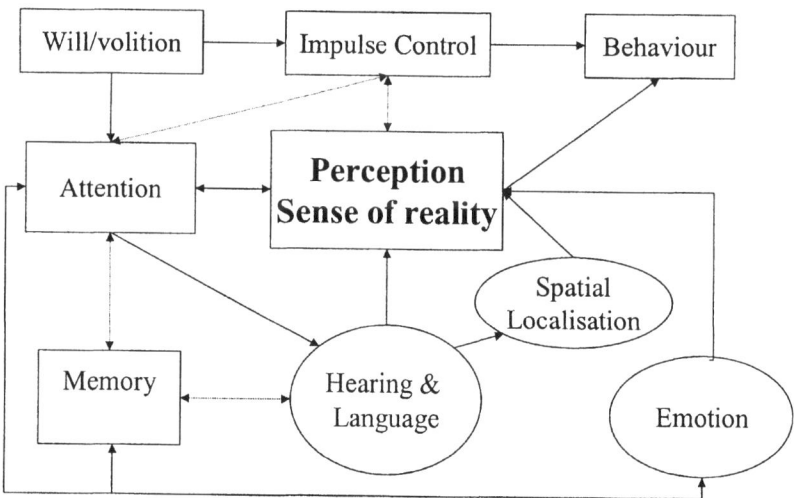

Figure 1. Auditory hallucinations and brain systems.

TABLE 2
Main brain areas activated during auditory hallucinations

Brain area
–Heschl's gyrus*
Superior temporal gyrus*
Broca's
Middle temporal gyrus*
–Planum temporale*
–Anterior cingulate*
Thalamus*
–Amygdala*
Insula
Parahippocampus
Hippocampus*
–Orbitofrontal

Studies: Musalek et al. (1989), Cleghorn et al. (1990), Suzuki et al. (1993), McGuire et al. (1993), Silbersweig et al. (1995), Woodruff et al. (1995), Dierks et al. (1999), Lennox et al. (2000), Shergill et al. (2000), Bentaleb et al. (2002). *Replicated study.

sentative sample of brain regions across these domains. They scanned six patients with schizophrenia whilst they were actually hallucinating, and also whilst not hallucinating, and compared brain activation between the two conditions. Within auditory and language regions, there was activation in the right superior temporal gyrus (STG) and middle temporal gyrus (MTG); auditory spatial localisation regions included the right superior and inferior parietal lobule and the middle frontal gyrus, as well as the right MTG (cf. Bushara et al., 1999); an "attentional network" which included the anterior cingulate and right thalamus; an "emotional network" of right and left insula, the parahippocampal gyrus (also possibly involved in self-monitoring); and finally, the prefrontal cortex involved broadly in executive function, and impulse control mechanisms.

Physiological theories and auditory processes

Penfield and Perot (1963) showed that direct brain stimulation lead to auditory hallucinations for simple sounds and words. Hence spontaneous cortical activity such as occurs during epileptic seizures, might be responsible for spontaneous auditory hallucinations. Naturally, there is a great difference between the experience of simple sounds and words and the complex auditory hallucinations that are experienced by patients.

Temporal cortical activation and language. The temporal cortex may be considered a final common path for the perception of complex speech with the features of auditory hallucinations. So, at some level the temporal cortex must be involved in the perception of auditory hallucinations. This hypothesis is borne out by a wealth of structural magnetic resonance imaging studies that show temporal lobe (STG and planum temporale, PT) abnormalities in schizophrenia (Pearlson, 1997; Levitan, Ward & Kats, 1999; Shapleske et al., 1999, 2001). Further, the finding of Barta, Pearlson, Powers, Richards, & Tune, (1990) (replicated by Rajarethinam, DeQuardo, Nalepa, & Tandon, 2000) of an inverse correlation between STG volume and auditory hallucination emphasises the central importance of this region in the pathogenesis of auditory hallucinations in schizophrenia.

In the functional domain, a number of studies report significant activation in language-related brain regions during auditory hallucinations (Table 3). Shergill et al. (2001) described the case of a patient who experienced concurrent auditory and somatosensory hallucinations of differing periodicity. Examination of brain areas active during hallucinations revealed right STG activation specific to the periodicity of auditory hallucinations.

If the temporal cortical activity is coincident with auditory hallucinations, how are its processing demands for other speech perception tasks affected? Does the temporal cortex process speech normally?

In our study (Woodruff et al., 1997), we tested the neural "saturation" hypothesis to probe how the auditory cortical response to speech alters with the experience of auditory hallucinations. A series of seven male patients were presented with external speech during scanning using functional magnetic resonance imaging (fMRI) on two occasions: first, whilst actively hallucinating,

TABLE 3
Neuroimaging studies that report significant activation in language-related brain regions during auditory hallucinations

	Author	Year	Scanning technique	Brain region activated
1	Matsuda et al.	1988	SPECT	Left STG
2	Suzuki et al.	1993	SPECT	Left STG
3	McGuire et al.	1993	SPECT	Broca's area
4	Woodruff et al.	1995	fMRI	STG, right MTG (in functionally defined auditory cortex)
5	Lennox et al.	1998	fMRI	STG (right > left)
6	Dierks et al.	1999	fMRI	Heschl's gyrus; STG; MTG
7	Shergill et al.	2000	fMRI	STG (bilateral); MTG (right > left)
8	Shergill et al.	2001	fMRI	Right STG/MTG
9	Bentaleb et al.	2002	fMRI	Left Heschl's gyrus; right MTG

SPECT = single photon emission computerised tomography; fMRI = functional magnetic resonance imaging; STG = superior temporal gyrus; MTG = middle temporal gyrus.

and second, after recovery. The external speech-induced activation in the temporal cortex (particularly the right MTG) was attenuated in the actively hallucinating patient group in comparison with the same patient group's response after treatment. Hence, auditory hallucinations drive the normal hearing apparatus (temporal cortex: STG and MTG) to the point where they compete with external speech for resources allocated to that apparatus. The fMRI case study by Bentaleb et al. (2002) also found evidence in favour of the saturation hypothesis. These studies are in keeping with an earlier study in the patients using magneto-encephalography (MEG) that reported response delays in the auditory cortex during auditory hallucinations (Tiihonen et al., 1992).

Although indirect, further evidence in support of the saturation hypothesis is the observation (in studies that include this region in their analyses) that the very regions that exhibit reduced response to external speech during auditory hallucinations (e.g., the STG and MTG) are those that activate during auditory hallucinations (Table 2).

Responsivity of auditory cortex to auditory stimuli and effects of attention. The *effect* of auditory hallucinations *on* sensory cortical response has been discussed. However, whatever the *origins* of the stimuli within the brain that lead to the *experience* of auditory hallucinations, it is likely that the final common path to that experience lies within the auditory cortex itself. If so, to what extent is the neuronal architecture of the temporal cortex such that it is *predisposed* to respond to certain auditory signals that may influence the subsequent experience? For example, is the temporal cortex predisposed to respond to certain emotional aspects of speech, that could be disturbed in those predisposed to develop auditory hallucinations?

Some insights about the predisposition of the temporal cortex to auditory signals come from work by Belin, Zatorre, & Lafaille, Ahad, and Pike (2000), who have shown that humans have regions of superior temporal gyrus including the left PT that respond specifically to voices as opposed to environmental sounds. Whether this differential responsivity reflects pre-attentive processes or higher cognitive influences remains to be explored. But whatever the modulating influences that may or may not act on the PT, this study demonstrates that responsivity of the PT varies according to "host-specific" qualities of auditory signals. In this case, that quality refers to signals of relevance to human social communication, and puts the PT at the heart of the neural processing of socially salient auditory signals.

Recent preliminary work in Sheffield (Woodruff et al., 2002) provides preliminary evidence to support the idea that the responsivity of the temporal cortex to passive perception of voices can be modulated by cortical stimulation across the skull using transcranial magnetic stimulation (TMS). In this example, the temporal cortical response to external speech (as detected using fMRI) was enhanced (doubled) by the addition of TMS to the left temporoparietal region above the left ear. TMS altered responsivity both ipsi- and contralateral to the site of TMS application, thus confirming the presence of distal effects to homotopically connected regions. This work parallels the additional neuroimaging observation that TMS alone induces cortical responses both directly underlying the site of application as well as distal to it (Nahas et al., 2001). In some clinical trials, TMS reduces the intensity of auditory hallucinations when delivered at frequencies of around 1 Hz to the left temporoparietal region (Hoffman et al., 2000, 2003). Hence, altered sensitivity of the auditory cortex provides a possible component pathophysiological brain mechanism for auditory hallucinations, and its modulation (by TMS) might have therapeutic implications.

Might it be, therefore, that an increased sensitivity to certain features of speech alters perception in subtle ways that increases the *liability* to develop auditory hallucinations? It is clinically observed that some patients with schizophrenia report increased sensitivity to noise; a feature that sometimes presages the occurrence of auditory hallucinations. Is this reflected in neuronal response? In some earlier work we showed that the responsivity of the auditory cortex appeared increased in those patients with schizophrenia who had a tendency to hallucinate, compared with those did not have such a tendency (Woodruff et al., 1998). On the understanding that the response of the auditory cortex to speech was modulated by attention to the auditory signal (Woodruff et al., 1996) we postulated that a tendency to hallucinate could be mediated by attentional processes that primed the auditory cortex to respond to certain features of speech preferentially (Figure 2).

One such "attentional preference" might be to certain emotional qualities in the sound of speech versus its semantic content. In addition to colouring the quality of auditory hallucinations for the hearer, such a mechanism could produce a sinister quality to how spoken speech is perceived and hence predispose to a paranoid interpretation. We know for instance, that in some studies (e.g., Woodruff et al., 1997), although not in all, the response of the auditory cortex is relatively right lateralised. And studies have shown that prosodic processing is processed mainly on the right (Buchanan et al., 2000). Could it be that some of the observed right lateralisation of speech activity in schizophrenia is due to a hyper-responsivity of the temporal cortex to emotional innuendo or other intonational properties? Mitchell, Elliott, Barry, Cruttenden, & Woodruff (2003) tested this hypothesis using fMRI. In healthy volunteers, passive listening to speech (filtered such that it contained only prosody without discernable semantic features) caused activation in the temporal cortex more on right than the left. Attending to happy-sounding versus happy-meaning sentences exaggerated this response on the right (Mitchell et al., 2003). In patients with schizophrenia, however, attending to the happy-sounding versus happy-meaning sentences enhanced activity in the left rather than the right temporal cortex (Mitchell & Woodruff, 2001). One possible explanation for this finding is that there is some

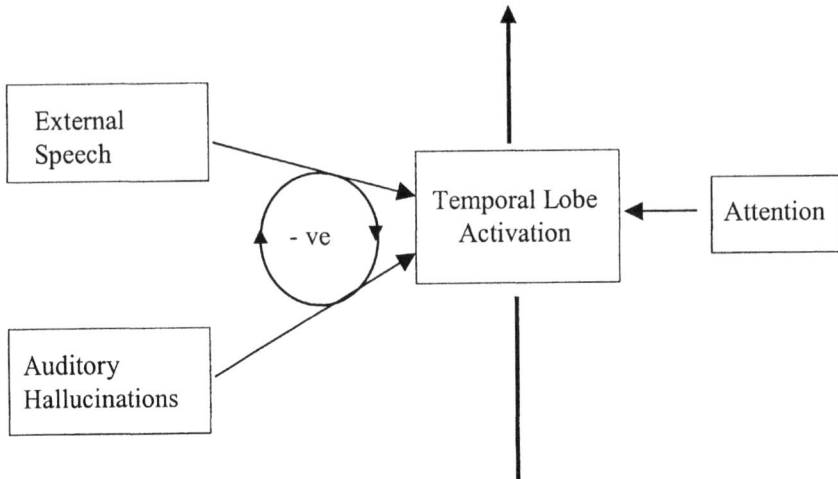

Figure 2. A model for attentional modulation of temporal cortical activation by both external speech and auditory hallucinations (which both compete for finite resources within the temporal cortex). The power of temporal lobe activation is represented by the vertical arrow in the centre of the figure. Both external speech and auditory hallucinations directly activate the temporal cortex (indicated by arrows). The circle between indicates the reciprocal relationship between the temporal cortical response to external speech versus that induced by auditory hallucinations (as predicted by the saturation hypothesis, see Woodruff et al., 1997). The extent to which these sources of stimuli actually result in temporal lobe activation is modulated by attention (arrow on the right). Attention may alter the threshold of response or general "responsivity" of temporal cortex to external speech or auditory hallucinations. Generally, the greater the attention to the sources of stimuli, the greater the temporal cortical activation. (See also Woodruff et al., 1997, 1998.)

reversal of function in schizophrenia in respect of prosody, but directed to the left rather than the right. This in turn could possibly interfere with normal semantic processes in left temporal cortex.

Altered sensitivity to emotional intonation, innuendo, and other aspects of speech that could perhaps predispose to auditory hallucinations and delusions need further investigation.

In the case study of a patient with bilateral auditory cortical damage following a stroke, Engelien et al. (2000) described temporal cortical activation induced by attention to sounds in the absence of auditory cortical function (that would lead to conscious perception of sound). Of note is that in this context MTG activation was prominent (an area that is commonly activated by auditory hallucinations). If auditory hallucinations are attentionally modulated, then it would seem from this work that the MTG is especially susceptible to such modulation. Of course, attention may lead to focus on features of speech to which the MTG predominantly responds (such as emotional prosody), or it may be that the MTG has a generally lower threshold of response to attentional modulation. Either way, presumably the auditory cortex has to be "switched on" by an auditory hallucination "trigger". Such a trigger could, for example, involve the posterior cingulate (an area of activation observed in the example above; and shown to respond to discerning emotional valency of emotional words; Maddock, Garrett, & Buonocore, 2003) or anterior cingulate, which may increase the person's awareness of the mind's "conscious content" (Posner & Rothbart, 1998). Other candidate regions could include the thalamus. In their pharmacologically modulated hearing case, Silbersweig and Stern (1998) noted that reduced conscious perception of continuous auditory stimulation induced by midazolam sedation was especially associated with decreased activity in the thalamus. The implication is that thalamic activity is necessary for conscious awareness of auditory signals. In this case, I do not distinguish between the origins of the stimuli (external or internal). However, thalamus activation as an accompaniment of conscious awareness of auditory hallucinations is a replicated finding (Table 2).

Imagery vs. reality. Auditory hallucinations often appear real to the person perceiving them. Their location as external to the hearer contributes to this sense of reality. Our work (Hunter et al., 2003; Hunter, 2004 this issue) explains how functional neuroimaging has been used to demonstrate how the brain detects the spatial location of speech, in the left posterior temporal cortex (planum temporale). Griffiths & Warren (2002) have argued that the planum temporale (PT) is a "computational hub" that allows us to integrate and make sense of a range of complex sound and speech features. It is quite possible that the PT provides the "computational hub" that allows the listener to compute where the voices come from, and through this, an appreciation of how real they are. The clinical observation that the location of the voice remains the same in relation to the head in around 65% of sufferers (does not become louder as the subject moves towards it) can be taken to support the idea that the internal "neural drive" that leads to the perception of auditory hallucinations also determines their spatial location fixed in relation to the head.

Auditory verbal imagery has been explored as a "proxy" marker for auditory verbal hallucinations but is, nevertheless, quite distinct from their actual experience. In a study of healthy volunteers, McGuire et al. (1996) used PET to distinguish the neural basis of auditory verbal imagery and inner speech. Some areas of activation overlapped with those regions subsequently described in other studies as engaged during auditory hallucinations (e.g., the anterior cingulate, posterior STG). Other regions, such as the SMA and DLPFC, were distinct from regions commonly described as active during auditory hallucinations (Table 2). Thus, there appears to be some distinction between the neural correlates of auditory verbal imagery and auditory hallucinations, in particular, the prominence of frontal lobe activation during imagery. Frontal lobe activation, it has been argued, represents the volitional control of imagery

(Silbersweig & Stern, 1998)—a feature that profoundly separates this "effortful" task from the effortless (or actively resisted) phenomena of auditory hallucinations. In the study of McGuire et al. (1996), and some other mental imagery studies (e.g., D'Esposito et al., 1997), the primary sensory cortex was not necessary for the conscious experience of imagery. Primary sensory cortical activation, commonly observed in neuroimaging studies of auditory hallucinations, may therefore be one of the key neural events that underpin the reality with which auditory hallucinations are experienced, as opposed to (consciously controlled) mental imagery. These factors (together with externality of auditory hallucinations) that lead to the heightened sense of reality of auditory hallucinations are a focus of intensive research in our laboratory.

Emotional response and auditory hallucinations. The personal, often derogatory content of auditory hallucinations in those suffering from psychotic disorders, would naturally be expected to cause a strong emotional response from the sufferer. Indeed, this response is the common clinical observation (see above). So, the emotional response is likely to result from distressing auditory hallucination content, as well as the disturbance caused by the form of the experience itself.

The evidence of structural abnormalities in "limbic" regions in those predisposed to auditory hallucinations, such as sufferers from schizophrenia, provides some neural basis for the emotional response. Hence, the insula has formed the focus of attention in this regard (Crespo-Facorro et al., 2000; Goldstein et al., 1999; Shapleske et al., 2002, Sigmundsson et al., 2001; Wright et al., 1999). The insula is a key relay station between the frontotemporal cortical areas and limbic regions, including MTG. The MTG has a role to play in verbal self-monitoring (see earlier) and is clearly activated by emotional processing such as empathy (Farrow et al., 2001). We have shown, using fMRI, that the right MTG acts as a key region that is modulated by attention to emotion as conveyed by the intonation of speech (emotional prosody; Mitchell et al., 2003). In patients with schizophrenia, however, attention to emotional prosody modulated activity in the MTG of the opposite (left) hemisphere (Mitchell & Warren, 2001; and see earlier).

It is recognised, but poorly understood, that emotion contributes significantly to the fixation of belief (Dolan, 2002). Here, the salience of emotional, self-referential content of auditory hallucinations experienced by those with schizophrenia may be linked to the frequently held strong belief in their external reality. Emotion may enhance perception and subsequent responses through pre-attentive or attentional mechanisms. An enhanced response to emotionally neutral targets is observed when associated with emotional cues (e.g., threat words), such as occur in auditory hallucinations in schizophrenia. Inappropriate activation of the orbitofrontal cortex (a possible site of interaction between targets and cues (Armony & Dolan, 2002), and site of activation during auditory hallucinations) could conceivably introduce inappropriate emotional salience to verbal hallucinations.

Memory. The involvement of memory systems in the pathogenesis of auditory hallucinations is little studied. It seems likely, however, that memory systems would be invoked by the need to access linguistic information. Whether they result from faulty memory retrieval however, is an interesting question.

The possible links between memory and emotion can be explored further. The amygdala is a region both activated during auditory hallucinations and implicated in linking perception (of emotionally salient events) to automatic emotional responses and (enhanced) memory (Dolan, 2002).

An intact amygdala is essential for acquiring and preserving implicit fear conditioning (LaBar, Le Doux, & Spencer, 1995). Its activation during auditory hallucinations may thus relate to the reinforcement or evocation of the adverse emotional response to auditory hallucinations themselves.

Abnormal endogenous language production and reception: Inner speech and verbal self-monitoring. A number of parallel lines of enquiry related to language systems have been examined by McGuire and colleagues. They have examined the idea that auditory hallucinations in schizophrenia are due to abnormalities of "inner speech" (the thinking to oneself in words) and self-monitoring deficits that are invoked by auditory verbal imagery (imaging someone speaking to you in an alien voice; McGuire et al., 1996; Shergill et al., 2000). The essential concept is that patients with schizophrenia have difficulties with monitoring their inner speech and misattribute their thoughts in some way to those arising from another person. They present some elegant neuroimaging studies, such as those of McGuire et al. (1996), which show differences in activation patterns of temporal cortical regions in patients with a strong tendency to hallucinate, those without this tendency, and healthy volunteers. They, and others, report activation, during auditory hallucinations, of systems in self-monitoring, such as the supplementary motor area (SMA), anterior cingulate (AC), and parahippocampus (see Table 2). What may be of interest to investigate further, is the functional relationship between regions such as the SMA and AC that Spence (2002) and others have studied in relation to disordered agency in the context of schizophrenia (and see Spence & Halligan, 2002). It may be that the breakdown of these and similar functional relationships leads to a loss of "ownership" and the misattribution of the source of voices. Spence (2002) has argued that inappropriate activation of the right inferior parietal lobe leads to the misattribution of ownership to another in the alien limb syndrome. Could there be a similarly specific inappropriate or deficient activation in an area responsible for the misattribution of a self-generated "voice" as belonging to another?

Johns et al. (2001) reported that hallucinating patients with schizophrenia misattributed their own voice (artificially distorted) to one belonging to another, more frequently than controls (although similarly to hallucination-free patients with delusions). A similarly conceived but quite differently designed study showed that hallucinating patients with schizophrenia failed to show a (normal) difference in perception between self-produced and externally produced tactile stimuli (Blakemore, Smith, Steel, Johnstone, & Frith, 2000). This, they argued, supported the existence of an abnormal self-monitoring system in those who experience auditory hallucinations with schizophrenia. On the other hand, Li, Chen, Yang, Chen, and Tsay (2002) tested the self-monitoring model in closely matched psychiatric control groups using an auditory detection and discrimination task, and found no differences in response bias between hallucinating and nonhallucinating patients with schizophrenia.

In an attempt to describe a neural correlate of the corollary discharge thought to relate to auditory self-monitoring, Curio, Neuloh, Numminen, Jousmäki, and Hari, (2000) performed a MEG study to measure auditory cortical activity that normally occurs around 100 ms after self-uttered syllables. These responses were delayed by 11 ms in the speech-dominant left hemisphere relative to the right, whereas listening to a replay of the same utterances produced a symmetric response. Hence, they argued, speaking "primes" the speech-dominant auditory cortex in a way that delays its response to expected utterances.

One essential question that arises from this body of work is how inner speech and imagery fit in with the phenomenology of auditory verbal hallucinations as *auditory **perceptions** in the absence of an external stimulus*. For instance, what is the link between inner speech and auditory verbal perception?

Impulse control. Impulsivity is linked to hypoactivity in serotonergic neurotransmitter systems within the amygdala and orbitofrontal cortex (Oquendo & Mann, 2000). Neuroimaging studies demonstrate abnormalities within this neural system in those neuropsychiatric conditions associated with deficits in impulse control, such as attention deficit disorder in children, and schizophrenia (Rubia, 2002). Further, in healthy volunteers, those engaged in tasks that demand impulse control (such as the Go-NoGo Task), activate specific brain regions including orbitofrontal gyrus (Horn, Dolan, Elliott, Deaken, & Woodruff, in press). On this basis, we could predict that continual auditory hallucinations, instructing a person to harm themselves, would engage brain regions involved in the inhibition of the response to obey the voices.

Corticocortical connectivity and auditory hallucinations. Less than 1% of cortical afferents are from the thalamus; the vast majority are from neighbouring regions of the cortex (corticocortical connections; Braitenberg, 1978, pp. 454). Of these connections, 40% are naturally remodelled and lost during adolescence; a phenomenon that clearly involves the language system. This natural remodelling may reduce a person's ability to learn a second language after adolescence, and usually also precedes the peak age of onset of schizophrenia.

Hoffman and McGlashan (1997) showed, using a computerised neural network model of working memory, that a 77% reduction of synaptic connections resulted in the detection of words in the absence of an input, i.e., hallucinations (see Hoffman and McGlashan, 1997, fig. 4). Some synaptic elimination enhanced performance of the mathematical model, as occurs in real life during brain maturation, until a threshold is reached that makes the experience of auditory verbal hallucinations more likely.

A recent fMRI study (Lawrie et al., 2002) examined specifically the functional connectivity between frontal and temporal cortex activations in patients with schizophrenia whilst performing a verbal task (sentence completion). A functional connectivity coefficient was computed from a correlation between activity in predefined regions of DLPFC and left MTG/STG. The higher the level of auditory hallucinations the lower was the correlation coefficient (i.e., those with less connection between the DLPFC working memory regions and language regions within the temporal cortex had more severe auditory hallucinations).

CONCLUSIONS

Functional domains implicated in the genesis of auditory verbal hallucinations include: (1) hearing and language; (2) "sense of reality", including externality of voices; (3) attention and salience; (4) emotional response; (5) memory; (6) volition and self-monitoring; (7) impulse control. Each of these domains can be mapped onto neural "systems" which comprise components that overlap with brain regions known to activate during the experience of auditory hallucinations. However, no studies have defined a model that explains why auditory hallucinations are *perceived* in the absence of an external stimulus. In the next phase of neuroimaging research into the pathogenesis of auditory hallucinations we need to examine component processes that lead to the patient's *perception* of them as *real*.

Manuscript accepted 3 April 2003

REFERENCES

Armony, J. L., & Dolan, R. J. (2002) Modulation of spatial attention by fear-conditioned stimuli: An event-related fMRI study. *Neuropsychologia, 40*, 817–826.

Barta, P. E., Pearlson, G. D., Powers, R. E., Richards, S. S., & Tune, L. E. (1990) Auditory hallucinations and smaller superior temporal gyral volume in schizophrenia. *American Journal of Psychiatry, 147*, 1457–1462.

Belin, P., Zatorre, R. J., Lafaille, P., Ahad, P., & Pike, B. (2000). Voice-selective areas in human auditory cortex. *Nature* 403: 309–312.

Bentaleb, L. A., Beuregard, M., Liddle, P., & Stip, E. (2002). Cerebral activity associated with auditory verbal hallucinations: A functional magnetic resonance imaging case study. *Journal of Psychiatry and Neuroscience, 27*, 110–5.

Blakemore, S-J., Smith, J., Steel, R., Johnstone, E. C., & Frith, C. D. (2000). The perception of self-produced sensory stimuli in patients with auditory hallucinations and passivity experiences: Evidence for a breakdown in self-monitoring. *Psychological Medicine, 30*, 1131–1139.

Braitenberg, V. (1978). Cortical architectonics: General and areal. In M. A. B. Brazier & H. Petsche (Eds.), *Cortico-cortical connections* (pp. 453–454). New York: Raven Press.

Buchanan, T. W., Lutz, K., Mirzade, S., Specht, K., Shah, N. J., Zilles, K., & Jancke, L. (2000). Recognition of emotional prosody and verbal components of spoken language: An fMRI study. *Brain Research: Cognitive Brain Research, 9*, 227–238.

Bushara, K. O., Weeks, R. A., Ishii, K., Catalan, M. J., Tian, B., Rauschecker, J. P., & Hallett, M. (1999). Modality-specific frontal and parietal areas for auditory and visual spatial localization in humans. *Nature Neuroscience, 2*, 759–66.

Cleghorn, J. M., Garnett, E. S., Nahmias, C., Brown, G. M., Kaplan, R. D., Szechtman, H., Szechtman, B., Franco, S., Dermer, S. W., & Cook, P. (1990). Regional brain metabolism during auditory hallucinations in chronic schizophrenia. *British Journal of Psychiatry, 157*, 562–570.

Crespo-Facorro, B., Kim, J. J., Andreasen, N. C., O'Leary, D. S., Bockholt, J., & Magnotta, V. (2000). Insular cortex abnormalities in schizophrenia: A structural magnetic resonance imaging study of first-episode patients. *Schizophrenia Research, 46*, 35–43.

Curio, G., Neuloh, G., Numminen, J., Jousmäki, V., & Hari, R. (2000) Speaking modifies voice-evoked activity in the human auditory cortex. *Human Brain Mapping, 9*, 183–191.

David, A. S. (1999). Auditory hallucinations: Phenomenology, neuropsychology and neuroimaging update. *Acta Psychiatrica Scandinavica Supplementum, 395*, 95–104.

D'Esposito, M., Detre, J. A., Aguirre, G. K., Stallcup, M., Alsop, D. C., Tippet, L. J., & Farah, M. J. (1997). A functional MRI study of mental image generation. *Neuropsychologia, 35*, 725–730.

Dierks, T., Linden, D. E. J., Jandl, M., Formisano, E., Goebel, R., Lanfermann, H., & Singer, W. (1999). Activation of Heschl's Gyrus during Auditory Hallucinations. *Neuron, 22*, 615–621.

Dolan, R. J. (2002). Emotion, cognition and behaviour. *Science, 298*, 1191–1194.

Engelien, A., Huner, W., Silbersweig, D., Stern, E., Frith, C. D., Döring, W., Thron, A., & Frackowiak, R. S. J. (2000). The neural correlates of 'deaf-hearing' in man. *Brain, 123*, 532–545.

Farrow, T. F., Zheng, Y., Wilkinson, I. D., Spence, S. A., Deakin, J. F., Tarrier, N., Griffiths, P. D., & Woodruff, P. W. R. (2001). Investigating the functional anatomy of empathy and forgiveness. *Neuroreport, 12*, 2433–2438.

Frith, C. D. (1987). The positive and negative symptoms of schizophrenia reflect impairments in the perception and initiation of action. *Psychological Medicine, 17*, 631–348.

Goldstein, J. M., Goodman, J. M., Seidman, L. J., Kennedy, D. N., Makris, N., Lee, H., Tourville, J., Caviness, V. S., Faraone, S. V., & Tsuang, M. T. (1999). Cortical abnormalities in schizophrenia identified by structural magnetic resonance imaging. *Archives of General Psychiatry, 56*, 537–547.

Griffiths, T. D., & Warren, J. D. (2002). The planum temporale as a computational hub. *Trends in Neurosciences, 25*, 348–353.

Hoffman, R. E., Boutros, N. N., Hu, S., Berman, R. M., Krystal, J. H., & Charney, D. S. (2000). Transcranial magnetic stimulation and auditory hallucinations in schizophrenia. *Lancet, 355*, 1073–1075.

Hoffman, R. E., Hawkins, K. A., Gueorguieva, R., Boutros, N. N., Rachid, F., Carroll, K., & Krystal, J. H. (2003). Transcranial magnetic stimulation of left temporoparietal cortex and medication-resistant auditory hallucinations. *Archives of General Psychiatry, 60*, 49–56.

Hoffman, R. E., & McGlashan, T. H. (1997). Synaptic elimination, neurodevelopment, and the mechanism of hallucinated "voices" in schizophrenia. *American Journal of Psychiatry, 154*, 1683–1689.

Horn, N. R., Dolan, M., Elliott, R., Deakin, J. F. W., & Woodruff, P. W. R. (in press). Response inhibition and impulsivity: An fMRI study. *Neuropsychologia*.

Hunter, M. D. (2004). Locating voices in space: A perceptual model for auditory hallucinations? *Cognitive Neuropsychiatry*, 9(1/2), 93–105.

Hunter, M. D., Griffiths, T. D., Farrow, T. F., Zheng, Y., Wilkinson, I. D., Hegde, N., Woods, W., Spence, S. A., & Woodruff, P. W. (2003). A neural basis for the perception of voices in external auditory space. *Brain*, 126, 161–169.

Johns, L. C., Rossell, S., Frith, C., Ahmad, F., Helmsley, D., Kuipers, E., & McGuire, P. K. (2001). Verbal self-monitoring and auditory verbal hallucinations in patients with schizophrenia. *Psychological Medicine*, 31, 705–715.

LaBar, K. S., LeDoux, J. E., Spencer, D. D., & Phelps, E. A. (1995). Impaired fear conditioning following unilateral temporal lobectomy in humans. *Journal of Neuroscience*, 15, 6846–6855.

Lawrie, S. M., Buechel, C., Whalley, H. C., Frith, C. D., Friston, K. J., & Johnstone, E. C. (2002). Reduced frontotemporal functional connectivity in schizophrenia associated with auditory hallucinations. *Biological Psychiatry*, 51, 1008–1011.

Lennox, B. R., Park, S. B., Medley, I. O., Morris, P. G., & Jones, P. B. (2000). The functional anatomy of auditory hallucinations in schizophrenia. *Psychiatry Research*, 100, 13–20.

Levitan, C. L., Ward, P. B., & Catts, S. V. (1999). Superior temporal gyral volumes and laterality correlates of auditory hallucinations in schizophrenia. *Biological Psychiatry*, 46, 955–962.

Li, C. S., Chen, M.-C., Yang, Y. Y., Chen, M. C., & Tsay, P. K. (2002). Altered performance of schizophrenic patients in an auditory detection and discrimination task: Exploring the 'self-monitoring' model of hallucination. *Schizophrenia Research*, 55, 115–128.

Maddock, R. J., Garrett, A. S., & Buonocore, M. H. (2003). Posterior cingulate cortex activation by emotional words: fMRI evidence from a valence decision task. *Human Brain Mapping*, 18, 30–41.

Matsuda, H., Gyobo, Y. Masayasu, I., & Hisada, K. (1988) Increased accumulation of N-isoropyl-(I-^{123}) p-iodoamphetamine on the left auditory area in a schizophrenic patient with auditory hallucinations. *Clinical Nuclear Medicine*, 13, 53–55.

McGuire, P. K., Shah, G. M. S., & Murray, R. M. (1993). Increased blood flow in Broca's area during auditory hallucinations in schizophrenia. *Lancet*, 342, 703–6.

McGuire, P. K., Silbersweig, D. A., Wright, I., Murray, R. M., Frackowiak, R. S., & Frith, C. D. (1996). The neural correlates of inner speech and auditory verbal imagery in schizophrenia: relationship to auditory verbal hallucinations. *British Journal of Psychiatry*, 169, 148–159.

Mitchell, R., & Woodruff, P. W. R. (2001). The functional neuroanatomy of emotional prosody in patients with schizophrenia. 7th Annual Meeting of the Organization for Human Brain Mapping. *NeuroImage*, 13, S1073.

Mitchell, R. L. C., Elliott, R., Barry, M., Cruttenden, A., & Woodruff, P. W. R. (2003) The neural response to emotional prosody as revealed by functional magnetic resonance imaging. *Neuropsychologia*, 41, 1410–1421.

Musalek, M., Podreka, I., Walter, H., Suess, E., Passweg, V., Nutzinger, D., Strobl, R., & Lesch, O. M. (1989). Regional brain function in hallucinations: A study of regional cerebral blood flow with 99m-Tc-HMPAO-SPECT in patients with auditory hallucinations, tactile hallucinations, and normal controls. *Comprehensive Psychiatry*, 30, 99–108.

Nahas, Z., Lomarev, M., Roberts, D. R., Shastri, A., Lorberbaum, J. P., Teneback, C., McConnell, K., Vincent, D. J., Li, X., George, M. S., & Bohning, D. E. (2001). Unilateral left prefrontal transcranial magnetic stimulation (TMS) produces intensity-dependent bilateral effects as measured by interleaved BOLD fMRI. *Biological Psychiatry*, 50, 712–720.

Nayani, T. H., & David, A. S. (1996). The auditory hallucination: A phenomenological survey. *Psychological Medicine*, 26, 177–189.

Oquendo, M. A., & Mann, J. J. (2000). The biology of impulsivity and suicidality. *Psychiatric Clinics of North America*, 23, 11–25.

Pearlson, G. D. (1997). Superior temporal gyrus and planum temporale in schizophrenia: A selective review. *Progress in Neuro-psychopharmacology and Biological Psychiatry, 21*, 1230–1229.
Penfield, W., & Perot, P. (1963). The brain's record of auditory and visual experience. *Brain, 86*, 596–696.
Posner, M. I., & Rothbart, M. K. (1998). Attention, self-regulation and consciousness. *Philosophical Transactions of The Royal Society of London, 353*, 1915–1927.
Rajarethinam, R. P., DeQuardo, J. R., Nalepa, R., & Tandon, R. (2000). Superior temporal gyrus in schizophrenia: A volumetric magnetic resonance imaging study. *Schizophrenia Research, 41*, 303–312.
Rubia, K. (2002). The dynamic approach to neurodevelopmental psychiatric disorders: Use of fMRI combined with neuropsychology to elucidate the dynamics of psychiatric disorders, exemplified in ADHD and schizophrenia. *Behavioural Brain Research, 130*, 47–56.
Shapleske, J., Rossell, S. L., Chitnis, X. A., Suckling, J., Simmons, A., Bullmore, E. T., Woodruff, P. W. R., & David, A. S. (2002). A computational morphometric MRI study of schizophrenia: Effects of hallucinations. *Cerebral Cortex, 12*, 1331–1341.
Shapleske, J., Rossell, S. L., Simmons, A., David, A. S., & Woodruff, P. W. R. (2001). Are auditory hallucinations the consequence of abnormal cerebral lateralisation? A morphometric MRI study of the Sylvian fissure and Planum Temporale. *Biological Psychiatry, 49*, 685–693.
Shapleske, J., Rossell, S., Woodruff, P. W. R., & David, A. S. (1999). The planum temporale: A systematic, quantitative review of its structural, functional and clinical significance. *Brain Research Reviews, 29*, 26–49.
Shergill, S. S., Brammer, M. J., Williams, S. C., Murray, R. M., & McGuire, P. K. (2000). Mapping auditory hallucinations in schizophrenia using functional magnetic resonance imaging. *Archives of General Psychiatry, 57*, 1033–1038.
Shergill, S. S., Cameron, L. A., Brammer, M. J., Williams, S. C., Murray, R. M., & McGuire, P. K. (2001). Modality specific neural correlates of auditory and somatic hallucinations. *Journal of Neurology, Neurosurgery and Psychiatry, 71*, 688–690.
Sigmundsson, T., Suckling, J., Maier, M., Williams, S. C. R., Bullmore, E. T., Greenwood, K., Fukuda, R., Ron, M. A., & Toone, B. K. (2001). Structural abnormalities in frontal, temporal and limbic regions and interconnecting white matter tracts in schizophrenia. *American Journal of Psychiatry, 158*, 234–243.
Silbersweig, D. A., & Stern, E. (1998). Towards a functional neuroanatomy of conscious perception and its modulation by volition: Implications of human auditory neuroimaging studies. *Philosophical Transactions of The Royal Society of London, 353*, 1883–1888.
Silbersweig, D. A., Stern, E., Frith, C., Cahill, C., Holmes, A., Grootoonk, S., Seaward, J., McKenna, P., Chua, S. E., Schnorr, L., Jones, T., & Frackowiak, R. S. J. (1995). A functional neuroanatomy of hallucinations in schizophrenia. *Nature, 378*, 176–179.
Spence, S. A. (2002). Alien motor phenomena: A window on to agency. *Cognitive Neuropsychiatry, 7*, 211–220.
Spence, S. A., & Halligan, P. W. (Eds.). (2002). *Pathologies of body, self and space*. Hove, UK: Psychology Press.
Suzuki, M., Yuasa, S., Minabe, Y., Murata, M., & Kurachi, M. (1993). Left superior temporal blood flow increases in schizophrenic and schizophreniform patients with auditory hallucination: A longitudinal case study using 123I-IMP SPECT. *European Archives of Psychiatry and Clinical Neurosciences, 242*, 257–261.
Tiihonen, J., Hari, R., Naukkarinen, H., Rimón, R., Jousmäki, V., & Kajola, M. (1992). Modified activity of the human auditory cortex during auditory hallucinations. *American Journal of Psychiatry, 149*, 255–257.
Weinberger, D. R., Aloia, M. S., Goldberg, T. E., & Berman, K. F. (1994). The frontal lobes and schizophrenia. *Journal of Neuropsychiatry and Clinical Neurosciences, 6*, 419–427.
Weis, A. P., & Heckers, S. (1999). Neuroimaging of hallucinations: A review of the literature. *Psychiatry Research, 92*, 61–74.

Woldorff, M. G., Gallen, C. C., Hampson, S. A., Hillyard, S. A., Pantev, C., Sobel, D., & Bloom, F. E. (1993). Modulation of early sensory processing in human auditory cortex during auditory selective attention. *Proceedings of the National Academy of Science USA, 90,* 8722–8726.

Woodruff, P. W. R., Benson, R. R., Bandettini, P. A., Kwong, K. K., Howard, R. J., Talavage, T., Belliveau, J., & Rosen, B. R. (1996). Modulation of auditory and visual cortex by selective attention is modality-dependent. *Neuroreport, 7,* 1909–1913.

Woodruff, P. W. R., Blackwood, N., Ha, Y., Wright, I. C., Bullmore, E. T., Brammer, M., Howard, R. J., Williams, S. C. R., Shapleske, J., Rossell, S., & Murray, R. M. (1998). Is cortical responsivity increased in schizophrenics predisposed to hallucinations? 9th Congress of Association of European Psychiatrists. *European Psychiatry, 13*(Suppl. 4), 133s.

Woodruff, P. W. R., Brammer, M., Mellers, J., Bullmore, E., Wright, I., Bullmore, E. T., & Williams, S. (1995). Auditory hallucinations and perception of external speech. *Lancet, 346,* 1035.

Woodruff, P. W. R., Wilkinson, I. D., Papadakis, N. G., Hunter, M. D., Zheng, Y., Farrow, T., Spence, S. A., & Barker, A. T. (2002). *Modulation of auditory cortical response by TMS demonstrated using fMRI.* 8th International Conference on Functional Mapping of the Human Brain. Sendai, Japan. [Published on the Internet and as a CD].

Woodruff, P., Wright, I., Bullmore, E., Brammer, M. J., Howard, R. J., Williams, S. C. R., Shapleske, J., Rossell, S., David, A., McGuire, P. K., & Murray, R. M. (1997) Auditory hallucinations and the temporal cortical response to speech in schizophrenia: A functional magnetic resonance imaging study. *American Journal of Psychiatry, 154,* 1676–1682.

Wright, I., Ellison, Z., Sharma, T., Friston, K., Murray, R. M., & McGuire, P. K. (1999). Mapping of grey matter changes in schizophrenia. *Schizophrenia Research, 35,* 1–14.

Wright, I. C., Rabe-Hesketh, S., Woodruff, P., David, A. S., Murray, R. M., & Bullmore, E. T. (2000). Meta-analysis of regional brain volumes in schizophrenia. *American Journal of Psychiatry, 157,* 16–25.

Locating voices in space: A perceptual model for auditory hallucinations?

Michael D. Hunter
University of Sheffield, UK

Introduction. Auditory hallucinations are often perceived as being located in external auditory space ("outside the head"), like real auditory perceptions, but in the absence of a speaker or other external stimulus.
Method. A selective literature review of the spatial phenomenology of auditory hallucinations and the cognitive neuroscience of locating real voices in external space was undertaken. An auditory-perceptual model of external auditory hallucinations was developed in healthy right-handed subjects using functional magnetic resonance imaging and the presentation of speech in virtual acoustic space.
Results. Karl Jaspers inextricably linked "reality" and "externality" of auditory hallucinations. Although these two properties do not always occur simultaneously in hallucinating patients, the issue of "externality" is important from both a clinical and neuroscientific perspective. In an auditory-perceptual model of auditory hallucinations, association cortex in the left planum temporale is critically involved in the perception of real voices as located in external space. Right-sided voice stimuli are associated with greater neural response in the dominant (left) auditory cortex than left-sided stimuli. Subjects are better at identifying the spatial location of voices presented on the right than on the left.
Conclusion. The auditory-perceptual model described helps identify candidate brain systems likely to be involved in the pathogenesis of auditory hallucinations in schizophrenia, and is distinct from other models, which use concepts of "internal monitoring" and "inner speech". Its application, in the cognitive neuroscientific investigation of the phenomenology of auditory hallucinations, may shed further light on the mechanisms underlying this distressing experience.

This paper is about the application of auditory spatial paradigms to understanding the phenomenology, and perhaps etiology, of auditory hallucinations.

Correspondence should be addressed to Michael D. Hunter, Sheffield Cognition and Neuroimaging Laboratory (SCANLab), Academic Department of Psychiatry, University of Sheffield, The Longley Centre, Norwood Grange Drive, Sheffield S5 7JT, UK; e-mail: m.d.hunter@shef.ac.uk

I am grateful to Professor Peter Woodruff and Dr Tim Griffiths for their scientific contributions to the virtual acoustic space/fMRI paradigm referred to in the paper. I am supported by a Wellcome Training Fellowship.

The fundamental premise is that auditory hallucinations are *perceived*, and that a model of auditory hallucinations should, therefore, be a *perceptual* one.

The first part of this paper reviews the spatial phenomenology of auditory hallucinations, drawing particularly on the work of Jaspers and Schneider, and on data from modern phenomenological surveys. The second part deals with the perception of real environmental sounds (such as voices) as external auditory "objects". I outline a cognitive neuropsychiatric project, which aims to identify candidate mechanisms for spatial aspects of auditory hallucinations by modelling these experiences in healthy subjects. This auditory-perceptual model is discussed with particular respect to its applicability to auditory hallucinations in schizophrenia and its distinction from theories involving "internal monitoring" of "inner speech" in the pathogenesis of auditory hallucinations.

SPATIAL PHENOMENOLOGY OF AUDITORY HALLUCINATIONS

In this section, I aim to describe a view of auditory hallucinations as perceptions that may arise in external auditory space, and contrast this with the concept of the pseudo-hallucination. Problems with defining the pseudo-hallucination will be discussed, and an alternative classification of auditory hallucinations as "external" or "internal" will be proposed.

Auditory hallucinations as perceptions

"*Hallucinations proper* are actual false perceptions which are not in any way distortions of real perceptions but spring up on their own as something quite new and occur simultaneously with and alongside real perceptions" (Jaspers, 1997, p. 66). Jaspers' assertion provides a useful starting point for exploring the spatial phenomenology of auditory hallucinations. In this account, he equates "hallucinations proper" with real sense-perception (*Wahrnehmung*), which is in contrast with his concept of "image or idea" (*Vorstellung*).

Jaspers listed the characteristics of *Wahrnehmung* and *Vorstellung*, in order that they could be phenomenologically separated (Table 1). Of the distinguishing characteristics identified, he considered the most important to be, first, that sense-perceptions arise with a quality of concrete reality and, second, that sense-perceptions are located in *external objective space*. Jaspers thought that these two (essential) characteristics divided perception from imagery "as by a gulf", whereas the remaining (nonessential) characteristics were "not so clear-cut" (Jaspers, 1997, p. 70).

Therefore, Jasperian auditory "hallucinations proper" must arise in external objective space, because they are like sense-perceptions. Furthermore, according to this description, there can be no transitional phase, either an experience is concrete and external, or it is not.

According to Schneider (1959), the sensation of hearing is "mainly object-bound" (p. 146). On the other hand, feelings are subjective "states of the ego"

TABLE 1
Jaspers' distinction between "sense-perception" and "image or idea" (adapted from Jaspers, 1997)

Sense-perception (Wahrnehmung)	*Image or idea* (Vorstellung)
Essential features	
Concrete reality	Figurative
External objective space	Internal subjective space
Nonessential features	
Clearly delineated, detailed	Incomplete
Full, fresh, and bright	Neutral toned
Constant and unaltered	Tend to dissipate
Independent of will, passive	Dependent on will, active

(p. 145). He goes on to say that, in exceptional circumstances, hearing sensations can also be subjective states (a ringing alarm clock produces a sound that is both linked to the object and piercing in the ears), but this is not generally the case.

In this context, Schneider also considered auditory hallucinations to be abnormalities of perception that are *sensed*. He states, "It cannot be too often repeated that the issue here is one of actual sense deception, which implies that the experience involved is one of sensing something to be there that is not, of *sensing*, not just *believing*" (p. 95). So, for Schneider, auditory hallucinations are disorders of hearing sensation, and normal hearing sensations are "mainly object-bound". However, the verbatim accounts of auditory hallucinations that Schneider gives are full of *subjective* impact. For example, a man with schizophrenia says, "When I try to think, my head gets full of noise; it's *as if* my brain were in an uproar with my thoughts" (p. 97; italics added).

Synthesising Schneider's ideas could lead to an account of auditory hallucinations as perceptual abnormalities that arise in the absence of an external stimulus and are experienced as an exceptional case of hearing sensation because they operate on a "double front" (p. 145) of objectivity and subjectivity. However, unlike Jaspers, Schneider does not explicitly equate objectivity (being "mainly object-bound") with spatial externality.

Pseudo-hallucinations

"Pseudo-hallucinations" have been variously conceptualised, but the Jasperian definition is predominant in British psychiatry, as outlined by Sims (1995). Specifically, Jaspers described pseudo-hallucinations as having some of the *nonessential* features of sense-perception, whilst never having the *essential* features of concreteness or objective externality (Table 1). This definition is quite different from the French concept of pseudo-hallucination, which regards the experience as an intermediate form that may or may not progress to authentic hallucinations (reviewed by Hamada, 1998). Jaspers' definition is also distinct from the idea that pseudo-hallucinations are hallucinations that can be "recognised" as such by the sufferer (Hare, 1973).

Practically speaking, these conflicting views lead to a tautological situation where the spatial phenomenology of pseudo-hallucinations is dependent on how the experience is defined. If the Jasperian account is accepted, then pseudo-hallucinations are, by definition, located in internal space. However, in their phenomenological survey, Oulis and colleagues described some auditory hallucinations as simultaneously internally located and possessing a quality of concrete reality, an experience that cannot be accommodated by Jaspers (Oulis, Mavreas, Mamounas, & Stefanis, 1995). Furthermore, even when pseudo-hallucinations are defined in the Jasperian sense, the clinical significance of the experience is inconsistently described. For example, the fourth edition of the *Diagnostic and Statistical Manual of Mental Disorders* states "experiences that lack the quality of an external percept ... are not considered to be hallucinations characteristic of schizophrenia" (DSM-IV; American Psychiatric Association, 1994, p. 275). This position is supported by Sims (1995) but not by Hamilton, editor of Fish's work, who claims that the distinction between hallucinations and pseudo-hallucinations is "purely of academic interest" (Hamilton, 1976, p. 47).

Given the uncertainty outlined above, it might be better to dissociate spatial phenomenology from the diagnosis of auditory hallucination versus pseudo-hallucination. This could allow auditory hallucinations to be simply defined, in the spirit of Jaspers and Schneider, as "perception-like", that is, *heard*. Furthermore, Jaspers' first essential feature of sense-perception (concrete reality) could still be applied to auditory hallucinations, without the need to invoke his second essential feature (location in external objective space). Such *heard* experiences might then be classified as "external" or "internal" dependent on their spatial projection at the moment of perception. The Schedule for Clinical Assessment in Neuropsychiatry (SCAN) accommodates this approach in its classification of "internal hallucinations" (World Health Organisation, 1992). An interesting question arises for auditory neuroscience: Why are some hallucinated voices perceived as external, like real environmental sounds, whereas others are not? This question is clinically important, because voices located solely "outside the head" may be the most typical form of the experience, and associated with worse reality testing and greater subjective distress than voices "inside the head" (Nayani & David, 1996).

MECHANISMS FOR THE PERCEPTION OF AUDITORY SPACE

Consider the situation where a real speaker is situated on the right-hand side of a real listener; speech arrives at the listener's right ear *before* her left ear, and with greater *intensity* at the right than the left ear, because of the acoustic "shadow" cast by the listener's head. Respectively, these are interaural *phase* and *amplitude* differences that represent binaural cues, involved in the perception of sounds as arising on one or other side of the head (Rayleigh, 1876). Neural processing of these binaural cues first occurs in the brainstem, and may utilise synaptic depression to preserve temporal information in the presence of potentially confounding intensity changes (Cook, Schwindt, Grande, & Spain, 2003). Disorders that affect the brainstem, such as multiple sclerosis, can cause derangement of sound laterality processing (Van der Poel, Jones, & Miller, 1988).

Binaural cues are, therefore, involved in localising sounds in the azimuthal plane (the horizontal plane through subjects' ears) but, alone, cannot explain how we are able to perceive sounds as truly external, that is, as situated in front of or behind the head, and with elevation in the vertical plane. The perception of speech as an *external* (not merely *lateral*) sound object is dependent upon filtering by the outer ear (Hofman, Van Riswick, & Van Opstal, 1998). This amounts to the imposition of a head-related transfer function on sounds that corresponds to a spatially dependent filter; the filter characteristics vary according to the direction of a sound from its origin (Wightman & Kistler, 1989). In other words, the shape of the ears imposes a spectrotemporal pattern on a sound that is determined by the spatial location of that sound. The perception of a sound's location in external auditory space putatively requires separation of the spectrotemporal pattern inherent in the sound (sound object characteristics) from the additional spectrotemporal effects of its location (sound location characteristics). Griffiths and Warren have called this task a "daunting computational problem" (Griffiths & Warren, 2002, p. 348), which may be addressed by auditory association cortex in the planum temporale (Westbury, Zatorre, & Evans, 1999). This region is located in the superior temporal plane, posterior to primary auditory cortex in Heschl's gyrus (Rademacher et al., 2001).

Functional neuroimaging has implicated the planum temporale in processing a number of different types of spectrotemporal pattern in sound. These include speech (Belin, Zatorre, Lafaille, Ahad, & Pike, 2000; Zatorre, Evans, Meyer, & Gjedde, 1992), melody (Griffiths, Buchel, Frackowiak, & Patterson, 1998; Zatorre, Evans, & Meyer, 1994), and sound movement (Baumgart, Gaschler-Markefski, Woldorff, Heinze, & Scheich, 1999; Warren, Zielenski, Green, Rauschecker, & Griffiths, 2002). Furthermore, activation in the planum temporale positively correlates with the spatial distribution of a number of simultaneously presented sound objects (Zatorre, Bouffard, Ahad, & Belin, 2002). Activation of the planum temporale by complex environmental sounds, and by spatially determined sound properties, suggests that it would be a suitable area for disentangling sound object and sound location characteristics; a candidate region for the perception of acoustic "externality".

MODELLING SPATIAL ASPECTS OF AUDITORY HALLUCINATIONS IN HEALTHY SUBJECTS

We have recently used functional magnetic resonance imaging (fMRI) and a virtual acoustic space paradigm (Wightman & Kistler, 1989) to test the hypothesis that the planum temporale enables the perception of real "hallucination-like" voices as external sound objects (located "outside the head"; Hunter et al., 2003). In that experiment, healthy subjects were presented with command hallucination-like voices (e.g., "close the door") via headphones in the fMRI scanner. Normally, presentation of sounds via headphones results in a percept that is spatially located inside the head. However, virtual acoustic space techniques utilise eardrum microphone recordings of free field sounds to derive digital filter characteristics that mimic the filtering effect of the outer ear; in our case the filter was a generic head-related transfer function. Convolution of stimuli with a generic head-related transfer function (above) enabled subjects to perceive voices as spatially located outside the head, despite presentation via

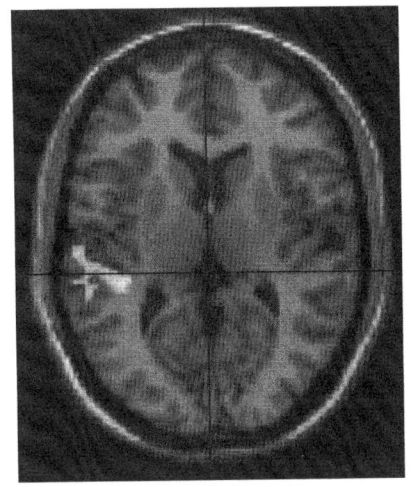

Figure 1. Hallucination-like voices in external auditory space. The brain area, shown in pale grey, (left planum temporale) that demonstrated greater activation during the perception of voice stimuli located in external space than during the perception of voices located inside the head (Hunter et al., 2003). Group data ($n = 12$) are displayed on an axial slice through a canonical T1 image, 10 mm above the line through the anterior commissure. Statistical threshold: $p < .001$, uncorrected, for height and extent of activation. The dark crosshair that runs left to right marks the anteroposterior maximum of the planum temporale, from the probabilistic map of Westbury and colleagues (1999). In this experiment the majority of both outside and inside head voice stimuli were on the right hand side; in other experiments we found that the left planum temporale was more activated by external stimuli regardless of precise spatial location.

headphones. Brain activation during the perception of external stimuli was contrasted with activation during the perception of identical, but unconvolved, stimuli that were perceived as located inside the head. We found that, regardless of precise spatial location, the left planum temporale (PT) demonstrated greater activation during the presentation of external stimuli (Figure 1). Furthermore, right-sided external voices were associated with much greater extent of activation in the left PT than left-sided external voices. This led us to directly examine the effect of stimulus laterality on the neural and behavioural correlates of perceiving "externality"—an exploration of "ear advantage" effects in auditory spatial processing of hallucination-like voices.

Correlates of right- and left-sided voices

The normal brain demonstrates functional asymmetry for auditory processes manifest as "ear advantage" effects (Kimura, 1967). The direction of ear advantage in a task is determined by the relative superiority of the contralateral (vs. ipsilateral) hemisphere for processing the type of information contained in the stimulus (Geffen & Quinn, 1984). This situation is thought to arise because the bilateral representation of the auditory system amounts to a functional decussation (crossing over) of afferents. For example, in right-handed subjects, right ear afferents are more directly connected to the language dominant (left) auditory cortex than left ear afferents, which travel via the language non-dominant (right) auditory cortex and corpus callosum.

We conducted a psychophysical experiment to test the hypothesis that healthy, right-handed, subjects are better at accurately identifying the spatial location of hallucination-like voices when the stimuli are presented on the right- versus the left-hand side (Hunter et al., 2002a). Using the same stimuli and virtual acoustic space techniques as Hunter et al. (2003), in a forced-choice paradigm we examined whether subjects could differentiate between "inside head" and "outside head" voice stimuli. Via headphones, subjects were presented with pairs of command hallucination-like voice stimuli; both elements of a pair were identical in content and laterality, but one element of each pair was "outside head" and the other "inside head". There were equal numbers of left- and right-lateralised stimuli overall. The position (first or second) of the "outside head" element varied randomly. Subjects were required to state which of the two elements was "outside head" for 200 trials. Using nonparametric statistics, we found that, although the overall psychophysical robustness of the virtual acoustic space technique was good (> 99% accuracy for identifying the "outside head" element in the group), accuracy was significantly greater when stimuli were presented on the right- (vs. left-) hand side. To test the specificity of the effect, we repeated the experiment in a group of left-handed subjects; we predicted that the superiority of one or other hemisphere for processing speech stimuli might not be clear-cut, and that this would be manifest as no overall ear advantage in the spatial task. In left-handed subjects, the overall psychophysical robustness of the external percept was still good, but there was no significant difference in accuracy for identifying the "outside head" voice between pairs of stimuli presented on the right- or left-hand side (unpublished data).

These behavioural results suggest two testable "laterality" hypotheses in right-handed subjects. Firstly, that the left auditory cortex is more sensitive (demonstrates greater physiological response to) right- than left-sided external voice stimuli. Secondly, that the converse does not occur in the right auditory cortex; it is not more sensitive to left- than right-sided voices. In a second fMRI experiment we found that this was indeed the case (Hunter et al., 2002b). Utilising the same right-handed subjects and "outside head" (convolved) stimuli as Hunter et al. (2003) we directly compared brain activation during the perception of external hallucination-like voice stimuli on the right- versus the left-hand side. The left auditory cortex demonstrated significantly greater activation during the perception of the right- versus left-sided stimuli. No brain areas demonstrated greater activation during perception of the left- versus right-sided stimuli.

In summary, the modelling work in healthy, right-handed, subjects suggests that:

1. The left planum temporale has a critical role in the perception of hallucination-like voices as spatially located "outside the head" that is not dependent on precise spatial location.
2. Notwithstanding (1), right-handed subjects are better at correctly identifying the spatial location of hallucination-like voices as "outside the head" when the stimuli are presented on the right-hand side.
3. The behavioural effect described in (2) could arise because, in right-handed subjects, the language dominant (left) auditory cortex is more sensitive to external hallucination-like voice stimuli presented on the right- than on the left-hand side.

APPLICATION OF THE AUDITORY-PERCEPTUAL MODEL TO ACTUAL HALLUCINATIONS IN SCHIZOPHRENIA

Our work predicts that externally located auditory hallucinations are associated with activation in the left planum temporale, the brain region that allows us to perceive real voices as external sound objects. Elsewhere in this issue, Woodruff (2004) has argued that auditory hallucinations are perceptions and has cited a number of functional imaging studies to support the hypothesis that primary and secondary auditory cortex must be involved in their pathogenesis. The prediction here is a specific case of Woodruff's argument—a particular region in secondary auditory cortex (planum temporale) subserves a particular phenomenological quality of auditory hallucinations ("externality").

Using fMRI, Dierks and colleagues demonstrated that the left planum temporale was activated during auditory hallucinations in two out of three patients with schizophrenia whom they studied (Dierks et al., 1999). In that study, the spatial location of auditory hallucinations was not described; we might speculate that the two patients with planum temporale activation had external voices whereas the third did not.

If the planum temporale was abnormally activated during the perception of external auditory hallucinations, then a question arises as to the nature of any structural abnormality that could underlie the functional problem. Imaging work has shown reversal of the normal left > right asymmetry for planum temporale surface area in schizophrenia (Barta et al., 1997) but another study has failed to demonstrate any association between auditory hallucinations in schizophrenia and pathological reversal of planum temporale laterality (Shapleske, Rossell, Simmons, David, & Woodruff, 2001). No published study has directly examined structural planum temporale abnormality and "externality" of auditory hallucinations, but Mathalon and colleagues have produced data suggesting that the region diminishes in size, over time, in schizophrenia (Mathalon, Sullivan, Lim, & Pfefferbaum, 2001) and a phenomenological survey has indicted that auditory hallucinations might become more internal in chronic psychotic disorders (Nayani & David, 1996).

At the behavioural level, external auditory hallucinations might also interfere with the ability to correctly identify the spatial location of real sounds. The psychophysical study of sound spatial localisation in schizophrenia constitutes a small literature. However, there is evidence to suggest that patients with schizophrenia perform worse than healthy controls on a sound localisation task (Guterman & Klein, 1992) and, specifically, that patients with auditory hallucinations are worse at correctly identifying the location of voice sounds than nonhallucinators (Heilburn, Blum, & Haas, 1983).

Turning to issues of stimulus laterality, our model suggests that in healthy right-handed subjects, the left temporal cortex is more sensitive to contralateral than ipsilateral speech, but that the right temporal cortex is not. The behavioural correlate of this effect may be right ear advantage in a speech spatial localisation task. Previous fMRI work indicates that the "healthy" model may be reversed in patients with schizophrenia. Woodruff and colleagues found that, compared to healthy controls, right-handed patients with schizophrenia demonstrated greater haemodynamic response in the right than the left temporal cortex when presented with speech via headphones; evidence of right hemisphere superiority (or left hemisphere dysfunction) for processing auditory speech stimuli (Woodruff et al., 1997). Furthermore, behavioural studies have shown that patients with psychoses and auditory hallucinations have *no* ear advantage in a dichotic listening task, whereas nonhallucinators have normal *right* ear advantage (Green, Hugdahl & Mitchell, 1994); and patients with schizophrenia have *left* ear advantage in an auditory acuity task (Aydin et al., 2001). A detailed discussion of brain lateralisation in schizophrenia is beyond the scope of this short paper (see Crow, 2004, this issue) but the current evidence suggests that a lateralised voice stimulus could be a useful way of probing lateralised brain function in schizophrenia.

The distinction between "auditory-perceptual" and "inner speech" models of auditory hallucinations

From a psychoanalytic point of view, the auditory system occupies an "exceptional position" in human mental life, because it is thought to be closely tied to self-consciousness, whereas the visual modality is tied to object-consciousness (Isakower, 1939). In cognitive neuroscience, previous models of auditory hallucinations have also focused on issues of "internal monitoring" (Frith, 1987) and neuroimaging data has been put forward to support a hypothesis that auditory hallucinations could result from dysfunction in brain areas that are involved in the generation and monitoring of "inner speech" (McGuire et al., 1996). In that model, a deficit in monitoring leads to a situation where the "willed intention" to think in inner speech is not recognised. However, the "corollary discharge" resulting from the selection of inner speech is still detected, leading to a mismatch between intention and (mental) action. Frith states that, in this situation, a patient with schizophrenia and auditory hallucinations might, "... describe the experience of *hearing* voices *inside* his head" (Frith, 1987, p. 639, italics added). However, thinking in inner speech is still *thinking*; the model does not directly address the issue of how defective monitoring of thoughts could lead to the experience of *auditory perceptions* that are often located *outside* the head, in external auditory space. It could be argued that a premise on which the "inner speech" model is built is that the brain *produces* auditory hallucinations.

In contrast, the phenomenological model that we have developed starts from a premise that the brain *perceives* auditory hallucinations. We regard auditory hallucinations as perceptions (because that is how patients describe them) and attempt to model phenomenological aspects of actual speech, in order to make predictions regarding the neural basis for the phenomenology of auditory hallucinations. Our regions of interest are in the auditory system. A possible link between the "auditory-perceptual" and "inner speech" models is the suggestion that auditory association cortex constructs a transient representation of the spectrotemporal pattern in speech sounds during retrieval from lexical memory (Wise et al., 2001). It seems likely that an experience as diverse and complex as auditory hallucinosis may require explanation by several cognitive neuroscientific models that might explicate different aspects of the phenomenon.

CONCLUSIONS AND FUTURE DIRECTIONS

In classical psychiatric phenomenology, auditory hallucinations have been defined as perceptions; the experience is one of *hearing*. This definition is supported by phenomenological surveys in psychiatric populations. A key feature of real auditory perceptions, and some auditory hallucinations, is their location in external auditory space. In the case of real speech, binaural phase and amplitude cues, and filtering by the external ear are important in the perception of spatial location. For auditory hallucinations, the quality of "externality" may be associated with impaired reality testing and subjective distress.

We have used fMRI and virtual acoustic space techniques to develop an auditory-perceptual model for spatial aspects of auditory hallucinations. The model implicates auditory association cortex in the left planum temporale in the false perception of external auditory hallucinations. The model also suggests that a lateralised auditory voice stimulus could be a useful way of probing lateralised brain function in schizophrenia, specifically, the behavioural and imaging correlates of asymmetry for language processing.

Future studies might examine the behavioural and imaging correlates of phenomenologically diverse auditory hallucinations in varied patient and nonclinical groups. Our knowledge may also benefit from the use of finegrained assessment tools that are able to detect subtle change in phenomenology (see Wykes, 2004, this issue).

The auditory-perceptual model is distinct from concepts of "internal monitoring" or "inner speech". A question arises as to whether the currently available data could be used to support an auditory hypothesis for the mechanism of auditory hallucinations.

Manuscript accepted 19 February 2003

REFERENCES

American Psychiatric Association (1994). *Diagnostic and statistical manual of mental disorders* (DSM-IV) (4th ed.). Washington DC: Author.

Aydin, N., Dane, S., Ozturk, I., Uslu, C., Gumustekin, K., & Kirpinar, I. (2001). Left ear (right temporal hemisphere) advantage and left temporal hemispheric dysfunction in schizophrenia. *Perceptual and Motor Skills, 93,* 230–238.

Barta, P. E., Pearlson, G. D., Brill, L. B., Royall, R., McGilchrist, I. K., Pulver, A. E., Powers, R. E., Casanova, M. F., Tien, A. Y., Frangou, S., & Petty, R. G. (1997). Planum temporale asymmetry in schizophrenia: Replication and relationship to gray matter abnormalities. *American Journal of Psychiatry, 154,* 661–667.

Baumgart, F., Gaschler-Markefski, B., Woldorff, M. G., Heinze, H-J., & Scheich, H. (1999). A movement-sensitive area in auditory cortex. *Nature, 400,* 724–726.

Belin, P., Zatorre, R. J., Lafaille, P., Ahad, P., & Pike, B. (2000). Voice-selective areas in human auditory cortex. *Nature, 403,* 309–312.

Cook, D. L., Schwindt, P. C., Grande, L. A., & Spain, W. J. (2003). Synaptic depression in the localization of sound. *Nature, 421,* 66–70.

Crow, T. J. (2004). Auditory hallucinations as primary disorders of syntax: An evolutionary theory of the origins of language. *Cognitive Neuropsychiatry, 9*(1/2), 125–145.

Dierks, T, Linden, D. E. J., Jandl, M., Formisano, E., Goebel, R., Lanfermann, H., & Singer, W. (1999). Activation of Heschl's gyrus during auditory hallucinations. *Neuron, 22,* 615–621.

Frith, C. D. (1987). The positive and negative symptoms of schizophrenia reflect impairments in the perception and initiation of action. *Psychological Medicine, 17*, 631–648.

Geffen, G., & Quinn, K. (1984). Hemispheric specialisation and ear advantage in processing speech. *Psychological Bulletin, 96*, 273–291.

Green, M. F., Hugdahl, K., & Mitchell, S. (1994). Dichotic listening during auditory hallucinations in patients with schizophrenia. *American Journal of Psychiatry, 151*, 357–362.

Griffiths, T. D., Buchel, C., Frackowiak, R. S. J., & Patterson, R. D. (1998). Analysis of temporal structure in sound by the human brain. *Nature Neuroscience, 1*, 422–427.

Griffiths, T. D., & Warren, J. D. (2002). The planum temporale as a computational hub. *Trends in Neurosciences, 25*, 348–353.

Guterman, Y., & Klein, E. (1992). The role of head movement and pinnae in auditory localisation in schizophrenia and psychosis. *Schizophrenia Research, 6*, 67–73.

Hamada, H. (1998). La pseudo-hallucination schizophrenique. *Annales Medico-Psychologiques, 156*, 236–243.

Hamilton, M. (1976). *Fish's schizophrenia.* Bristol, UK: John Wright.

Hare, E. H. (1973). A short note on pseudo-hallucinations. *British Journal of Psychiatry, 122*, 469–476.

Heilburn, A. B., Blum, N., & Haas, M. (1983). Cognitive vulnerability to auditory hallucination: Preferred imagery mode and spatial location of sounds. *British Journal of Psychiatry, 143*, 294–299.

Hofman, P. M., Van Riswick, J. G. A., & Van Opstal, A. J. (1998). Relearning sound localization with new ears. *Nature Neuroscience, 1*, 417–421.

Hunter, M. D., Farrow, T. F. D., Zheng, Y., Wilkinson, I. D., Woods, W., Spence, S. A., Griffiths, T.D., & Woodruff, P.W.R. (2002b). A laterality effect in brain response to simulated auditory verbal hallucinations in external space. *Schizophrenia Research, 53*(Suppl.), 91.

Hunter, M. D., Griffiths, T. D., Farrow, T. F. D., Zheng, Y., Wilkinson, I. D., Hegde, N., Woods, W., Spence, S. A., & Woodruff, P. W. R. (2003). A neural basis for the perception of voices in external auditory space. *Brain, 126*, 161–169.

Hunter, M. D., Smith, J. K., Taylor, N., Woods, W., Spence, S. A., Griffiths, T. D., & Woodruff, P. W. R. (2002a). A laterality effect in the perception of simulated auditory verbal hallucinations in external space. *Schizophrenia Research, 53*(Suppl.), 91.

Isakower, O. (1939). On the exceptional position of the auditory sphere. *International Journal of Psycho-Analysis, 20*, 340–348.

Jaspers, K. (1997). *General psychopathology* (J. Hoenig, & M. W. Hamilton, Trans.). Baltimore, MD: Johns Hopkins University Press.

Kimura, D. (1967). Functional asymmetry of the brain in dichotic listening. *Cortex, 3*, 417–432.

McGuire, P. K., Silbersweig, D. A., Wright, I., Murray, R. M., Frackowiak, R. S., & Frith, C. D. (1996). The neural correlates of inner speech and auditory verbal imagery in schizophrenia: Relationship to auditory verbal hallucinations. *British Journal of Psychiatry, 169*, 148–159.

Mathalon, D. H., Sullivan, E. V., Lim, K. O., & Pfefferbaum, A. (2001). Progressive brain volume changes and the clinical course of schizophrenia in men: A longitudinal magnetic resonance imaging study. *Archives of General Psychiatry, 58*, 148–157.

Nayani, T. H., & David, A. S. (1996). The auditory hallucination: A phenomenological survey. *Psychological Medicine, 26*, 177–189.

Oulis, P. G., Mavreas, V. G., Mamounas, J. M., & Stefanis, C. N. (1995). Clinical characteristics of auditory hallucinations. *Acta Psychiatrica Scandinavica, 92*, 97–102.

Rademacher, J., Morosan, P., Schormann, T., Schleicher, A., Werner, C., Freund, H-J., & Zilles, K. (2001). Probabalistic mapping and volume measurement of human primary auditory cortex. *Neuroimage 2001, 13*, 669–683.

Rayleigh (Lord). (1876). On our perception of the direction of a source of sound. *Nature, 14*, 32–33.

Schneider, K. (1959). *Clinical psychopathology.* New York: Grune & Stratton.

Shapleske, J., Rossell, S. L., Simmons, A., David, A. S., & Woodruff, P. W. R. (2001). Are auditory hallucinations the consequence of abnormal cerebral lateralization? A morphometric MRI study of the sylvian fissure and planum temporale. *Biological Psychiatry*, *49*, 685–693.

Sims, A. (1995). *Symptoms in the mind*. London: W. B. Saunders.

Van der Poel, J. C., Jones, S. J., & Miller, D. H. (1988) Sound lateralisation, brainstem auditory evoked potentials and magnetic resonance imaging in multiple sclerosis. *Brain*, *111*, 1453–1474.

Warren, J. D., Zielinski, B. A., Green, G. G. R., Rauschecker, J. P., & Griffiths, T. D. (2002). Perception of sound source motion by the human brain. *Neuron*, *34*, 139–148.

Westbury, C. F., Zatorre, R. J., & Evans, A. C. (1999). Quantifying variability in the planum temporale: A probability map. *Cerebral Cortex*, *9*, 392–405.

Wightman, F. L., & Kistler, D. J. (1989). Headphone simulation of free-field listening: I. Stimulus synthesis. *Journal of the Acoustical Society of America*, *85*, 858–67.

Wise, R. J., Scott, S. K., Blank, S. C., Mummery, C. J., Murphy, K., & Warburton, E. A. (2001). Separate neural subsystems within "Wernicke's area". *Brain*, *124*, 83–95.

Woodruff, P. W. R. (2004). Auditory hallucinations: Insights and questions from neuroimaging. *Cognitive Neuropsychiatry*, *9*(1/2), 73–91.

Woodruff, P. W. R, Wright, I. C., Bullmore, E. T., Brammer, M., Howard, R. J., Williams, S. C. R., Shapleske, J., Rossell, S., David, A. S., McGuire, P. K., & Murray, R. M. (1997). Auditory hallucinations and the temporal cortical response to speech in schizophrenia: A functional magnetic resonance imaging study. *American Journal of Psychiatry*, *154*, 1676–1682.

World Health Organisation. (1992). *Schedules for clinical assessment in neuropsychiatry*. Geneva: Author.

Wykes, T. (2004). Psychological treatment for voices in psychosis. *Cognitive Neuropsychiatry*, *9*(1/2), 25–41.

Zatorre, R. J., Bouffard, M., Ahad, P., & Belin, P. (2002). Where is "where" in the human auditory cortex? *Nature Neuroscience*, *5*, 905–909.

Zatorre, R. J., Evans, A. C., & Meyer, E. (1994). Neural mechanisms underlying melodic perception and memory for pitch. *Journal of Neuroscience*, *14*, 1908–1919.

Zatorre, R. J., Evans, A. C., Meyer, E., & Gjedde, A. (1992). Lateralization of phonetic and pitch discrimination in speech processing. *Science*, *256*, 846–849.

The cognitive neuropsychiatry of auditory verbal hallucinations: An overview

Anthony S. David

Institute of Psychiatry, London, UK

Introduction. The cognitive neuropsychiatric approach to auditory verbal hallucinations (AVHs) attempts to explain the phenomena in cognitive or information-processing terms and ultimately their brain bases.
Methods. A narrative review of the literature and an overview of this special issue of *Cognitive Neuropsychiatry*.
Results. First, an operational definition of AVHs is offered. Next, clues to etiology are derived from a detailed consideration of the clinical phenomenology of "voices", their form and content. Functional and structural neuroimaging studies suggest the importance of left-side language areas in the generation/perception of AVHs.
Conclusions. Existing cognitive neuropsychiatric models provide a useful framework for the understanding of AVHs. However, data need to be applied more specifically to these models so that they may be refined.

The cognitive neuropsychiatry approach attempts to explain in cognitive terms psychiatric phenomena—such as hallucinations, thought disorder, delusions. Put another way, it seeks to uncover the underlying cognitive processes for these phenomena and ultimately their brain bases. This aim is greatly facilitated if there is a well understood candidate cognitive mechanism for a "normal" process that forms a credible basis upon which the psychiatric symptom develops. In the case of auditory verbal hallucinations (AVHs) there are a number of putative cognitive mechanisms, each of which can explain some but not all of the features of the phenomena. Examples include: short-term memory/inner speech; reality or source monitoring; abnormal mental imagery. These all overlap considerably and have two components. They have in common the notion that mental contents (thoughts, memories, plans, etc.) are translated into an auditory verbal form, and second, that this auditory representation becomes

---

Correspondence should be addressed to Anthony S. David, Section of Cognitive Neuropsychiatry, PO Box 68, Institute of Psychiatry, DeCrespigny Park, London, SE5 8AF, UK; email: a.david@iop.kcl.ac.uk

somewhat detached from subjective ownership[1]. A third component can be added: An often elaborate system of beliefs and attributions concerning the supposed origin of the auditory verbal representation or "voice" (see Frith, 1996).

The typical content of AVHs in clinical settings is not explained by these theories, but some researchers have proposed that emotional and arousing thought content might disrupt underlying cognitive processes more than neutral content. The intermittent and stereotyped nature of AVHs remains largely unexplained. Alternative theories propose that hallucinations are entirely due to attributional processes and are not fundamentally sensory. Neurological theories start from the opposite premise—that hallucinations are aberrant sensory phenomena normally detected (see David, 1994a), reasoning by analogy from the experiments using externally applied electrical stimulation to the cortex described by Penfield and Perot (1963). Evidence for neurological views will be reviewed with reference to neuroimaging studies.

What is it we are trying to explain?

First of all, we hardly need to remind ourselves that the topic of this collection of papers is "voices" rather than an experience in another or multiple sensory modalities. The fact that in the major psychiatric disorders the hallucinations take this form, while in overtly neurological conditions visual hallucinations predominate, is important (e.g., Barnes & David, 2001). Of course, visual (and indeed, olfactory, tactile, gustatory) hallucinations do occur in people with schizophrenia (as do auditory hallucinations in people with neurological conditions, such as Alzheimer's disease and Parkinson's disease). However, they seem to be hierarchically organised, that is to say that visual, olfactory, and gustatory hallucinations are in my experience, almost never observed in the absence of auditory hallucinations in schizophrenia while, auditory hallucinations are seldom seen in, say people with Parkinson's disease on dopamine agonist treatment, in the absence of visual hallucinations (Inzelberg, Kiperwasser, & Korczyn, 1998). I interpret this to indicate that in each case, "organic" and "functional" hallucinations have their own unique pathophysiologies but that each may also involve additional or generic mechanisms which render the individual vulnerable to hallucinations *per se*. Such additional mechanisms operate in a dose-related manner. These may be physiological, for example, related to arousal, or psychological, related to reality monitoring. In any event, it has proven useful to explore mechanisms underlying both visual and auditory hallucinations with similar paradigms (Barnes, Boubert, Harris, Lee, & David, 2003; Ffytche et al., 1998; Howard et al., 1995).

---

[1] A case has been described (Kobayashi & Kato, 2000) who showed a contrary pattern (i.e., the subject believed that he was speaking out loud when in fact he was not).

There are types of auditory hallucination other than "voices". Musical hallucinations have attracted attention recently (Griffiths, 2000). These seem to have a specific association with auditory sensory impairment, and become more common with age (Keshavan, David, Steingard, & Lishman, 1992). A mechanism for this has been proposed which draws on ideas of "de-afferentation" and the experience of phantom limb (Schultz & Melzack, 1991). A weak association between sensory problems and schizophrenia has been demonstrated (David et al., 1995) but they are not consistently related to AVHs except in the case of unilateral hallucinations where ipsilateral sensory or contralateral neurological lesions have been reported (Almeida, Forstl, Howard, & David, 1993; Doris, O'Carroll, Steele, & Ebmeier, 1993; Takebayashi, Takei, Mori, & Suzuki, 2002).

Definitions

A satisfactory definition of hallucination is surprisingly difficult to come by and continues to arouse debate. Aleman and DeHaan (1998) discussed this issue and came up with the following, which in turn is a modification of that offered by Slade and Bentall (1988):

> A sensory experience which occurs in the absence of external stimulation of the relevant sensory organ, but has the compelling sense of reality of a true perception, is not amenable to direct and voluntary control by the experiencer, and occurs in the awake state.

I would suggest some further modifications. First, the notion of "absence of external stimulation" requires qualification. It is there in the definition, presumably to help distinguish between an illusion—wherein the perception of an external object undergoes some distortion, which may be extreme but not so much that the experiencer, or an observer party to the experiencer's description, cannot still infer its origin. However, this part of the definition might be interpreted as "*complete* absence" so that an auditory hallucination can only occur in silence. Further, the relationship of some form of sensory stimulation and the hallucination—either as a trigger, a source of noise (Hoffman, Rapaport, Ameli, McGlashen, & Harcherik, 1995) or some nonspecific arouser or cue—is still a topic of research so cannot be excluded from the field of interest. From patients' accounts, auditory hallucinations may occur when the individual is watching television or in a crowded room where the presence of speech (even as background noise) may be etiologically significant.

Another modification I would proffer concerns the phrase regarding a "compelling sense of reality of a true perception". The problem with this is that it precludes the frequent questioning that people in the midst of psychosis often perform as to whether the sensation is indeed real or of a similar kind to a true or "ordinary" perception, a process that might be called insight (David, 1990).

Further, what if the perception is supernatural in some way, like the voice of God, with what does the experiencer compare this in order to decide that this is real or true? Again, the purpose of this clause is to exclude fleeting and vague sensations, which might be seen as trivialising the study of "genuine" hallucinations.

Finally, there is the issue of "direct voluntary control". Here, the qualification is inserted to exclude voluntary mental imagery. Patients may discover "coping strategies", such as talking, thinking certain thoughts, physical activities, etc., which ameliorate the hallucinations (Cockshutt, 2004, this issue; Fallon & Talbot, 1981; Nayani & David, 1996; Shergill, Murray, & McGuire, 1998; Wykes, 2004, this issue) although this would not count as "direct control". Similarly, a few patients seem to be able to "bring them on" by carrying out certain actions or thoughts. Hence, it may be, possibly, that they are indeed subject to voluntary control but that the individual might not be fully aware that he or she has such control. That is to say, the key concept is that the voice hearer does not *feel* as if he or she has direct voluntary control over their perception.

In the light of the above discussion, my preferred definition is as follows:

> A sensory experience which occurs in the absence of corresponding external stimulation of the relevant sensory organ, has a sufficient sense of reality to resemble a veridical perception, over which the subject does not feel s/he has direct and voluntary control, and which occurs in the awake state.

Clues to etiology

Auditory verbal hallucinations (AVHs) are a highly specific phenomenon, which immediately places etiological explanations in the realm of language perception and expression (see David, 1994a for a full treatment of this). We can be even more specific when we consider the commonest form we encounter in psychiatric practice, namely, the voice addressing the individual directly (in the second person). This lacks the diagnostic specificity for schizophrenia of the third person AVHs of Schneider, which though rare, demand explanation (Crow, 2004, this issue). The voice is often personalised and personified—that is, it comes from a specific being with their own biography, either in the experiencer's life now or previously. Indeed, parental or dominant figures predominate suggesting some relationship to early memories as well as ongoing perceptions of power relationships (Chadwick & Birchwood, 1994). If not immediately recognisable, the voice may take on a persona. Another characteristic of "voices" is that they often occur inside subjective space—within the mind or head. The distinction between this and the externally located "true" hallucination used to be emphasised. In our definition above, the issue is avoided since some experiencers find the distinction difficult to make (presumably all perceptions are "in the mind" but then projected outwards in some way, back to the object). As long as the experience "seems real" we can call it a hallucination. That is not to say that the internal/external distinction is not a genuine one and may not offer clues to etiology (Hunter et al., 2003; Hunter, 2004, this issue); but for this very reason it is appropriate to include internal and external sensations within the rubric of hallucinations pending further empirical work (see also Stephane, Thuras, Nasralla, & Georgopoulos, 2003).

Another point regarding etiology as well as the cognitive models to be discussed below, is the claim that hallucinations occur in a surprisingly large proportion of "normal" individuals. This observation has been noted in the scientific literature for over a century now but has been boosted recently by a number of methodologically sound population surveys (see Johns & Van Os, 2001). As noted in the introduction, cognitive neuropsychiatry as an approach relies on the existence of a spectrum of "normal" cognitive processes upon which to model abnormal phenomena. The high prevalence of auditory hallucinations in nonclinical groups (including 84% of psychiatric nurses; Millham & Easton, 1998) appears to justify this. However, in my opinion, it would be wrong to conclude that there is nothing inherently pathological about "hearing voices", and hence no need to add a psychiatric or neuropsychiatric dimension, except in cases where the consequences of "voices" are disadvantageous, for example, acting on voices that encourage self-harm (see Leuder & David, 2001 for a debate on this issue). My reading of the research is that many of the phenomena reported in surveys are responses to questions in which the hallucination is explicitly described as an "as if" phenomenon (Peters, Joseph, & Garety, 1999). For example: "Do you ever feel as if your own thoughts were being echoed back to you?" Similarly, work from the same authors, suggesting that it is only the distress and preoccupation concomitant with psychotic symptoms that marks them out as pathological, raises the question of whether a truly experienced, nonfleeting event, meeting the definition of hallucinations given above could ever be treated with the indifference with which normal subjects seem to treat them. A "softer" conclusion from these data is that phenomena somewhat akin to AVHs are indeed part and parcel of everyday, nonpathological, mental activity, but may be risk factors for mental disorder. The data also show the importance of auditory imagery in a number of cognitive functions (speech and language, judgement, affect regulation, etc.). But that is a world apart from claiming that true hallucinations are "normal". Searching for neural correlates of AVHs or pathological processes that distort the normal cognitive architecture to produce them, is a legitimate endeavour.

The "content" of AVHs has previously been derided by phenomenolgists but may also be important, not only to the experiencer, but also to the cognitive neuropsychiatrist. The content of the "voices" is mostly meaningful but may be mundane and repetitive (see Bracken et al., 2004, this issue). The most obvious example of the latter is the commenting voice—again said to have particular diagnostic significance according to Kurt Schneider. Such voices are usually context-dependent, context here including affective state as well as physical

TABLE 1
Features of auditory hallucinations that suggest physiological or psychological causation

Neurophysiological	*Psychological*
Modality consistent within different disorders. Possibly some general propensity to hallucination	Auditory hallucinations seldom seen following brain damage (cf. visual)
Nonpropositional content, may be lateralised. Points to right hemisphere origin (Ellis et al., 1989)	Not random: Meaningful, sometimes valued
Unbidden	Resemble inner speech and may be associated with "subvocal" speech (Gould, 1949; Green & Kinsbourne, 1990)
Responds well to antipsychotic drugs if part of schizophrenic illness	Responds poorly to antipsychotic drugs if not part of schizophrenic illness
Related to arousal	Related to affect and possibly memory
Related to brain structures (e.g., superior temporal gyrus volume) (Stephane et al., 2001)	Found in lesser forms in nonclinical subjects (Peters et al., 1999; Johns & Van Os, 2001)

surroundings. They are, by definition unbidden and, in the clinical context, usually unpleasant and unwanted but may be positive and valued (Miller, O'Connor, & Dipasquale, 1993).

Simply by considering these and related clinical observations, we can derive clues to the etiology of "voices", in particular, whether they conform to a pathophysiological process with minimal or only subsequent psychological effects versus a primary psychological process embedded within "normal" physiology (see Table 1).

Auditory hallucinations and brain structure

There has been considerable interest in relating the propensity to experience auditory hallucinations to certain brain structures, particularly those related to language processes (see Crow, 2004, this issue). The structure that has attracted most attention in this regard is the left temporal lobe, particularly the superior temporal gyrus (STG), known to be activated during speech perception. In a review by Stephane, Barton, and Boutros (2001) there were 10 studies that examined the STG, five of which found some association with hallucinations. Three studies (Barta, Pearlson, Powers, Richards, & Tune, 1990; Levitan, Ward, & Catts, 1999; Rajarethinam, DeQuardo, Napela, & Tandon, 2000) found a negative correlation between STG volume and AH severity. Many of these used *ad-hoc* clinical ratings of hallucinations. In contrast, Shapleske et al. (2001, 2002) recruited patients on the basis of their experiencing marked or little propensity to AVHs and examined various brain structures. No difference was found in planum temporale surface area or volume—a structure with particular importance in language perception and production (Shapleske et al., 2001) or for that matter the corpus callosum (Rossell et al., 2001). However, using voxel-based morphometric methods, Shapleske et al. (2002) found a reduction in grey matter density in the left insula and adjacent temporal cortex in hallucinators. In summary, there are clues that relevant brain structures are implicated in the pathogenesis of AVHs, at least in the context of schizophrenic disorders. The data are not overwhelming but indicative of disruption to language-relevant circuits.

Auditory hallucinations and brain function

These are discussed by Woodruff (2004, this issue), David (1999), and also in part by Seal and colleagues (2004, this issue). In summary, the evidence is accumulating in favour of mechanisms involving language perception and production, less so for auditory sensory activation. The first pioneering study using high resolution functional imaging techniques was that published by Silbersweig and colleagues (1995) using positron emission tomography (PET) with radio-labelled water. In retrospect, the extent and combination of sub-cortical and cortical areas revealed to be active during the experience of hallucinations in comparison to the "resting state", is not easy to assimilate into current theories (see also Shergill, Bullmore, Simmons, Murray, & McGuire, 2000). A major focus of increased regional cerebral blood flow over the pre-motor cortex, for example, was unexplained and may have been related to the idiosyncrasies of the subjects' hallucinations. Interestingly, several studies (Bar, Nenadic, & Sauer, 2002; Musalek et al., 1989; Shergill, Brammer, Williams, Murray, & McGuire, 2001) have now shown somato-sensory cortical involvement in somatic hallucinations.

Techniques that do not require the active generation or monitoring of auditory perceptions do allow the inference that extensive auditory linguistic and sensory cortical areas are active during hallucinations (David et al., 1996; Tiihonen et al., 1992; Woodruff et al., 1997). In these longitudinal studies the responsiveness of the superior temporal cortex bilaterally to externally delivered meaningful speech appeared to be inhibited, perhaps competitively, during the experience of hallucinations. However, the additional factors responsible for the alien nature of the perceived speech remain less well elucidated. Self-generated auditory verbal imagery and audible (external) speech activate at least some areas in common (McGuire et al., 1995, 1996a, 1996b), but areas of executive control and self-monitoring seem to form the basis of the added ingredients for distinguishing thoughts from hallucinations. A recent report by Copolov et al. (2003) should be added to this body of work. These authors compared relative regional cerebral blood flow (CBF) using the methods developed by Silbersweig et al. (1995). They studied patients actively hallucinating plus patient and healthy controls presented with multispeaker babble. Both control groups indicated their perception of speech with a button press. The hallucinators showed activation in the superior temporal gyrus as well as right frontal and temporal regions and left hippocampus. Broca's area and other motor areas were not activated during hallucinations. There was considerable intersubject variation. The authors favour a model of AVHs in which memory processes are more central than language (see also Busatto et al., 1995). Indeed many "voices" represent salient figures from an individual's past (see Thomas and colleagues, 2004, this issue).

Finally, those functional imaging studies which, like structural imaging, are more relevant to understanding the propensity to auditory hallucinations within the schizophrenia syndrome, again tend to draw attention to frontotemporal (language-related) regions and their lack of normal connectivity (Lawrie et al., 2002). And there are other imaging and neurophysiological techniques that point to frontotemporal language regions. For example, repetitive transcranial magnetic stimulation (Hoffman et al., 2003; Schreiber et al., 2002) and electroencephalography (EEG) (Ishii et al., 2000).

Cognitive models of auditory hallucinations

A variety of plausible cognitive models has been developed and tested over recent years and these models are thoroughly reviewed by Seal and colleagues (2004, this issue). They have been stimulated by neuropsychologist Chris Frith's ideas about defective self-monitoring being the fundamental cognitive abnormality underlying psychosis (Frith 1992). Frith and colleagues have developed cybernetic models in which intentions give rise to a corollary discharge or efference copy (also known as a feed-forward model) which then serves as a comparison against the ensuing perceived action. Put simply, the presence of a perceived action (including a speech act) or its precursor, in the absence of an efference copy, is interpreted as being of external (alien) origin. This applies particularly well to the case of passivity phenomena or "made actions" (Blakemore, Smith, Steel, Johnstone, & Frith, 2000). Frith (1996) interprets auditory hallucinations in the same way. I have adapted his model to be more specific to auditory language processing merely as a way of illustrating and classifying experimental cognitive neuropsychiatric approaches to AVHs (see Figure 1). One can postulate several different points at which an efference copy is sent. For example, at the point of formulating a thought—a lack of feed-forward model leading to the experience of thought insertion—or later at the point of preparing an utterance, leading to the more familiar AVH. Evidence for two-way communication between the various output levels comes from phenomena, such as priming and on-line error correction.

Earlier work on AVHs concentrated on auditory imagery (see Slade & Bentall, 1988) while more recent research implicates source memory and verbal

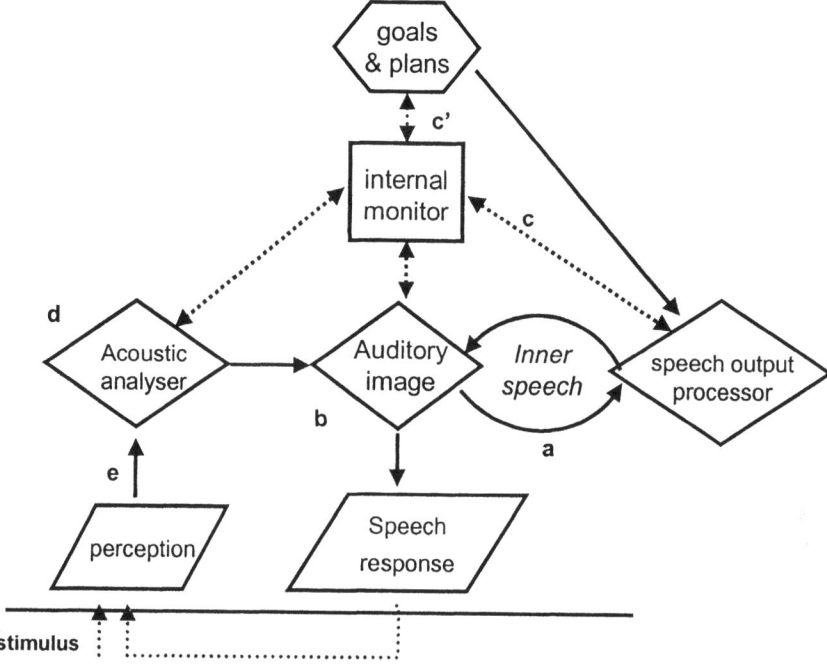

Figure 1. Cognitive neuropsychiatric model of auditory verbal hallucinations (adapted from Frith, 1992).

a and b: Inner speech
Studies investigating phonological similarity and word length effects; verbal transformations; pitch, phoneme, rhyme, homophone judgements. No abnormalities during hallucinations (David & Lucas, 1993) but abnormalities in people with schizophrenia (Haddock et al., 1996); No difference between hallucination-prone and nonhallucinating patients (Evans et al., 2000). Early studies of auditory imagery *per se*, are inconsistent (see Slade & Bentall, 1988; Seal and colleagues, 2004, this issue).

c: Reality/source monitoring (Seal and colleagues, 2004, this issue)
This is the site of the disconnection between willed intentions and selected actions advanced by Frith (1992) to account for positive psychotic symptoms. C' is an alternative more proximal site also suggested by Frith. Several studies have investigated this (cognitive and ERPs, PET and fMRI). Interpretation of results is hampered by problems with memory *per se*, general problems with source and context (see Keefe et al., 2002); relationship to IQ (Seal et al., 1997) and poorly correlated with hallucinations; misattribution of thoughts to heard speech not found consistently. Recent ERP work is supportive (Ford et al., 2001).

d: Delayed/distorted auditory feedback
Internal monitoring is violated by external input which comes in through auditory perceptual routes but could have effects at any point d, b or even a. The assumption is that the effects will be lessened if there is a lack of expectation caused by failure at point c. Results from delayed feedback are inconsistent with abnormal monitoring (Goldberg et al., 1997). Distorted feedback (Cahill et al., 1996; Johns et al., 2001) again assumes a problem with monitoring at point c but in fact may produce its effects at the acoustic analysis stage or within the internal monitor itself. Some evidence of monitoring failure from these experiments, but related to delusions and hallucinations.

e: Ectopic production/misperception of sound
Some evidence of misperception but hallucinations tend to be worse during silence (see Margo et al., 1981). Functional imaging evidence supports on "ectopic" origin of hallucinations, including right hemisphere source (i.e., *physiological* rather than cognitive explanation). However, attributional processes and content are unexplained by a "lesion" at this level alone.

self-monitoring. All these models have face validity but none has enjoyed consistent experimental support (see caption to Figure 1). Novel applications of event-related potentials (ERPs) have, however, given a boost to the notion of impaired verbal self-monitoring with a specific failure in marking self-generated speech as distinct from other generated speech (Ford et al., 2001; Ford, Mathalon, Whitfield, Faustman, & Roth, 2002).

The more specific language-based theories have hardly fared better. The notion that AVHs were akin to the inner speech of phonological short-term memory has been effectively excluded by the description of a single case who had normal phonological short-term memory (STM) function, that is she showed the predicted phonological superiority effect and word length effects, despite continuous AVHs (David & Lucas, 1993; cf. thought echo, David, 1994b). This was replicated in a more recent group study showing no substantial differences between schizophrenia patients with and without AVHs on a battery of phonological STM tests, plus those of verbal and musical imagery putatively testing the "inner voice" and the "inner ear" (Smith, Wilson, & Reisberg, 1995), including the verbal transformation effect ("life" becoming "fly" on repetition) (Evans, McGuire, & David, 2001; cf. Haddock, Slade, & Bentall, 1995). Nevertheless, such models of STM may be overly simplistic and fail to account for multiple streams of information within the phonological store. We can, however, say that theoretically, coherent AVHs depend on intact language production (speech output processes in the model) and this seems to be confirmed in practice (Thompson & Copolov, 1998).

Another small group of studies has investigated delayed or distorted auditory feedback. In the case of the former, speech output is usually rendered dysfluent because, it is argued, that the delayed feedback interferes with or "violates" the normal internal feedback between intentions and "the monitor" which maintains and corrects speech errors "on-line". Goldberg, Gold, Coppola, & Weinberger (1997) proposed that if the internal feedback is lacking then the effect of delay should be somewhat attenuated. This was not observed. Leuder, Thomas, and Johnstone (1994) suggested that people with schizophrenia rely more on external feedback to correct speech errors because, by implication, internal feedback routes are impaired in some way. Another variant on this design has been explored by Cahill, Silbersweig, and Frith (1996) and Johns and colleagues (2001) using immediate but distorted feedback, such that the participant's speech sounded "alien". A strong sense of self, supported by intact monitoring should overcome the accompanying sensation that someone else is speaking. In contrast, the authors found both hallucinating and nonhallucinating patients with schizophrenia tended to make more misattribution errors although hallucinators were more likely to attribute the voice to the "other" category. How this fits into the feed-forward model advanced by Frith (1992) is not entirely clear. Presumably, the individual is generating speech and receiving some "confirmation" of the output, if not from the efference copy then from bone conduction, or, if this is blotted out by the distorted speech, by kinaesthetic feedback from the speech musculature. Hence, the problem is not failure to recognise self-generated actions as such but in dealing with near simultaneous contradictory information. It appears that people with psychotic symptoms are forced into making errors in this situation plus, perhaps, a bias toward nonself attributions under conditions of uncertainty (see below). It could be that the internal monitor is not capable of adjudicating under these circumstances or that some higher cognitive control is lacking.

Despite its naivety, the notion that external or ectopic activation of speech perception modules could underlie AVHs, finds apparent support in much of the functional imaging reviewed above (Ait-Bentaleb, Beuregard, Liddle, & Stip, 2002; Stephane, Folstein, Mathew, & Hill, 2000; Woodruff, 2004, this issue). Indeed, in the early days of neuroimaging using single photon emission computerised tomography (SPECT), several studies uncovered "hot spots" in the left temporal and frontotemporal regions in people with AVHs which disappeared along with the hallucinations (Matsuda, Gyobo, Masayasu, & Hisada, 1988, McGuire, Shah, & Murray, 1993; Suzuki, Yuasa, Minabke, Murata, & Kurachi, 1993). The basic notion still holds sway albeit with the caveat that a dysfunctional "network" is to blame rather than a single aberrant "centre" (see Shergill et al., 2001).

Even if both the sensory experience and experience of alien source can be explicated in terms of neuropsychological function or dysfunction, there remains a great deal to be explained in terms of the personification and meaningful content of the hallucinatory dialogue (see Leuder & Thomas, 2000; Nayani & David, 1996; Thomas et al., 2004, this issue). Cognitive psychology has taken up the challenge to do so—leaving aside the neural correlates for the time being. This has mainly come from the cognitive therapy field where models involving biases rather than deficits appear to have more explanatory power (Bentall, Baker, & Havers, 1991; Bentall, Haddock, & Slade, 1994 were first to articulate this view; see Beck & Rector, 2003 for a comprehensive review and Wykes, 2004, this issue). For example, notions that the source-monitoring of heard or remembered speech could be faulty would, on its own, leave the individual in a state of confusion about whether he/she had heard certain statements or whether he/she had said or thought them him/herself but would not on the face of it necessarily lead to auditory hallucinations. This requires a more consistent tendency (or bias) to attribute self-generated thoughts to an alien speech source. Similarly, this process does not appear to occur at random but more often in association with hostile or derogatory thoughts (see Morrison & Haddock, 1997). So the disrupted mechanism is selective in terms of content and the nature of its attributions. Similarly, hostile thoughts or statements are more likely to be remembered (or resisted) and to recur at times of low mood or anxiety—providing a mechanism for their perpetuation (see Chaturvedi & Sinha, 1990).

As in anxiety disorders, the hallucinatory experience may lead to avoidance of real or feared precipitants which may in turn increase their salience (Persaud & Marks, 1995). Various coping strategies from talking back to the voices, subservience to them or simply distraction, may be useful but may also perpetuate the experience (Morrison, 1998). The personification of the voices may owe less to the primary experience itself but more to the sufferer's attempt to make sense of it in terms of past or current life experience or as a consequence of longstanding engagement and dialogue. The growth of support groups and forums where "voice hearers" can discuss their experiences may reduce the stigma and fear associated with voices although it may also tend to reinforce them (see Leuder & David, 2001; Cockshutt, 2004, this issue). Many voice hearers do indeed value their "voices" especially where they make positive utterances. These may in some way be a construction by the voice hearer to combat the other "negative" voices, which grows out of a conscious attempt to demystify the alien voice by talking back to it (Nayani & David, 1996).

CONCLUSION

Cognitive neuropsychiatry is a direct descendant of phenomenology. In the case of AVHs, it is very likely that phenomenology is giving us important clues to etiology and pathophysiology. There are demonstrable cerebral correlates of AVHs affecting auditory cortex evident from structural and functional neuroimaging, so these cannot be dismissed and they too can help us formulate hypotheses regarding etiology and mechanism. Models of language production/perception with internal/source monitoring suggest many sites for the production of hallucinations (see Figure 1) but the extant models are insufficiently precise, or allow for multiple sites of abnormality to result in similar phenomena. Perhaps we now have to consider further subcategorisations of hallucinations and hallucination-like phenomena. Those that seem to represent past experiences replayed may have their origin in source memory processes while the more immediate commenting and instructional voices may be related to on-line self-monitoring. Thought echo and broadcast may reflect inner speech but with an additional component of heightened auditory imagery. Externally perceived voices may be most likely to correlate with excessive neural activation in speech perceptual areas but with appraisal functions adding a necessary ingredient. A simple "neural excitatory" model of AVHs, which functional neuroimaging encourages and indeed tends to support, is inadequate on its own to explain all that is entailed in "hearing voices". An integrated account is needed, which must take account of the characteristic content and "behaviour" of voices. The collected papers in this issue represent a first such attempt at integration.

Manuscript accepted 9 June 2003

REFERENCES

Ait-Bentaleb, L., Beauregard, M., Liddle, P., & Stip, E. (2002). Cerebral activity associated with auditory verbal hallucinations: A functional magnetic resonance imaging case study. *Journal of Psychiatry and Neuroscience, 27*, 110–115.

Aleman, A., & DeHaan, E. H. F. (1998). On redefining hallucination. *American Journal of Orthopsychiatry, 68*, 656–658.

Almeida, O., Forstl, H., Howard, R., & David, A. (1993). Unilateral auditory hallucinations. *British Journal of Psychiatry, 162*, 262–264.

Bär, K-J., Gaser, C., Nenadic, I., & Sauer, H. (2002). Transient activation of a somatosensory area in painful hallucinations shown by fMRI. *Neuroreport, 13*, 805–808.

Barnes, J., Boubert, L., Harris, J., Lee, A., & David, A. S. (2003). Reality monitoring and visual hallucinations in Parkinson's disease. *Neuropsychologia, 41*, 565–574.

Barnes, J., & David, A. S. (2001). Visual hallucinations in Parkinson's disease: A review and phenomenological survey. *Journal of Neurology, Neurosurgery, and Psychiatry, 70*, 727–733.

Barta, P. E., Pearlson, G. D., Powers, R. E., Richards, S. S., & Tune, L. E. (1990). Auditory hallucinations and smaller superior temporal gyral volume in schizophrenia. *American Journal of Psychiatry, 147*, 1457–1462.

Beck, A. T., & Rector, N. A. (2003). A cognitive model of hallucinations. *Cognitive Therapy and Research, 27*, 19–52.

Bentall, R., Baker, G., & Havers, S. (1991). Reality monitoring and psychotic hallucinations. *British Journal of Clinical Psychology, 30*, 213–222.

Bentall, R. P., Haddock, G., & Slade, P. D. (1994). Cognitive behavior therapy for persistent auditory hallucinations. From theory to therapy. *Behavior Therapy, 25*, 51–66.

Blakemore, S. J., Smith. J., Steel, R., Johnstone, C. E., & Frith C. D. (2000). The perception of self-produced sensory stimuli in patients with auditory hallucinations and passivity experiences: Evidence for a breakdown in self-monitoring. *Psychological Medicine, 30*, 1131–1139.

Busatto, G. F., David, A. S., Costa, D. C., Ell, P. J., Pilowsky, L. S., Lucey, J. V., & Kerwin, R. W. (1995). Schizophrenic auditory hallucinations are associated with increased regional cerebral blood flow during verbal memory activation in a study using single photon emission computed tomography. *Psychiatry Research, 61*, 255–264.

Cahill, C., Silbersweig, D., & Frith C. D. (1996). Psychotic experiences induced in deluded patients using distorted auditory feedback. *Cognitive Neuropsychiatry, 1*, 201–211.

Chadwick, P., & Birchwood, M. (1994). The omnipotence of voices: A cognitive approach to auditory hallucinations. *British Journal of Psychiatry, 164*, 190–201.

Chaturvedi, S., & Sinha, V. (1990). Recurrence of hallucinations in consecutive episodes of schizophrenia and affective disorder. *Schizophrenia Research, 3*, 103–106.

Cockshutt, G. (2004). Choices for voices: A voice hearer's perspective on hearing voices. *Cognitive Neuropsychiatry, 9*(1/2), 9–11.

Copolov, D. L., Seal, M. L., Maruff, P., Ulusoy, R., Wong, M. T., Tochon-Danguy, H. J., & Egan, G. F. (2003). Cortical activation associated with the experience of auditory hallucinations and perception of human speech in schizophrenia: A PET correlation study. *Psychiatry Research, 122*, 139–152.

Crow, T. J. (2004). Auditory hallucinations as primary disorders of syntax: An evolutionary theory of the origins of language. *Cognitive Neuropsychiatry, 9*(1/2), 125–145.

David, A. S. (1990). Insight and psychosis. *British Journal of Psychiatry, 156*, 798–808.

David, A. S. (1994a). The neuropsychology of auditory-verbal hallucinations. In A. S. David & J. C. Cutting (Eds.), *The neuropsychology of schizophrenia* (pp. 269–312). Hove, UK: Psychology Press.

David, A. S. (1994b). Thought echo reflects the activity of the phonological loop. *British Journal of Clinical Psychology, 33*, 81–83.

David, A. S. (1999). Auditory hallucinations: Phenomenology, neuropsychology and neuroimaging update. *Acta Psychiatrica Scandinavica. Supplementum, 395*, 95–104.

David, A. S., & Lucas, P. (1993). Auditory–verbal hallucinations and the phonological loop: A cognitive neuropsychological study. *British Journal of Clinical Psychology, 32*, 431–441.

David, A. S., Malmberg, A., Lewis, G., Brandt, L., & Allebeck, P. (1995), Are there neurological and sensory risk factors for schizophrenia? *Schizophrenia Research, 14*, 247–251.

David, A. S., Woodruff, P. W. R., Howard, R., Mellers, J. D. C., Brammer, M., Bullmore, E., Wright, I., Andrew, C., & Williams, S. C. R. (1996). Auditory hallucinations inhibit exogenous activation of auditory association cortex. *Neuroreport, 7*, 932–936.

Doris, A., O'Carroll, R. E., Steele, J. D., & Ebmeier, K. P. (1995). Single photon emission computed tomography in a patient with unilateral auditory hallucinations. *Behavioural Neurology, 8*, 145–148.

Ellis, A. W., Young, A. W., & Critchley, E. M. R. (1989). Intrusive automatic or nonpropositional inner speech following bilateral cerebral injury. *Aphasiology, 3*, 581–585.

Evans, C. L., McGuire, P. K., & David, A. S. (2000). Is auditory imagery defective in patients with auditory hallucinations? *Psychological Medicine, 30*, 137–148.

Falloon, I. R., & Talbot, R. E. (1981). Persistent auditory hallucinations: Coping mechanisms and implications for management. *Psychological Medicine, 11*, 329–339.

Ffytche, D. H., Howard, R. J., Brammer, M. J., David, A. S., Woodruff, P. W. R., & Williams, S. C. R. (1998). The anatomy of conscious vision: An fMRI study of visual hallucinations. *Nature Neuroscience, 1*, 738–742.

Ford, J. M., Mathalon, D. H., Kalba, S., Whitfield, S., Faustman, W. O., & Roth W. T. (2001). Cortical responsiveness during talking and listening in schizophrenia: An event-related brain potential study. *Biological Psychiatry, 50*, 540–549.

Ford, J. M., Mathalon, D. H., Whitfield, S., Faustman, W. O., & Roth, W. T. (2002). Reduced communication between frontal and temporal lobes during talking in schizophrenia. *Biological Psychiatry, 51*, 485–92.

Frith, C. D. (1992). *The cognitive neuropsychology of schizophrenia*. Hove, UK: Psychology Press.

Frith, C. D. (1996). The role of the prefrontal cortex in self-consciousness: The case of auditory hallucinations. *Philosophical Transactions of the Royal Society of London. Series B: Biological Sciences, 351*, 1505–1512.

Goldberg, T. E., Gold, J. M., Coppola, R., & Weinberger, D. R. (1997). Unnatural practices, unspeakable actions: A study of delayed auditory feedback in schizophrenia. *American Journal of Psychiatry, 154*, 858–860.

Gould, L. N. (1949). Auditory hallucinations and subvocal speech. *Journal of Nervous and Mental Disease, 109*, 418–427.

Green, M. F., & Kinsbourne, M. (1990). Subvocal activity and auditory hallucinations: Clues for behavioral treatment. *Schizophrenia Bulletin, 16*, 617–625.

Griffiths, T. D. (2000). Musical hallucinosis in acquired deafness: Phenomenology and brain substrate. *Brain, 123*, 2065–2076.

Haddock, G., Slade, P. D., & Bentall, R. P. (1995). Auditory hallucinations and the verbal transformation effect: The role of suggestions. *Personality and Individual Differences, 19*, 301–306.

Haddock, G., Slade, P. D., Prasaad, R., & Bentall, R. P. (1996). Functioning of the phonological loop in auditory hallucinations. *Personality and Individual Differences, 20*, 753–760.

Hoffman, R. E., Hawkins, K. A., Gueorguieva, R., Boutros, N. N., Rachid, F., Carroll, K., & Krystal, J. H. (2003). Transcranial magnetic stimulation of left temporoparietal cortex and medication-resistant auditory hallucinations. *Archives of General Psychiatry, 60*, 49–56.

Hoffman, R. E., Rapaport, J., Ameli, R., McGlashan, T. H., & Harcherik, D. (1995). A neural network simulation of hallucinated "voices" and associated speech perception impairments in schizophrenic patients. *Journal of Cognitive Neuroscience, 7*, 479–496.

Howard, R., Williams, S., Bullmore, E., Brammer, M., Mellers, J., Woodruff, P. W. R., & David, A. S. (1995). Cortical response to exogenous visual stimulation during visual hallucinations. *Lancet*, *345*, 70.

Hunter, M. D. (2004). Locating voices in space: A perceptual model for auditory hallucinations? *Cognitive Neuropsychiatry*, *9*(1/2), 93–105.

Hunter, M. D., Griffiths, T. D., Farrow, T. F., Zheng, Y., Wilkinson, I. D., Hegde, N., Woods, W., Spence, S. A., & Woodruff, P. W. R. (2003). A neural basis for the perception of voices in external auditory space. *Brain*, *126*, 161–169.

Inzelberg, R., Kipervasser, S., & Korczyn, A. D. Auditory hallucinations in Parkinson's disease. *Journal of Neurology, Neurosurgery, and Psychiatry*, *64*, 533–535.

Ishii, R., Shinosaki, K., Ikejiri, Y., Ukai, S., Yamashita, K., Iwase, M., Mizuno-Matsumoto, Y., Inouye, T., Yoshimine, T., Hirabuki, N., Robinson, S. E., & Takeda, M. (2000). Theta rhythm increases in left superior temporal cortex during auditory hallucinations in schizophrenia: A case report. *Neuroreport*, *11*, 3283–3287.

Johns, L. C., Rossell, S., Frith, C. D., Ahmad, F., Hemsley, D., Kuipers, E., & McGuire, P. K. (2001). Verbal self-monitoring and auditory verbal hallucinations in patients with schizophrenia. *Psychological Medicine*, *31*, 705–715.

Johns, L. C., & Van Os, J. (2001). The continuity of psychotic experiences in the general population. *Clinical Psychology Review*, *21*, 1125–1141.

Keefe, R. S., Arnold, M. C., Bayen, U. J., McEvoy, J. P., & Wilson, W. H. (2002). Source-monitoring deficits for self-generated stimuli in schizophrenia: Multinomial modeling of data from three sources. *Schizophrenia Research*, *57*, 51–67.

Keshavan, M. S., David, A. S., Steingard, S., & Lishman, W. A. (1992). Musical hallucinations: A review and synthesis. *Neuropsychiatry, Neuropsychology, and Behavioral Neurology*, *3*, 211–223.

Kobayashi, T., & Kato, S. (2000). Hallucination of soliloquy: Speaking component and hearing component of schizophrenic hallucinations. *Psychiatry and Clinical Neurosciences*, *54*, 531–536.

Lawrie, S. M., Buechel, C., Whalley, H. C., Frith, C. D., Friston, K. J., & Johnstone, E. C. (2002). Reduced frontotemporal functional connectivity in schizophrenia associated with auditory hallucinations. *Biological Psychiatry*, *51*, 1008–1011.

Leudar, I., & David, A. S. (2001). Is hearing voices a sign of mental illness? *Psychologist*, *14*, 256–259.

Leudar, I., & Thomas P. (2000). *Voices of reason, voices of insanity*. London: Routledge.

Leudar, I., Thomas, P., & Johnston, M. (1994). Self-monitoring in speech production: Effects of verbal hallucinations and negative symptoms. *Psychological Medicine*, *24*, 749–761.

Levitan, C., Ward, P. B., & Catts, S. V. (1999). Superior temporal gyral volumes and laterality correlates of auditory hallucinations in schizophrenia. *Biological Psychiatry*, *46*, 955–962.

Margo, A., Hemsley, D. R., & Slade, P. D. (1981). The effects of varying auditory input on schizophrenic hallucinations. *British Journal of Psychiatry*, *139*, 122–127.

Matsuda, H., Gyobo, T., Masayasu, I., & Hisada, K. (1988). Increased accumulation of N-isopropyl-(I-123) p-iodoamphetamine in the left auditory area in a schizophrenic patient with auditory hallucinations. *Clinical Nuclear Medicine*, *13*, 53–55.

McGuire, P. K., Shah, G. M. S., & Murray, R. M. (1993). Increased blood flow in Broca's area during auditory hallucinations in schizophrenia. *Lancet*, *342*, 703–706.

McGuire, P. K., Silbersweig, D. A., & Frith, C. D. (1996a). Functional neuroanatomy of verbal self-monitoring. *Brain*, *119*, 907–917.

McGuire, P. K., Silbersweig, D. A., Murray, R. M., David, A. S., Frackowiak, R. S. J., & Frith, C. D. (1996b). The functional anatomy of inner speech and auditory imagery. *Psychological Medicine*, *26*, 29–38.

McGuire, P. K., Silbersweig, D. A., Wright, I., Murray, R. M., David, A. S., Frackowiak, R. S. J., & Frith, C.D. (1995). Abnormal monitoring of inner speech: A physiological basis for auditory hallucinations. *Lancet*, *346*, 596–600.

Miller, L. J., O'Connor, E., & DiPasquale, T. (1993). Patients' attitudes toward hallucinations. *American Journal of Psychiatry, 150*, 584–588.

Millham, A., & Easton, S. (1998). Prevalence of auditory hallucinations in nurses in mental health. *Journal of Psychiatric and Mental Health Nursing, 5*, 95–9.

Morrison, A. P. (1998). A cognitive analysis of the maintenance of auditory hallucinations: Are voices to schizophrenia what bodily sensations are to panic? *Behavioural and Cognitive Psychotherapy, 26*, 289–302.

Morrison, A. P., & Haddock, G. (1997). Cognitive factors in source monitoring and auditory hallucinations. *Psychological Medicine, 27*, 669–679.

Musalek, M., Podreka, I., Walter, H., Suess, E., Passweg, V., Nutzinger, D., Strobl, R., & Lesch, O. M. (1989). Regional brain function in hallucinations: A study of regional cerebral blood flow with ^{99m}Tc-HMPAO-SPECT in patients with auditory hallucinations, tactile hallucinations and normal controls. *Comprehensive Psychiatry, 30*, 99–108.

Nayani, T. H., & David, A. S. (1996). The auditory hallucination: A phenomenological survey. *Psychological Medicine, 26*, 177–189.

Penfield, W., & Perot, P. (1963). The brain's record of auditory and visual experience: A final summary and conclusion. *Brain, 86*, 568–693.

Persaud, R., & Marks, I. (1995). A pilot study of exposure control of chronic auditory hallucinations in schizophrenia. *British Journal of Psychiatry, 167*, 45–50.

Peters, E. R., Joseph, S. A., & Garety, P. A. (1999). Measurement of delusional ideation in the normal population: Introducing the PDI (Peters et al. Delusions Inventory). *Schizophrenia Bulletin, 25*, 553–576.

Rajarethinam, R. P., DeQuardo, J. R., Napela, R., & Tandon, R. (2000). Superior temporal gyrus in schizophrenia: A volumetric magnetic resonance imaging study. *Schizophrenia Research, 41*, 303–312.

Rossell, S. L., Shapleske, J., Fukuda, R., Woodruff, P. W. R., Simmons, A., David, A. S. (2001). Corpus callosum area and functioning in schizophrenic patients with auditory-verbal hallucinations. *Schizophrenia Research, 50*, 9–17.

Schultz, G., & Melzack, R. (1991). The Charles Bonnet syndrome: 'Phantom visual images'. *Perception, 20*, 809–825.

Schreiber, S., Dannon, P. N., Goshen, E., Amiaz, R., Zwas, T. S., Grunhaus, L. (2002). Right prefrontal rTMS treatment for refractory auditory command hallucinations: A neuroSPECT assisted case study. *Psychiatry Research: Neuroimaging, 116*, 113–117.

Seal, M. L., Aleman, A., & McGuire, P. K. (2004). Compelling imagery, unanticipated speech and deceptive memory: Neurocognitive models of auditory verbal hallucinations in schizophrenia. *Cognitive Neuropsychiatry, 9*(1/2), 43–72.

Seal, M. L., Crowe, S. F., & Cheung, P. (1997). Deficits in source monitoring in subjects with auditory hallucinations may be due to differences in verbal intelligence and verbal memory. *Cognitive Neuropsychiatry, 2*, 273–290

Shapleske, J., Rossell, S. L., Chitnis, X., Suckling, J., Simmons, A., Bullmore, E. T., Woodruff, P. W. R., & David, A. S. (2002). A computational morphometric MRI study of schizophrenia: Effects of hallucinations. *Cerebral Cortex, 12*, 1331–1341.

Shapleske, J., Rossell, S. L., Simmons, A., David, A. S., & Woodruff, P. W. R. (2001). Are auditory hallucinations the consequence of abnormal cerebral lateralization? A morphometric MRI study of the sylvian fissure and planum temporale. [Erratum appears in *Biological Psychiatry, 50*, 394]. *Biological Psychiatry, 49*, 685–693.

Shergill, S. S., Brammer, M. J., Williams, S. C., Murray, R. M., & McGuire, P. K. (2000). Mapping auditory hallucinations in schizophrenia using functional magnetic resonance imaging. *Archives of General Psychiatry, 57*, 1033–1038.

Shergill, S. S., Bullmore, E., Simmons, A., Murray, R. M., & McGuire, P. K. (2000). Functional anatomy of auditory verbal imagery in schizophrenic patients with auditory hallucinations. *American Journal of Psychiatry, 157*, 1691–1693.

Shergill, S. S., Cameron, L. A., Brammer, M. J., Williams, S. C., Murray, R. M., & McGuire, P. K. (2001). Modality specific neural correlates of auditory and somatic hallucinations. *Journal of Neurology, Neurosurgery, and Psychiatry, 71*, 688–690.

Shergill, S. S., Murray, R. M., & McGuire, P. K. (1998). Auditory hallucinations: A review of psychological treatments. *Schizophrenia Research, 32*, 137–150.

Silbersweig, D. A., Stern, E., Frith, C. D., Cahill, C., Holmes, A., Grootoonk, S., Seaward, J., McKenna, P., Chua, S. E., Schnorr, L., Jones, T., & Frackowiak, R. S. J. (1995). A functional neuroanatomy of hallucinations in schizophrenia. *Nature, 378*, 176–179.

Slade, P., & Bentall, R. (1988). *Sensory deception: A scientific analysis of hallucination*. London: Croom Helm.

Smith, J. D., Wilson, M., & Reisberg, D. (1995). The role of subvocalization in auditory imagery. *Neuropsychologia, 33*, 1433–1454.

Stephane, M., Barton, S., & Boutros, N. N. (2001). Auditory verbal hallucinations and dysfunction of the neural substrates of speech. *Schizophrenia Research, 50*, 61–78.

Stephane, M., Folstein, M., Matthew, E., & Hill, T. C. (2000). Imaging auditory verbal hallucinations during their occurrence. *Journal of Neuropsychiatry and Clinical Neurosciences, 12*, 286–287.

Stephane, M., Thuras, P., Nasrallah, H., Georgopoulos, A. P. (2003). The internal structure of the phenomenology of auditory verbal hallucinations. *Schizophrenia Research, 61*, 185–193.

Suzucki, M., Yuasa, S., Minabe, Y., Murata, M., & Kurachi, M. (1993). Left superior temporal blood flow increases in schizophrenic and schizophreniform patients with auditory hallucinations: A longitudinal case study using 123I-IMP SPET. *European Archives of Psychiatry and Clinical Neuroscience, 242*, 257–261.

Takebayashi, H., Takei, N., Mori, N., & Suzuki S. (2002). Unilateral auditory hallucinations in schizophrenia after damage to the right hippocampus. *Schizophrenia Research, 58*, 329–331.

Thomas, P., Bracken, P., & Leudar, I. (2004). Hearing voices: A phenomenological-hermeneutic approach. *Cognitive Neuropsychiatry, 9*(1/2), 13–23.

Tiihonen, J., Hari, R., Naukkarinen, H., Rimón, R., Jousmäki, V., & Kajola, M. (1992). Modified activity of the human auditory cortex during auditory hallucinations. *American Journal of Psychiatry, 149*, 255–257.

Thompson, I. M., & Copolov D. L. (1998). The psycholinguistics of auditory hallucinations. *Aphasiology, 12*, 919–932.

Woodruff, P. W. R. (2004). Auditory hallucinations: Insights and questions from neuroimaging. *Cognitive Neuropsychiatry, 9*(1/2), 73–91.

Woodruff, P. W., Wright, I. C., Bullmore, E. T., Brammer, M., Howard, R. J. Williams, S. C., Shapleske, J., Rossell, S., David, A. S., McGuire, P. K., & Murray R. M. (1997). Auditory hallucinations and the temporal cortical response to speech in schizophrenia: A functional magnetic resonance imaging study. *American Journal of Psychiatry, 154*, 1676–1682.

Wykes, T. (2004). Psychological treatment for voices in psychosis. *Cognitive Neuropsychiatry, 9*(1/2), 25–41.

Auditory hallucinations as primary disorders of syntax: An evolutionary theory of the origins of language

Timothy J. Crow

SANE POWIC, Warneford Hospital, Oxford, UK

A theory of the evolutionary origins of language is built around: (1) the notion that language is a *sapiens*-specific capacity that arose in the speciation event that separated modern *Homo sapiens* from a prior hominid species, and (2) Broca's concept of asymmetry (subsequently recognised as a "torque" from right frontal to left occipital cortices) as the defining characteristic of the human brain. The four chambers of human association cortex thus created allow the separation of "thought" from the speech output and "meaning" from the speech input, these abstractions representing the associations in the nondominant hemisphere of the motor and sensory phonological representations in the dominant hemisphere. The nuclear symptoms of schizophrenia are conceived as manifestations of the breakdown of the boundaries between these four compartments, and as indicating the necessity of the separation of motor and sensory speech engrams as the basis for the speaker-hearer distinction. They further illustrate a requirement for a "deictic core" to the cerebral organisation of language as Mueller and Buehler proposed. In this sense the nuclear symptoms are disorders of the syntax of universal grammar.

The gradualist theory

When Charles Darwin published his *Origin of Species by Means of Natural Selection* in 1859 he was notably reticent about the origins of man. In the last chapter entitled 'Recapitulation and Conclusion' he confined himself to one paragraph:

> In the distant future I see open fields for far more important researches. Psychology will be based on a new foundation, that of the necessary acquirement of each mental power and capacity by gradation. Light will be thrown on the origin of man and his history.

Correspondence should be addressed to Timothy J. Crow, SANE POWIC, Warneford Hospital, Oxford OX3 7JX, UK.

The reticence is curious because with the publication of Darwin's M and N notebooks (Barrett & Gruber, 1974) it is clear that Darwin had been preoccupied with the origins of human psychological faculties at least since 1829. The explanation that is offered (Gruber, 1974) is that Darwin was impressed (perhaps dating back to the events at the Plinian Society meeting in Edinburgh on 27 March 1827 when W.A.F. Browne's presentation on the material basis of mind was struck from the record as heretical) with the social opprobrium that might attach to an evolutionary account of human origins. The fear of this disapproval and scandal may, it is suggested, have contributed to the long delay in the publication of *The Origin of Species*.

The form of words—"that of the necessary acquirement of each mental power and capacity by gradation"—is also of note because it expresses clearly Darwin's predilection for a gradualist account of the origin of human faculties, as of other evolutionary innovations. The paradox has been noted that the issue on which *The Origin of Species* is weak is—the origin of species. One figure appears in the book (see Figure 1 below).

The point of the figure is to show how within one genus different varieties and species emerge over aeons of time. Darwin states that the horizontal lines can be taken as separating thousands or tens of thousands of generations. The species under consideration have a common origin as indicated by the convergence of the lines below the diagram. Within the diagram are branch points. These represent the origins of varieties or sometimes species. Some lineages, for example A and I, are highly divergent; others, for example E to G, are unchanged. Some lineages die out and some survive to the present (i.e., beyond epoch XIV).

The implication of the figure is that variation within species (represented as movement along the x-axis) is qualitatively the same as variation between species, hence the absence of a clear differentiation of varieties and species. This can be understood in the light of Darwin's aim to establish that species have a common origin, they are not the subjects of independent creations. Species can arise, subject to favourable environmental circumstance, out of the variation that is present in the natural world at any point in time. The theory is gradualist. That gradualism was preserved into the "Evolutionary Synthesis" of the Darwinian theory of natural selection with Mendel's laws of genetic inheritance in the 1940s (Mayr & Provine, 1998).

In 1863, T.H. Huxley addressed the question in *Evidence of Man's Place in Nature* (Huxley, 1863). In this book he mounted a powerful case that on a series of anatomical comparisons the distance between man and any one of the great apes was no greater than that between any pair of the great apes compared on their own. Huxley thus fitted man into the framework of the Darwinian theory of natural selection of which he was so powerful an advocate. But on the issue of speciation he did not see entirely eye to eye with his mentor. After the publication of *The Origin of Species* he wrote to Darwin that he was ready to go to the stake for the theory but added that he thought that Darwin had loaded

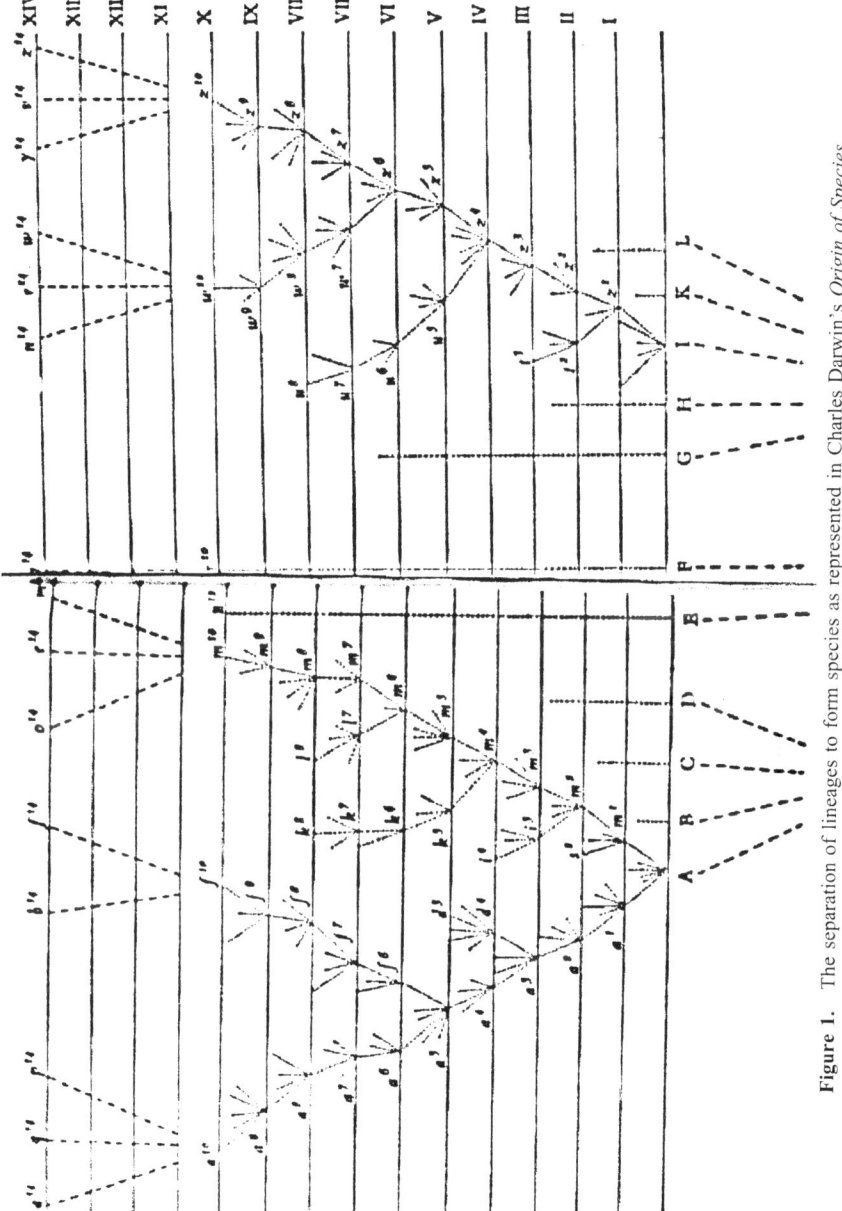

Figure 1. The separation of lineages to form species as represented in Charles Darwin's *Origin of Species*.

himself with "an unnecessary difficulty in adopting Natura *non facit saltum* so unreservedly".

In 1871, Darwin addressed himself to the problem of human origins in *The Descent of Man* (1871). This publication linked in a single volume, *The Descent of Man*, and *Selection in Relation to Sex*, the anatomical and palaeontological case with Darwin's theory of sexual selection. In his Introduction, Darwin writes that:

> During many years it has seemed to me highly probable that sexual selection has played an important part in differentiating the races of man; but in my *Origin of Species* I contented myself by merely alluding to this belief. When I came to apply this belief to man, I found it indispensable to treat the whole subject in full detail (pp. 4–5).

Some passages in the second part of the book indicate that Darwin considered the two arguments to be related in a more fundamental way. Thus:

> ... Sexual selection has apparently acted on both the male and the female side, causing the two sexes of man to differ in body and mind ... [and] has indirectly influenced the progressive development of various bodily structures and of certain mental qualities. Courage, pugnacity, perseverance, strength and size of body ... have all been indirectly gained by one sex or the other, through the influence of love or jealousy, through the appreciation of the beautiful in sound, colour and form, and through the exertion of choice ... (p. 402).

But Darwin nowhere specifies exactly how sexual selection and the descent of man are related. The fact remains that these are separate books.

Language and the case for saltation

In 1873, within two years of the publication of *The Descent of Man*, Friedrich Max Mueller (1873), who held the chair of Philology in the University of Oxford, delivered a series of three lectures at the Royal Institution in which he drew attention to the problems that language raises for Darwin's theory:

> My object is simply to point out a strange omission, and to call attention to one kind of evidence—I mean the evidence of language—which has been most unaccountably neglected, both in studying the development of the human intellect, and determining the position which man holds in the system of the world.

Mueller objected that Darwin's theory that:

> man being the descendant of some lower animal, the development of the human mind out of the mind of animals, or out of no mind, is a mere question of time, is certainly enough to make one a little impatient.

The problem in Mueller's view was that the contents of human consciousness were not merely, as maintained by Locke and Hume, those that arose from the sensations but also from the framework (the "pure intuitions") of space and time that according to Kant is intrinsic to the human mind:

> If we are to become conscious of anything ... we must place all phenomena side by side, or in space; and we can accept them only as following each other in succession, or in time. If we wanted to make it still clearer, that Time and Space are subjective, or at all events determined by the Self, we might say that there can be no There without a Here, there can be no Then without a Now, and that both Here and Now depend on us as recipients, as measurers, as perceivers.

In other words, there must be a deictic frame, and that frame is intrinsic to the capacity for language.

In the second lecture Mueller addresses the problem:

> There is one difficulty which Mr Darwin has not sufficiently appreciated ... There is between the whole animal kingdom on the one side, and man, even in his lowest state, on the other, a barrier which no animal has ever crossed, and that barrier is—*Language* ... If anything has a right to the name of specific difference, it is language, as we find it in man, and in man only ... If we removed the name of *specific difference* from our philosophic dictionaries, I should still hold that nothing deserves the name of man except what is able to speak ... a speaking elephant or an elephantine speaker could never be called an elephant. Professor Schleicher, though an enthusiastic admirer of Darwin, observed once jokingly, but not without a deep meaning, 'If a pig were ever to say to me, "I am a pig" it would ipso facto cease to be a pig'.

Thus, language is the species-defining characteristic. Mueller considers how far Darwin had gone towards conceding the point:

> 'Articulate language is peculiar to man' (Darwin, 1871) and 'It is not the mere power of articulation that distinguishes man from other animals, for, as everyone knows, parrots can talk; but it is his large power of connecting *definite sounds with definite ideas.*'

> Here, then, we might again imagine that Mr Darwin admitted all that we want, viz. that some kind of language is peculiar to man, and distinguishes man from the other animals ... but, no, there follows immediately ... 'This obviously depends upon the development of the mental faculties'.

Mueller asks:

> What can be the meaning of this sentence? ... If it refers to the mental faculties of man, then no doubt it may be said to be obvious. But if it is meant to refer to the

mental faculties of the gorilla, then whether it be true or not, it is, at all events, so far from being obvious, that the very opposite might be called so—I mean the fact that no development of the mental faculties has ever enabled one single animal to connect one single definite idea with one single definite word.

I confess that after reading again and again what Mr Darwin has written on the subject of language; I cannot understand how he could bring himself to sum up the subject as follows: 'We have seen that the faculty of articulate speech in itself does not offer any insuperable objection to the belief that man has been developed from some lower animal'.

The role of sexual selection

Thus, on the one hand we have Charles Darwin committed to the view that humans are descended from the great apes by the process of natural selection with a strong intuition that the ancillary process of sexual selection also has something to do with it, but unable to integrate these processes. On the other hand, we have Friedrich Max Mueller complaining that language has characteristics that are present in the communicative abilities of no animal other than man and that Darwin has given no account of its origins. The solution to this dispute that I have offered (Crow, 1998b; 2000a, 2002b) is that the Darwinian gradualist account indeed has to give ground to a saltational version of speciation as argued strongly for example by Goldschmidt (1940) and Gould (2002). Speciation events have a reality that is obscured in *The Origin of Species*. But that there is a relationship between speciation and sexual selection as Kaneshiro (1980) and Carson (1997) amongst others have argued; species are distinguished by characteristics that are often sexually dimorphic. The possibility is that the first change in the process of speciation occurs in one sex, generally the male, and that this change is then subject to mate choice to define what Paterson (1985) has called a specific mate recognition system. My proposal is that changes on the sex chromosomes, including chromosomal rearrangements and subsequent epigenetic modifications of gene control, play a critical role in these transitions. This concept of the nature of speciation comes from a consideration of the problem that vexed Max Mueller—the origins of language and its relationship to the origin of man—and its relevance to the central paradox of psychosis: The universal persistence in human populations of a genetic predisposition in the face of a biological disadvantage (Crow, 2000b).

Paul Broca and cerebral asymmetry

The key to a solution lies in the asymmetry or torque that appears to be characteristic of the human brain. After he had convinced himself (Broca, 1861) of the reality of the earlier observations of Marc Dax that language in the frontal lobes is localised on the left side, Paul Broca (1877) came to the conclusion that:

> Man is, of all the animals, the one whose brain in the normal state is the most asymmetrical. He is also the one who possesses the most acquired faculties. Among these faculties ... the faculty of articulate language holds pride of place. It is this that distinguishes us most clearly from the animals.

A further point of historical interest is how and when it became clearly established that directional asymmetry distinguishes the brain of Homo sapiens from that of other primates. While it is clear that there are directional asymmetries (e.g., of the habenular nucleus) that are ancient in vertebrate phylogeny, these are presumably unrelated to those associated with language that are expressed in the cortex. Such specificity would have been no surprise to Broca (see Harrington, 1987, pp. 49–51 for his views on the "essence" of human nature), but the assumption that directional asymmetry on a population level is present in other primates, perhaps based upon Darwinian gradualist principles, has been widespread in the literature. Annett introduced a discussion of the issue in her earlier volume (Annett, 1985, pp. 169–173) with reference to the work of Finch (1941) who found no evidence of directional handedness in a group of 30 chimpanzees. Subsequent studies (e.g., Annett & Annett, 1991) of 31 lowland gorillas in European zoos, and (Byrne & Byrne, 1991) of 38 mountain gorillas in Rwanda, have reinforced this conclusion. Recently, Marchant and McGrew (1996) conducted a systematic study of 42 chimpanzees in the Gombe National Park and reviewed the primate literature to conclude that "non human primate hand function has not been shown to be lateralized at the species level—it is not the norm for any species, task, or setting, and so offers no easy model for the evolution of human handedness" (McGrew & Marchant, 1997; see also Holder, 1999, for congruent conclusions in a field survey of primates in Africa). Thus, we have evidence that the putative correlate of the capacity for language that Mueller and Chomsky identify as the defining characteristic of *Homo sapiens* demonstrates a discontinuity in the primate phylogenetic tree. (See Figure 2.)

Thus, at some point in the course of hominid evolution the dimension of asymmetry was introduced into the sequence of brain development and this dimension, or some modification of it, is the obvious correlate of language.

The nuclear symptoms of schizophrenia and the central paradox

These considerations have implications for our understanding of the nature of schizophrenia. The core nuclear symptoms of schizophrenia, according to Kurt Schneider, and defined by the glossary of the Present State Examination (Wing, Cooper, & Sartorius, 1974) are:

Thought echo or commentary (item 57): The subject experiences his own thought as repeated or echoed with very little interval between the original and the echo.

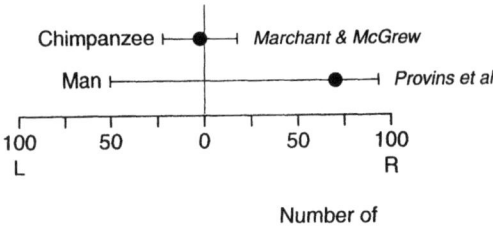

Figure 2. Hand preference in humans and chimpanzees compared. Data for chimpanzees refer to a community of wild chimpanzees in the Gombe National Park (Marchant & McGrew, 1996). Data for *Homo sapiens* were collected by questionnaire from populations of students by Provins, Milner, and Kerr (1982). Medians and boundary values (95%) have been extracted from the graphs of the original publications.

Voices commenting (item 62): A voice or voices heard by the subject speaking about him and therefore referring to him in the third person.

Passivity (delusions of control: item 71): The essence of the symptom is that the subject experiences his will as replaced by that of some other force or agency.

Thought insertion (item 55): The essence of the symptom is that the subject experiences thoughts *which are not his own* intruding into his mind. The symptom is not that he has been caused to have unusual thoughts (e.g., if he thinks the Devil is making him think evil thoughts) but that the thoughts *themselves* are not his. In the most typical case the alien thoughts are said to have been inserted into the mind from outside, by means of radar or telepathy or some other means.

Thought withdrawal (item 58): The subject says that his thoughts have been removed from his head so that he has no thoughts.

Thought broadcast (item 56): The subject experiences his thoughts actually being shared with others.

Primary delusions (item 82): Based upon sensory experiences [delusional perceptions] in which a patient suddenly becomes convinced that a particular set of events has a special meaning.

What is striking about these symptoms is that they can hardly be conceived except within the framework of language. Auditory hallucinations (items 57 and 62) are self-evidently an anomaly of the perception of the spoken word. The primary experiences of thought insertion, withdrawal, and broadcast (items 55, 58, and 56) can be considered as disturbances in the subjective experience of thought and of the transition from thought to speech production. Primary delusions (item 82) constitute the most discrete deviation in the attachment of meaning to symbolic representations, that is to say that they are a disturbance of semantics. Only delusions of control (item 71) are not immediately recognisable as a disturbance of speech, but these cannot be described except with the use of language; they can be understood as anomalies of the identification and experience of the self in relation to the rest of the universe of symbols.

Aside from their significance as disturbances of the structure of language, nuclear symptoms are important in that it was through these features that the authors of the World Health Organisation Ten Country Study of the Incidence and Manifestations of Schizophrenia (Jablensky et al., 1992) reached their conclusion that "schizophrenic illnesses are ubiquitous, appear with similar incidence in different cultures, and have clinical features that are more remarkable by their similarity across cultures than by their difference". Thus, schizophrenia is constant across populations that differ widely in geographic, climatic, industrial, and social environment; it seems it is a characteristic of human populations. It is a disease (perhaps *the* disease) of humanity.

If the core of the syndrome is a characteristic of populations it must somehow be intrinsic (i.e., genetic in origin). This raises the central paradox—why, if the disease is associated with a biological disadvantage (Essen-Moller, 1959; Haverkamp, Propping, & Hilger, 1982; MacSorley, 1964; Penrose, 1991; Stevens; 1969; Vogel, 1979), is this genetic variation not selected out? About the existence of the fecundity deficit there is little doubt—it is of the order of 70% in males and 30% in females. To balance such a disadvantage a substantial and universal advantage must be invoked. But what could such an advantage be, and who might carry it? These questions were first clearly formulated in a paper (Huxley, Mayr, Osmond, & Hoffer, 1964) that is notable in that its authorship includes J. S. Huxley and E. Mayr, two progenitors of the "modern evolutionary synthesis" of Mendelian genetics and Darwinian theory. The first paragraph identifies these two as the originators of the notion that schizophrenia must be balanced by an evolutionary advantage. Yet the theory they proposed—that the balance lay in resistance to wound shock and stress—was clearly mistaken, as Kuttner, Lorincz, and Swan (1967) were quick to point out. It makes no sense to suppose that the advantage of a particular genetic variation lies in a field that is unrelated to the disadvantage. Kuttner et al. considered three advantages—intelligence, language and complex social ability—and favoured the last. But these three are clearly related and one—language—is both of more obvious adaptive significance and is more readily defined in terms of neural function than the other two. As the characteristic that is associated with the success of the species (Bickerton, 1995) it is a correlate of the universality of psychosis. Genetic variation associated with and inseparable from this evolutionary innovation provides an answer to Huxley et al.'s question.

The cerebral torque

But why should the capacity for language be variable between individuals? Perhaps only when we understand the nature of the genetic mechanism will we have a clear answer to this question (Crow, 2002a). The important point is that Broca's hypothesis—that language is lateralised in the brain—provides an indication of the neurophysiological basis and an approach to its pathophysiology. Buxhoeveden, Switala, Litaker, Roy, and Casanova (2001) have recently documented the anatomical correlate of population bias to right-handedness. Through a statistical analysis of the minicolumn structure of the cerebral cortex they demonstrated asymmetries (e.g., of minicolumn width and separation) that are present in the planum temporale of man but absent in those of the chimpanzee and rhesus monkey.

The form of the asymmetry—from right frontal to left occipital, described as the cerebral torque—has implications for function and pathophysiology. There is now evidence that aspects of anatomical asymmetry are deviant in individuals who suffer from psychosis (see Crow, 1990, 1997; Petty, 1999) and evidence also from a study of handedness in childhood that they are lateralising less or more slowly (Crow, Done, & Sacker, 1996). In postmortem studies the anatomical changes appear to be more posterior in the brain; losses or reversals of asymmetry have been detected in fusiform, parahippocampal, and superior temporal gyri (Highley, McDonald, Walker, Esiri, & Crow, 1999; McDonald et al., 2000). In frontal regions no gross asymmetry and no change in volume was detected in schizophrenia (Highley et al., 2001) but in the density of cells in the cortex (in Brodmann area 9) there was an asymmetry (greater cell density) to the left in controls and loss or reversal of this asymmetry in patients (Cullen et al., 2003).

How are the symptoms to be explained? On the basis that the anatomical changes reflect an alteration in connectivity and that the asymmetry of the human brain (the torque) is the foundation of the faculty of language one can construct a theory of nuclear symptoms—that these are primary disorders of the structure of language, and that they reveal the way in which the constituent elements relate to each other within and between heteromodal areas of the cerebral cortex.

The linguistic sign is bihemispheric

De Saussure (1916) maintained that the linguistic sign (the word) was characteristically bipartite, comprising a signifier (the sound pattern or phonological engram) and a signified (the associated concept or meanings). The association between the sound pattern and its meanings according to de Saussure is arbitrary—any sound pattern can be associated with any concept or meaning (the first principle). This is what is distinctive about the human use of words and what makes language so flexible.

There is a two-way relationship between the two components—with movement from the sound pattern to the meanings in speech reception, and from the concepts to sound patterns in speech production. One can ask what is the neural basis of the separation of the two components? If asymmetry is what is characteristic of the human brain it seems that there must be a relationship between specialisation of function of the hemispheres and the feature that de Saussure identifies as the key to language. The most parsimonious hypothesis is that the components are (at least in part) segregated to the two hemispheres.

From Broca's observations it is clear that what is localised in the dominant hemisphere is the phonological engram. It follows that some part of the signifieds must be assumed to be located in the nondominant hemisphere. For each phonological engram there must be a corresponding engram—a mirror image—in the nondominant hemisphere, but one that is systematically transformed by the differing terminations of the interhemispheric connexions in that hemisphere.

De Saussure's second principle is that speech is linear—just a "ribbon of sound". Allied to this is the notion that there must be a speaker and a hearer—speech is necessarily communicative—and the ribbon of sound is what travels between them. (See Figure 3.)

One envisages therefore that speech is encoded, and this is a bihemispheric process, by the speaker from his concepts or thoughts into phonological engrams that are then transformed into the ribbon of sound, and that this is received by the hearer, and decoded into his own meanings or concepts, and that this decodification takes place partly by interhemispheric interactions. Communication depends upon the hearer sharing at least some of the speaker's signifier-signified associations, in other words that they speak the same language.

Deixis and the significance of the indexical

The system works straightforwardly so long as the speaker refers to the world outside him/herself and the hearer. But a complication arises when he/she refers to him/herself. As Hurford (1992) points out, such a referral necessitates further

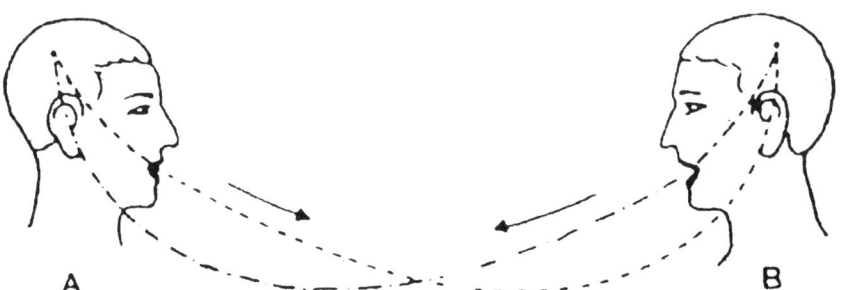

Figure 3. The relationship between speaker and hearer according to de Saussure (1916).

decoding on the part of the hearer—that the "I" that the speaker refers to, relates not to the "I" of the hearer but to the "you" (to him/her) of the speaker. This class of symbols—the "indexicals"—referring to the speaker or hearer belongs to the wider class of "deictic" symbols that include reference to the "here" of the present place and the "now" of the present moment in time.

Deixis—the necessity to define this class of symbols by pointing—has a special status in philosophy and, it was suggested by Buehler (1934), echoing Mueller, in the structure of language. According to Buehler this triad of terms defining the present moment and the location and identity of the speaker can be considered as a coordinate origin around which language is structured—this place, at the present moment in time, defined by the "I" of the speaker. Without this, language has no point of reference and loses its capacity to convey meaning.

The concept of the indexical has relevance to the nature of psychotic symptoms. While it is true that there is no general misuse of the first person pronoun in individuals with psychosis it is interesting that those with early onset developmental disorders such as autism and Asperger's syndrome sometimes have difficulty in acquiring the distinction between the use of "I" and "you". The more general significance arises in relation to Hurford's point that these symbols relate to what is self-generated in speech and what is other-generated—that there is a fundamental dichotomy between speech production and speech perception—and that this dichotomy can be understood in terms of the brain torque (see Figure 4.)

The human brain as a four-chambered organ

The point is often overlooked that the asymmetry of the human brain is not a simple left-right difference but a deviation across the fronto-occipital axis that transforms the human brain from the standard primate and vertebrate pattern of two chambers (anterior and posterior corresponding to motor and sensory compartments) into a four-chambered organ in which motor and sensory compartments are distinguished on the left and the right sides. The torque has the effect of differentiating the two sides of the brain by influencing the relative surface area of the cerebral cortex, but it does so in different directions in the anterior (motor) and posterior (sensory) halves. It is a remarkable fact that the volumes of the two hemispheres are closely similar. What has changed relative to other primates is either the distribution of tissue between the two sides along the anteroposterior axis or more subtly the sulcogyral folding of the cortical surface. The effect must be assumed to be that the distribution of interhemispheric connetions is different on the two sides and it is this that allows the spread of neural activity to be systematically different on one side compared to the other. But the direction of the difference is opposite in the motor and sensory halves of the brain—converging from right to left anteriorly and from left to right posteriorly.

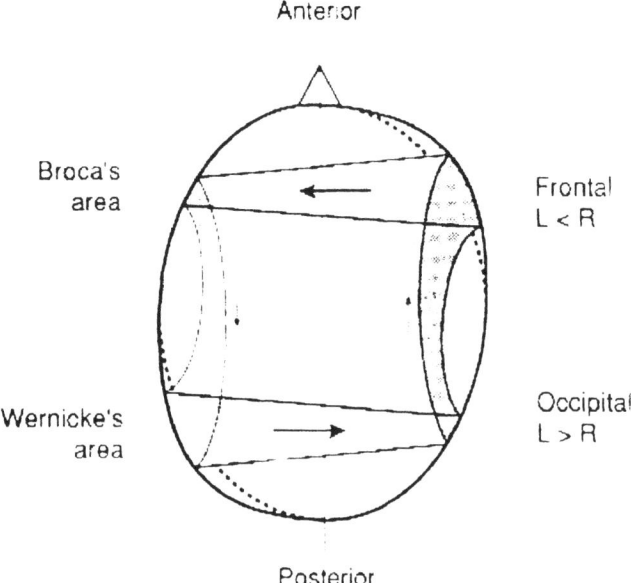

Figure 4. The torque of the human brain and its implication for the connections between areas of heteromodal association cortex on the two sides of the brain from Crow (1998a).

If the torque is what is characteristic of the human brain these changes, and no others, are critical to the evolution of language. The interconnections between areas of heteromodal cortex have altered and these changes alone must account for what is characteristic of the capacity for language. Two features are suggested—the arbitrariness of the association between the signifier and the signifieds, the phonological engram and its meanings (de Saussure, 1916), and universal grammar, a mechanism that generates the structure of the sentence (Chomsky, 1988). But the striking fact about the evolution of language is that it occurred relatively abruptly, in the transition to modern *Homo sapiens*, and all of a piece (Bickerton, 1990, 1995) along with the capacity for symbolic representation (Mellars, 2002). It does not make sense to suppose that there were two sequential innovations each contributing a revolution to brain function. These two features must reflect different aspects of the same change and that change must be either the introduction of the torque or some modification of a torque that was introduced earlier in hominid evolution.

Perhaps the key change is the separation of a phonological engram from its associations. The human cortex is not qualitatively different from that of the chimpanzee or any other primate. It must presumably have the same capacity to receive inputs and to transform them into outputs. What is different about the human brain is the interaction between areas of (particularly heteromodal) cortex on the two sides. Thus, if we can assume that what is segregated in the dominant hemisphere is the phonological engram—that is to say, a collection of simple but heavily interconnected motor sequences—this leaves open the possibility that each of these motor patterns has connections with engrams that are systematically different (either more diffuse or more restricted) in the nondominant hemisphere.

But here is the key consequence of the torque—whether the connections are more diffuse or more restricted depends on whether they are in the motor or sensory halves of the brain. The convergences are in different directions in the anterior and posterior heteromodal association cortices and this has an obvious implication for the organisation of the capacity for language. Whatever transformation takes place from right to left in the dorsolateral prefrontal cortex is reversed in sense in the transition from left to right in the occipitoparietotemporal cortex. This can be regarded as the *first principle* in the neural organisation of language.

The *second principle* is that the sensory phonological engram is distinct from the motor engram. These engrams are obviously located in Wernicke's and Broca's areas, respectively. But it is not so obvious that the form of the engram must be different—the motor engram can be relatively directly associated with pyramidal tract neurones and with the output, but the sensory engram is one step removed from the acoustic input—word traces need to be filtered out from the totality of incoming sensory information.

Nonetheless, there is a relationship between the two. Words that are heard are recognised as related if not identical to those that are spoken. The form of the relationship presumably is what is established in the course of language acquisition. Conversely, some aspect of the distinction between the two is what is lost in the case of auditory hallucinations—what is clearly intrinsically generated (whether in the process of thought or in motor planning) has activated engrams that are normally accessible only to incoming acoustic stimuli. In this distinction, and in the association of the signifier and the signifieds, lies the puzzle of psychosis.

The four chambers of the human brain are the framework within which the problem can be solved—in the separation of the motor from the sensory by the central sulcus, and in the segregation of the signifier (the phonological engram) in its two forms in the dominant hemisphere from its primary associations in the nondominant, by the bias of the torque. The key to the solution is to specify the nature of the difference between what is motor and what is sensory and what is intrinsic to the signifier and what is arbitrarily associated with it—on the one hand in its sensory form, and on the other in its motor configuration.

The simplest approach to the problem is to assume that contiguous functions are dealt with in anatomically related areas. Thus, if the phonological engrams of the output are assembled in the association areas of cortex that are focused on Broca's area in the left hemisphere one must assume that the processes that are related to this assembly, but differ from it in the crucial respect that they confer upon it its arbitrariness and flexibility, are located in the homologous regions in the right hemisphere. In functional terms these engrams can be loosely referred to as "thought"—the precursor of, or the plans for, speech. Thought has a relationship to speech in that each element has an associated phonological engram in the left hemisphere, but it is not speech in that without the linear sequence that forms the output on the left the association between elements is to a certain degree random and arbitrary. This presumably is related to the fact that each phonological engram on the left is associated with a number of less well-structured engrams on the right. The relationship from right to left is many-to-one.

In the parietotemporo-occipital junction association areas the convergence is in the opposite direction. From the phonological engrams that have been extracted from the primary acoustic signal in the auditory association areas on the left there is a convergence to a smaller area of homologous cortex on the right. Thus the many-to-one transition in this case is from left to right, and the process of simplification may be identified as the distillation of "meaning" from the linear sequence of phonology on the left.

According to this concept the transition from thought to speech takes place from right to left in the dorsolateral prefrontal cortex and from perceived speech to meaning from left to right in parietotemporo-occipital association cortex. But what is the relationship between perceived meaning and the thought that is the plan for speech? Both are concepts or associations (signifieds) removed from the phonological engram—but one is sensory and one is motor. There is a connection between them and that connection is mediated by the uncinate and arcuate bundles in the right hemisphere. The patterns of activity in the right parieto-temporo-occipital cortex are thus accessible to the thought processes in the right dorsolateral prefrontal cortex but the activities are distinct, and the distinction differs from that between the activity in the association cortices around Broca's and Wernicke's areas in the left hemisphere.

The deictic origin and the performative hypothesis

The key here is syntax—the ability to relate the self to the outside world—and to use words to do it. According to Buehler, as noted above, language is built around a coordinate framework with an origin in the self, the present location and the present moment in time defined by the deictic symbols "I", "here" and "now". Without this, language loses its structure. In this context the function of language is to mediate the individual's relationship with the outside world including, particularly, other individuals. In every linguistic interaction there is a speaker and a hearer; sentences are the substance of the negotiation between them. The distinction between what is self- and what is other-generated and the meanings of these two classes of symbol is critical, and this distinction clearly relates to the division between the motor and sensory association cortices in the right hemisphere.

The nuclear symptoms of schizophrenia tell us what happens when this distinction breaks down. Thought, the precursor of speech, loses its characteristic of independence from the outside world—thoughts are inserted into or removed from the individual's mind—whilst retaining the features of thought they have lost the relationship to self-generated acts that is a defining feature of thought as a precursor of speech. The obvious interpretation is that they are influenced by activity in posterior association cortex in a way that differs from the "normal" exchange between posterior and anterior regions. Conversely, auditory hallucinations such as thoughts spoken aloud or running commentary presumably represent self-generated neural activity (thoughts or plans for action) that activates phonological engrams (perhaps in the superior temporal cortex on the left side) that are normally activated by speech from another individual. In each case, there is a loss of the boundary in symbolic communication (words) between what is self- and what is other-generated. In each case we can see that the boundary has something to do with what is located in anterior and what in posterior association cortices. But we cannot suppose that what is abnormal is simply that some neural activity crosses this boundary. Activity must normally be transmitted between posterior and anterior, along, for example, arcuate and uncinate bundles. The problem is to specify what is normal and what is abnormal. The nature of nuclear symptoms is the clue that we have.

Buehler's formulation of the structure of language—that it is intrinsically organised around a deictic core—and the distinction between what is self- and what is other-generated, that is illustrated by the nature of the nuclear symptoms, may both be necessary to a solution of the problem of syntax. In his thesis of *How to Do Things with Words*, J. L. Austin (1962) made the case that many uses of language are not simply to convey information but to have an effect, that is to say, to bring about a state of affairs according to the speaker's intention. Such utterances Austin referred to as "performatives" to distinguish them from the "constatives", the utterances, more usually the subject of linguistic and philosophic analyses, which convey information, generally about the external world. Later, he generalised the concept of the performative into the notion that all utterances have an "illocutionary force" in the sense that they are formulated towards some objective of the speaker.

In the linguistic literature there is an interesting parallel to Austin's concept in the "performative hypothesis". Ross (1970) defines the theory as stating that declarative sentences (constatives) "must also be analysed as being implicit performatives, and must be derived from deep structures containing an explicitly represented performative main verb". Perfomative sentences he says "must have first person subjects and usually have second person direct or indirect objects in deep structure. They must be affirmative and non-negative, they must be in the present tense, and that their main verb must belong to the class that includes verbs such as advise, ask, command, declare, inform, say, write...'', in other words the class that designates the transmission of information, instructions, orders etc. The implication of the perfomative hypothesis is that a declarative sentence has an implicit (unstated) superordinate clause of the form 'I say unto you' in the first person and the present tense.

Austin's concept and the performative hypothesis bear a relationship to Buehler's notion of a deictic origin to the coordinate frame of language, and to de Saussure's insistence that language can only be understood in terms of the relationship between the speaker and the hearer. Without the deictic frame, Buehler insists, the structure of language dissolves. This may be what happens in the case of thought disorder—the determining focus is lost. What the nuclear symptoms of schizophrenia are telling us is what happens when the distinction between the indexicals, "I" and "you", of the speaker and the hearer begins to dissolve. Thus conceived they are disorders of the foundations of syntax. They tell us that the phonological engram for the perception of speech is quite separate from the phonological engram for speech production. They tell us that "thoughts" as the precursor to speech are distinct from the meanings that are extracted from perceived speech in the nondominant hemisphere. They draw attention to the obscure process of interaction between the motor and sensory elements of the associations (the signifieds) that takes place in the nondominant hemisphere. In each case the phenomena of psychosis provide evidence on the neural organisation of language through what happens when the mechanism goes wrong. We can begin to understand this through the structure of the torque.

CONCLUSION

1. The faculty of language as a defining feature of *Homo sapiens* with characteristics absent in the communicative systems of the great apes challenges Darwinian gradualism, as Friedrich Max Mueller in 1873 and Noam Chomsky (1959) clearly explained. It is more readily assimilated to a saltational account of speciation as suggested by T.H. Huxley and developed by R. Goldschmidt.
2. Broca's hypothesis that cerebral asymmetry is the characteristic that defines the human brain and has enabled the evolution of language is supported by recent cross-species comparisons for directional handedness and anatomical asymmetry.
3. The paradox of psychosis is that interindividual variation that is apparently genetic in origin persists at approximately the same frequency in all populations in the face of a fecundity disadvantage; it is suggested that this variation represents a component of the variation associated with the capacity for language.
4. Two characteristics of human language have been suggested—the arbitrariness of the association between the signifier and its associations

(de Saussure) and universal grammar (Chomsky); neither on its own has led to a clear exposition of the neural components of language and neither has been related to cerebral asymmetry.

5. It is suggested that the cerebral torque (the bias from right frontal to left occipital across the anteroposterior axis) defines the human brain as a four-chambered organ by comparison with the two chambers (anterior motor and posterior sensory) of the brains of other primates, and that it dictates a reversal of sign of the convergence of interhemispheric connections (from left to right posteriorly and from right to left anteriorly).
6. These transitions are proposed as critical to the separation of the sensory and motor phonological engrams in the dominant left hemisphere from some of their associated signifiers (the sensory "meanings" and the motor "thoughts") in the nondominant hemisphere.
7. Critical to the distinction between the speaker and the hearer and to what is motor and what is sensory in the neural representation of speech is the notion (associated with K. Buehler) of a deictic origin ("I, here, now") to the coordinate system of speech. Related to this is the performative hypothesis that every sentence has a (usually unexpressed) superordinate clause ("I say unto you") in the first person and the present tense.
8. The nuclear symptoms of schizophrenia (e.g., thoughts spoken aloud, running commentary, thought insertion) are interpreted as anomalies of segregation of the components of language into the four compartments of association cortex, anomalies that illustrate the importance of the separation of the motor and sensory aspects of the spoken word and of the two types of phonological engram from some of their associations.
9. The deictic origin is identified in Broca's area and defined by its interaction through the uncinate and arcuate bundles with Wernicke's area.
10. According to this concept the nuclear symptoms of schizophrenia are the primary disorders of syntax.

Manuscript accepted 9 June 2003

REFERENCES

Annett, M. (1985). *Left, right, hand and brain: The right shift theory*. Hove, UK: Lawrence Erlbaum Associates Ltd.

Annett, M., & Annett, J. (1991). Handedness for eating in gorillas. *Cortex, 27*, 269–275.

Austin, J. L. (1962). *How to do things with words*. Oxford: Oxford University Press.

Barrett, P. H. & Gruber, H. E. (1974). *Metaphysics, materialism and the evolution of mind: Early writings of Charles Darwin*. Chicago: University of Chicago.

Bickerton, D. (1990). *Language and species*. Chicago: University of Chicago.

Bickerton, D. (1995). *Language and human behavior*. Seattle: University of Washington.

Broca, P. (1861). Remarques sur la siegé de la faculté du langue. *Bulletin de la Société Anatomique de Paris* (2nd series), *6*, 330–357.

Broca, P. (1877). Rapport sur un memoire de M. Armand de Fleury intitulé: De l'inegalité dynamique des deux hemisphères cerébraux. *Bulletins de l'Academie de Medicine, 6*, 508–539.

Buehler, K. (1934). *Sprachtheorie* (Trans. D. W. Goodwin, 1990, as *Theory of language: The representational function of language*). Amsterdam: J. Benjamins.

Buxhoeveden, D., Switala, A. E., Litaker, M., Roy, E., & Casanova, M. F. (2001). Lateralization of minicolumns in human planum temporale is absent in nonhuman primate cortex. *Brain Behavioural Evolution, 57*, 349–358.

Byrne, R. W., & Byrne, J. M. (1991). Hand preference in the skilled gathering tasks of mountain gorillas (*Gorilla g. berengei*). *Cortex, 27*, 521–546.

Carson, H. L. (1997). Sexual selection: A driver of genetic change in Hawaiian Drosophila. *Journal of Heredity, 88*, 343–352.

Chomsky, N. (1959). A review of B. F. Skinner's verbal behavior. *Language, 35*, 26–58.

Chomsky, N. (1988). *Language and the problems of knowledge: The Managua lectures.* Cambridge, MA: MIT Press.

Crow, T. J. (1990). Temporal lobe asymmetries as the key to the etiology of schizophrenia. *Schizophrenia Bulletin, 16*, 433–443.

Crow, T. J. (1997). Schizophrenia as failure of hemispheric dominance for language. *Trends in Neurosciences, 20*, 339–343.

Crow, T. J. (1998a). Nuclear schizophrenic symptoms as a window on the relationship between thought and speech. *British Journal of Psychiatry, 173*, 303–309.

Crow, T. J. (1998b). Sexual selection, timing and the descent of Man: A genetic theory of the evolution of language. *Current Psychology of Cognition, 17*, 1079–1114.

Crow, T. J. (2000a). Did Homo sapiens speciate on the Y chromosome? *Psycoloquy, 11*. Retrieved from http://psycprints.ecs.soton.ac.uk/archive/00000001/

Crow, T. J. (2000b). Schizophrenia as the price that Homo sapiens pays for language: A resolution of the central paradox in the origin of the species. *Brain Research Reviews, 31*, 118–129.

Crow, T. J. (2002a). Handedness, language lateralisation and anatomical asymmetry: Relevance of protocadherinXY to hominid speciation and the aetiology of psychosis. *British Journal of Psychiatry, 181*, 295–297.

Crow, T. J. (2002b). Sexual selection, timing and an X-Y homologous gene: Did *Homo sapiens* speciate on the Y chromosome? In T. J.Crow (Ed.), *The speciation of modern* Homo sapiens (pp. 195–216). Oxford, UK: Oxford University Press.

Crow, T. J., Done, D. J., & Sacker, A. (1996). Cerebral lateralization is delayed in children who later develop schizophrenia. *Schizophrenia Research, 22*, 181–185.

Cullen, T. J., Walker, M. A., Eastwood, S. L., Esiri, M. M., Harrison, P. J., & Crow, T. J. (2003). *Neuronal density in the DLPFC in schizophrenia is anomalously asymmetrical but not increased.* Manuscript submitted for publication.

Darwin, C. (1871). *The descent of man, and selection in relation to sex.* London: J. Murray. (Facsimile of original published in 1981 by Princeton University Press, New Jersey).

De Saussure, F. (1916). *Course in general linguistics* (Trans R. Harris 1983 and published by Open Court, Illinois). Paris: Payot.

Essen-Moller, E. (1959). Mating and fertility patterns in families with schizophrenia. *Eugenics Quarterly, 6*, 142–147.

Finch, G. (1941). Chimpanzee handedness. *Science, 94*, 117–118.

Goldschmidt, R. (1940). *The material basis of evolution.* New Haven, CT: Yale University Press.

Gould, S. J. (2002). *The structure of evolutionary theory.* Cambridge, MA: Belknap.

Gruber, H. E. (1974). *Darwin on man: A psychological study of scientific creativity.* Chicago: University of Chicago.

Harrington, A. (1987). *Medicine, mind and the double brain.* Princeton, NJ: Princeton University Press.

Haverkamp, F., Propping, P., & Hilger, T. (1982). Is there an increase in reproductive rates in schizophrenics? I. Critical review of the literature. *Archiv für Psychiatrie und Nervenkrankheiten, 232*, 439–450.

Highley, J. R., McDonald, B., Walker, M. A., Esiri, M. M., & Crow, T. J. (1999). Schizophrenia and temporal lobe asymmetry: A post mortem stereological study of tissue volume. *British Journal of Psychiatry, 175*, 127–134.

Highley, J. R., Walker, M. A., Esiri, M. M., McDonald, B., Harrison, P. J., & Crow, T. J. (2001). Schizophrenia and the frontal lobes: A post mortem stereological study of tissue volume. *British Journal of Psychiatry, 178*, 337–343.

Holder, M. K. (1999). Influences and constraints on manual asymmetry in wild African primates: Reassessing implications for the evolution of human handedness and brain lateralization (Dissertation Abstracts International Section A). *Humanities and Social Sciences, 60*, 0470. PhD thesis, Rutgers University, NJ (pp. 1–535).

Hurford, J. R. (1992). An approach to the phylogeny of the language faculty. In J. A. Hawkins & M. Gell-Mann (Eds.), *The evolution of human languages* (pp. 273–303). Reading, UK: Addison-Wesley.

Huxley, J., Mayr, E., Osmond, H., & Hoffer, A. (1964). Schizophrenia as a genetic morphism. *Nature, 204*, 220–221.

Huxley, T. H. (1863). *Evidence of man's place in nature*. London: Williams & Norgate.

Jablensky, A., Sartorius, N., Ernberg, G., Anker, M., Korten, A., Cooper, J. E., Day, R., & Bertelsen, A. (1992). Schizophrenia: Manifestations, incidence and course in different cultures. A World Health Organization Ten Country Study. *Psychological Medicine* (Suppl 20), 1–97.

Kaneshiro, K. Y. (1980). Sexual isolation, speciation and the direction of evolution. *Evolution, 34*, 437–444.

Kuttner, R. E., Lorincz, A. B., & Swan, D. A. (1967). The schizophrenia gene and social evolution. *Psychological Reports, 20*, 407–412.

MacSorley, K. (1964). An investigation into the fertility rates of mentally ill patients. *Annals of Human Genetics, 27*, 247–256.

Marchant, L. F., & McGrew, W. C. (1996). Laterality of limb function in wild chimpanzees of Gombe National Park: comprehensive study of spontaneous activities. *Journal of Human Evolution, 30*, 427–443.

Mayr, E., & Provine, W. B. (1998). *The evolutionary synthesis*. Cambridge, MA: Harvard University Press.

McDonald, B., Highley, J. R., Walker, M. A., Herron, B., Cooper, S. J., Esiri, M. M., & Crow, T. J. (2000). Anomalous asymmetry of fusiform and parahippocampal gyrus grey matter in schizophrenia: a post-mortem study. *American Journal of Psychiatry, 157*, 40–47.

McGrew, W. C., & Marchant, L. F. (1997). On the other hand: Current issues in and meta-analysis of the behavioral laterality of hand function in nonhuman primates. *Yearbook of Physical Anthropology, 40*, 201–232.

Mellars, P. (2002). Archaeology and the origins of modern humans: European and African perspectives. In T. J. Crow (Ed.), *The speciation of modern* Homo sapiens (pp. 31–48). Oxford, UK: Oxford University Press.

Mueller, F. M. (1873). Lectures on Mr Darwin's philosophy of language. *Fraser's Magazine* (Vols. 7 & 8). [Reprinted in R. Harris (Ed.). (1996). *The origin of language* (pp. 147–233). Bristol, UK: Thoemmes Press.]

Paterson, H. E. H. (1985). The recognition concept of species. In E. S.Vrba (Ed.), *Species and Speciation* (pp 21–29). Pretoria: Transvaal Museum Monograph.

Penrose, L. S. (1991). Survey of cases of familial mental illness. *European Archives of Psychiatry and Neurological Science, 240*, 315–324.

Petty, R. G. (1999). Structural asymmetries of the human brain and their disturbance in schizophrenia. *Schizophrenia Bulletin, 25*, 121–139.

Provins, K. A., Milner, A. D., & Kerr, P. (1982). Asymmetry of manual preference and performance. *Perceptual and Motor Skills, 54*, 179–194.

Ross, J. R. (1970). On declarative sentences. In R. A. Jacobs, P. S. Rosenbaum (Eds.), *Readings in English Transformational grammar* (pp. 222–272). Waltham, MA: Ginn.

Stevens, B. C. (1969). *Marriage and fertility of women suffering from schizophrenia and affective disorders*. London: Oxford University Press.

Vogel, H. P. (1979). Fertility and sibship size in a psychiatric patient population. *Acta Psychiatrica Scandinavica, 60*, 483–503.

Wing, J. K., Cooper, J. E., & Sartorius, N. (1974). *The measurement and classification of psychiatric symptoms: An instruction manual for the PSE and Catego program*. Cambridge, UK: Cambridge University Press.

Subject Index

Abusive voices, 7, 19, 66
Acceptance, 10
Alzheimer's disease, 108
Ambiguous auditory perceptions, 48
Amphetamines, 66
Amygdala, 76, 85, 86
Angels, 2, 15
Anosognosia, 17
Anterior cingulate, 78, 83, 85
Anxiety, 27, 29, 37
Aphasia, 18
Arcuate bundle, 139, 140
Asperger's syndrome, 136
Association areas, 139, 140
Attention, 75–76, 80–83
Attributions, 108
Auditory association areas, 139, 140
Auditory cortex, 80–83
Auditory feedback, 116
Auditory imagery, 45–49
Auditory perception, 48
Auditory-perceptual model, 100–102
Auditory processing, 74–77
Auditory response bias, 48
Auditory space perception, 96–97
Auditory verbal hallucinations (AVHs)
   content, 111–112
   definition, 26, 109–110
   etiology, 110–112
   hearer's perspective, 9–11
   history, 1
   normal population, 7, 27, 111
   predisposing factors, 66
   prevalence, 27
   treatment-resistant, 25
Auditory verbal imagery, 83–84
Autism, 136

Autonoetic agnosia, 60

Behavioural approaches, 28–29
Beliefs, 27, 30, 33–36, 37, 38, 84, 108
Beliefs about Voices Questionnaire (BAVQ-R), 32
Bereavement, 19–21
Blackman, L., 18–19
Body–mind dualism, 14, 17
Brain
   asymmetry, 130–131
   four-chambered organ, 136–139
   inter-hemispheric transfer, 29, 136
   stimulation, 78, 80–81
   structure and function, 52–53, 61–62, 77–87, 112–114
   torque, 134
Brainstem disorders, 97
Brief Psychiatric Rating Scale (BPRS-E), 32
Brightness, 1–2
Broca, P., 130–131

Cartesianism, 14
Cerebellar activation, 53
Cerebral asymmetry, 130–131
Cerebral torque, 134
Changes in voice, 7, 19, 26
Character of voice, 7, 19
Charles VI (France), 3
Charles VII (France), 2–3
Cingulate, 78, 83, 85
Circumstantial speech, 18
Cognitive approaches, 31–32
Cognitive behaviour therapy (CBT), 6, 33–38
Cognitive biases, 44, 117

Cognitive differences, 28
Cognitive interference, 61
Cognitive models, 114–118
Cognitive neuropsychiatry, 107–123
Cognitive processing speed, 60
Cognitive scientists, 14
Cognitivism, 14, 15
Commenting voice, 111–112
Comparator, 63
Compartmentalising, 10
Computational hub, 83
Constatives, 140
Constructive memory, 53–60
Context, 2
    commenting voices, 111–112
    culture, 16
    ethical, 19
    meaning, 15
    ontological phenomenology, 18,
Coping strategies, 9, 10–11, 18, 30–31,
    32–33, 38, 66, 110, 118
Coping Strategy Enhancement (CSE), 33
Corollary discharge, 114
Corpus callosum, 113
Corticocortical connectivity, 86–87
Csordas, T., 18
Culture, 16, 27, 31
Cybernetic models, 114

Daemons, 15
Dan, 18
Darwin, C., 125–126, 128
Davies, P., 15
Deafferentation, 109
Definitions, 26, 109–110
Deixis, 135–136, 139–141
Delta-9-tetrahydrocannabinol (THC), 66
Delusions, 62
Descartes, R., 14
Descent of Man (Darwin), 128
Devils, 15
Diagnosis, 2
Diagnostic group differences, 27–28
Discursive turn, 14
Distraction techniques, 9, 76
Distress, 7, 27, 30, 66
Dominant figures, 110
Dopaminergic system, 6
Dorsolateral prefrontal cortex (DLPFC),
    76, 83, 87, 139
Dreyfus, H., 16

Drug-induced hallucinations, 66
Drug treatment breaks, 10

Ear advantage, 29, 99–100, 101
Ear plugs, 29
Efference copy, 62, 114
Embodiment, 17–19, 21
Emotional intonation, 81–82
Emotional response, 76, 84–85
Encoding, 60
Engagement, 37
Episodic memory, 53–60
Epistemological phenomenology, 16
Ethical context, 19
Etiology, 110–112
Event-related potentials, 116
Evidence of Man's Place in Nature
    (Huxley), 126, 128
Evolutionary theory, 125–145
Executive control, 113
External/internal voices, 110–111
External object space, 94

Feed-forward model, 63–64, 114
Focusing, 29–30
Frontal cortex, 83–84, 114, 134
Frontotemporal region, 114, 117
Fusiform gyrus, 134

God, 1–2
Gradualist theory, 125–128
Group cognitive behaviour therapy,
    33–38
Gustatory hallucinations, 108

Hallucinations
    definition, 109–110
    different sensory modalities, 108
    measurement, 32
Hearing Voices Network, 19, 35
Heidegger, M., 16–17
Hermeneutic phenomenology, 16–17
Heschl's gyrus, 97
Hippocampus, 76, 114
History, 1
Hope, 10
Humming, 29, 31
Husserlian phenomenology, 16
Huxley, J.S., 133
Huxley, T.H., 126, 128
Hyperreligiosity, 18

Illocutionary force, 140
Image or idea, 94
Imagery, 45–49, 83–84
Impulse control, 77, 86
Indexical, 135–136, 141
Information sources, 11
Inner speech, 29, 49, 53, 65, 76–77, 85–86, 102, 116
Innuendo, 81–82
Insight, 109
Insula, 76, 78, 84, 113
Intentional motor control, 62–64
Inter-hemispheric transfer, 29, 136
Internal/external voices, 110–111
Isolation, 34, 38
Item memory, 53, 54

Joan of Arc, 1–3

Language
  disturbances, 18
  evolutionary theory, 125–145
  involvement in hallucinations, 74–75
  perception and production, 113
  temporal cortex, 78–80
Lifetime prevalence, 27
Limbic system, 76, 84
Linguistic sign, bihemispheric, 134–135

Made actions, 114
Maintenance therapy, 37
Mayr, E., 133
Meanings, 14, 15
Measurement
  hallucinations, 32
  outcome, 35–36
Memory, 17, 53–60, 76, 85, 110, 114, 116
Mental Health Research Institute Unusual Perceptions Schedule (MUPS), 32
Mental imagery, 45–49, 84
Merleau-Ponty, M., 16, 17–19
Michael, 35
Middle frontal gyrus, 78
Middle temporal gyrus (MTG), 76, 78, 80, 82–83, 84, 87
Mind–body dualism, 14, 17
Misperception, thought, 64, 65
Monitoring voices, 35
Motor control, 62–64

Motor engram, 138
Motor self-monitoring, 61, 63–64
Mueller, F.M., 128–130
Multiple sclerosis, 97
Mundane voices, 111
Musical hallucinations, 109

Neural drive, 83
Neurocognitive deficits, 44
Neurocognitive models, 43–72
Neuroscientists, 14
Neurotransmitters, 6
Nonpreferred modality, 45, 48
'Normal' population, hallucinations, 7, 27, 111
Nuclear symptoms, 131–133

Object-bound sensations, 94–95
Olfactory hallucinations, 108
Omnipotence, 30
Ontological phenomenology, 16–17, 18
Orbitofrontal cortex, 84, 86
Origin of Species by Means of Natural Selection (Darwin), 125–126
Other–self distinction, 52, 85–86, 136, 139–140
Outcome measures, 35–36

Parahippocampal gyrus, 78, 134
Parahippocampus, 52, 85
Parental voices, 110
Parietal lobule, 78, 85
Parietotemporal-occipital association cortex, 139
Parkinson's disease, 108
Passivity phenomena, 114
Perception
  auditory space, 96–97
  auditory verbal hallucinations, 74, 94–95, 100–102
Performative hypothesis, 140–141
Personal stereos, 10
Personalised/personified voice, 110, 117, 118
Phantom limb, 17–18, 109
Phencyclidine (PCP), 66
Phenomenology, 2, 11, 14, 16–17, 18, 74–77, 94–96
Philosophical frameworks, 14
Phonological engram, 135, 137–139, 141
Phonological short-term memory, 116

Planum temporale (PT), 79, 80, 83, 97, 98–99, 100–101, 113, 134
Point prevalence, 27
Positive symptoms, 6
Posterior cingulate, 83
Power, 27, 30, 110
Pragmatics of Voices Interview, 15
Predisposing factors, 66
Prefrontal cortex, 76, 78, 83, 87, 139
Premotor cortex, 113
Present State Examination (PSE), 32
Prevalence, hallucinations, 27
Primary sensory cortex, 84
Prosodic processing, 81–82
Protopsychiatry, 15
Pseudo-hallucinations, 95–96
Psychiatry, 14, 16
Psychoactive substances, 66
Psychological predisposing factors, 66
Psychological treatment, 25–41
Psychosocial factors, 66
Psychosocial intervention (PSI), 11
Psychotic Symptom Rating Scale (PSYRATS), 32, 36
Pub approach, 10

"Quasi-present", 18

Reading aloud, 66
Re-afference, 63
Reality, 9, 11, 16, 75, 83–84
Relaxation, 10–11
Religion, 15, 18, 31
Repetitive voices, 111
Response bias, 53–54, 55

Sacks, O., 21–22
Salience, 75–76
Saltation, 128–130
Saturation hypothesis, 79–80
Schedule for Clinical Assessment in Neuropsychiatry (SCAN), 96
Self-esteem, 37
Self-generated action, 63–65, 114
Self-monitoring, 28–29, 76–77, 113, 114
  motor, 61, 63–64
  verbal, 49–53, 61, 85–86, 116
Self–other distinction, 52, 85–86, 136, 139–140
Sense perception, 94
Sensing, 95

Sensory phonological engram, 138
Sensory problems, 109
Sensory stimulation, 109
Serotonergic system, 6
Sexual selection, 128, 130
Shared formulation, 37
Short-term memory, 116
Signifier/signified, 134–135, 137, 138, 141
Situation of voices, 1–2, 14–15, 19, 20
Social anxiety, 29
Social isolation, 34, 38
Social predisposing factors, 66
Social skills, 38
Social support, 35
Socrates, 7, 15
Somatic hallucinations, 113
Somato-sensory cortex, 113
Source memory, 53, 54–55
Source-monitoring, 117
Spatial location, 75, 98–100
Speech
  comprehension, 29
  coping mechanism, 18, 31, 35, 66
  perception, 65
  perception modules, external/ectopic activation, 117
  self–other distinction, 52, 85–86, 136, 139–140
Spiritualism, 11, 15, 18
Subvocalisation, 29, 31, 45, 65
Sue, 19–21
Superior temporal gyrus (STG), 78, 79, 80, 87, 112–113, 114, 134
Supplementary motor area (SMA), 83, 85
Support groups, 118
Symbolic representation, 137
Syntax, 125–145

Tactile hallucinations, 108
Temporal cortex, 113, 114, 117
  language, 78–80
  self-monitoring, 52
Tetrahydrocannabinol (THC), 66
Thalamus, 78, 83
Thought, 139, 140, 141
  misperception, 64, 65
  suppression, 66
Top-down processes, 48, 65
Transcranial magnetic stimulation, 80–81

Uncinate bundle, 139, 140
Unintendedness, 64–65
Universal grammar, 137

Verbal self-monitoring, 49–53, 61, 85–86, 116
Verbal transformation effect, 116
Verbosity, 18
Visionary artists, 7

Visual hallucinations, 108
Vivid imagery, 45, 48–49
Volition, 76–77
Voluntary control, 110
Vorstellung, 94

Wahrnehmung, 94
Walkman use, 10
Working memory, 76